Cognitive Approaches
to Automated Instruction

COGNITIVE APPROACHES TO AUTOMATED INSTRUCTION

Edited by

J. WESLEY REGIAN
VALERIE J. SHUTE
Brooks Air Force Base
San Antonio, Texas

LEA LAWRENCE ERLBAUM ASSOCIATES, PUBLISHERS
1992   Hillsdale, New Jersey   Hove and London

Lawrence Erlbaum Associates, Inc., Publishers
365 Broadway
Hillsdale, New Jersey 07642

Library of Congress Cataloging-in-Publication Data

Cognitive approaches to automated instruction / edited by J. Wesley Regian, Valerie J. Shute.
    p.   cm.
    Revised papers presented at a conference held July 1990, at San Antonio, Texas.
    Includes bibliographical references and index.
    ISBN 0-8058-0992-9
    1. Learning, Psychology of—Congresses.   2. Programmed instruction—Psychological
aspects—Congresses.   3. Individualized instruction—Psychological aspects—Congresses.
4. Cognitive psychology—Congresses.   I. Regian, J. Wesley.   II. Shute, Valerie J.
(Valerie Jean), 1953– .
BF318.C65   1992
371.3′34′019—dc20   92-18722
                                                            CIP

Printed in the United States of America
10 9 8 7 6 5 4 3 2 1

Contents

Preface

This volume is about the design of automated instructional systems. It is intended to provide a snapshot of the state-of-the-art in this research area and should be useful to researchers as well as practitioners looking for guidance on designing automated instruction. The focus of the volume lies at the intersection of our respective interests in the area of automated instruction: diagnosis of the student's current level of understanding or performance (Shute's interest in learning); and selection of the appropriate intervention that would transition the student toward expert performance (Regian's interest in instruction). We set out to identify and clarify a set of principled approaches to automated instruction, diagnosis, and remediation, so that the approaches might be systematically applied, compared, and evaluated. Our first step was to organize a conference and invite a very select group of cognitive psychologists to come to San Antonio and share their ideas and research in this area.

The chapters in this volume are elaborations of the various talks presented at the July, 1990 conference. Following each chapter is a transcription of the discussion that ensued at the conference. In order to provide cohesion and focus to the talks (and the chapters), we asked the authors to address a specific set of questions in addition to describing their instructional approach. Within each of the chapters, the following questions are addressed:

1. What is your approach to cognitive diagnosis for automated instruction?
2. What is the theoretical basis of your approach?
3. What data support the utility of your approach?
4. What is the range of applicability of your approach?

5. What knowledge engineering or task analysis methods are required to support your approach?

We are indebted to a lot of people for making the conference and resulting volume a reality. First, we would like to acknowledge the contributions of Mike Young and Tom Killion for starting the Cognitive Skill Acquisition Workshop several years ago. We also extend heartfelt thanks to Mark Miller and Systems Explorations, Incorporated. Mark handled all of the logistics, large and small, that were involved with the organization of the conference and the volume. We applaud and appreciate the time and toil of all the speakers/contributors. Without them, of course, there would have been no conference or book. We truly appreciate the help of our astute friends who took time to review and critique final drafts of these chapters: Scott Chaiken, Ray Christal, Lisa Gawlick, Pat Kyllonen, and Bill Tirre.

J. W. Regian
V. J. Shute
San Antonio, Texas

1 Automated Instruction as an Approach to Individualization

J. Wesley Regian
Valerie J. Shute
Armstrong Laboratory, Brooks Air Force Base, Texas

We are interested in *automated instruction,* instruction that is delivered on any microprocessor-based system. The term as we use it may include, but is not limited to, computer-assisted instruction, computer-based training, intelligent tutoring, simulator-based training, interactive videodisk-based training, computerized part-task training, and embedded training. We believe that it is possible for automated instructional systems to be more effective than they currently are. Specifically, we believe that by using artificial intelligence programming techniques, it is possible for automated instructional systems to emulate the desirable properties of human tutors in one-on-one instruction.

Gamble and Page (1980; see also O'Neil & Baker, 1991) speculated that effective human tutors:

1. cause the heuristics of the student to converge to those of the tutor;
2. choose appropriate examples and problems for the student;
3. can work arbitrary examples chosen by the student;
4. are able to adjust to different student backgrounds;
5. are able to measure the student's progress; and
6. can review previously learned material with the student as the need arises.

Automated instructional systems have been built with various subsets of these capabilities (see Wenger, 1987). Moreover, we believe it is possible, in principle, for automated instructional systems to surpass the instructional effectiveness of human tutors due to certain inherent properties of automated systems. Automated systems are relentless in their persistence, being unable to "burn out" or become

1

unmotivated to help the student succeed. Automated instructional systems have the capability to graphically and behaviorally simulate desired learning and transfer contexts.[1] Finally, such systems can simulate psychomotor aspects of the transfer context (such as with simulators and virtual world environments). The goal of this book is to outline a set of principled approaches to tapping the potential of automated instructional systems to individualize instruction.

THE PROMISE OF INDIVIDUALIZED INSTRUCTION

Three overlapping streams of research provide the historical opportunity for this book: (a) research into individualized instructional approaches often called mastery learning approaches, (b) research into interactions between subject variables and instructional treatments called aptitude-treatment interactions, and (c) research into advanced computer-based instructional systems called intelligent tutoring systems (ITS). The common thread through these research streams is the belief that individually tailored instruction is superior to group-oriented instruction.

The idea that teaching is best accomplished by tailoring instruction to individual students is both ancient and ubiquitous among instructional theorists. Corno and Snow (1985) found the idea detailed in the 4th century B.C. Chinese Xue Ji, in the ancient Hebrew Haggadah of Passover, and in the 1st century Roman De Institutione Oratoria. Today the basic idea still forms the core of several important streams of research on instruction. The promise of individualized instruction is the basis of research on mastery learning (e.g., Bloom, 1956; Carroll, 1963; Cohen, Kulik, & Kulik, 1982), aptitude-treatment interactions (e.g., Corno & Snow, 1985; Cronbach & Snow, 1977; Shute, chapter 2, this volume, in press), and intelligent tutoring systems (e.g., Burton & Brown, 1982; Lewis, McArthur, Stasz, & Zmuidzinas, 1990; Woolf, 1987). The idea also has strong empirical support. A great deal of data indicates that carefully individualized instruction is superior to conventional group instruction (Bloom, 1984; Woolf, 1987). A consistent finding is that when using traditional stand-up instruction, other things being equal, smaller class sizes produce superior learning outcomes. The most common interpretation of this result is that smaller classes enable instructors to be more aware of, and responsive to, the instructional needs of individual students.

There is not full agreement on the best way to be responsive to the needs of individual students. The research streams introduced here represent relatively distinct ways to think about individualized instruction. In one approach, individuals are thought to differ primarily on learning rate. For example, enthusiasts

---

[1]Examples include jet engines, nuclear reactors, orbital dynamics, principles of economics, laws of physics, and steam turbines.

of programmed instruction (Skinner, 1957) believed that learning rate was the only individual difference worthy of attention. They believed that over time, however, learning-rate differences produce differences in readiness to learn because of failure to have learned previous material in the allotted time. Mastery learning enthusiasts seem to have been heavily influenced by this school of thought (see Carroll, 1963).

In a second approach to individualized instruction, learners are thought to differ on various dimensions, or aptitudes. According to this way of thinking, an aptitude is any characteristic of the individual that is supportive of future achievement in some situation. Thus, aptitudes may be learned or innate. Aptitude-treatment interaction researchers (see Cronbach & Snow, 1977) look for interactions between these aptitudes and instructional approaches, or treatments.

In a third approach to individualized instruction, individuals are characterized in terms of information-processing models of task performance. Instructional interventions are planned after comparing a model of trainee performance (the student model) to a model of expert performance (the expert model). Alternatively, no effort may be expended in developing a student model. In this case, instructional interventions are planned after comparing student performance to the expert model (see Anderson, 1990).

The three approaches (rate, aptitude, model-based) make different assumptions about how to design and implement individualized instruction. The research agenda for rate theorists is to make teachers and students aware of the student's progress toward mastery and to provide each student with ample time to learn. The research agenda for aptitude theorists is to identify the critical aptitudes along with the instructional approaches that are most suitable for levels of these aptitudes. And finally, model-based theorists work to develop models of expert performance and then identify the best approach to moving the student's performance toward the expert model. There are hybrid approaches. Shute (chapter 2, this volume), for example, describes an intelligent tutoring system using a combination of model-based and aptitude approaches. In the following sections we review each of the three approaches in greater detail.

MASTERY LEARNING

The Approach.   Several innovative models of classroom instruction originating in the 1970s sought to allow teachers in group instructional settings to approximate individualized instruction from a slightly elaborated rate perspective. In general, these programs were based on a combination of clear instructional objectives and periodic diagnostic evaluations, allowing teachers to be aware of and responsive to students' knowledge levels throughout the learning process (Stallings & Stipek, 1986). The most influential of these programs were Learning for Mastery (LFM; Bloom, 1968) and the Personalized System of

Instruction (PSI) or the Keller plan (Keller, 1968). These, and related programs, came to be known collectively as mastery learning. The basic premise of mastery learning programs is as follows: Rather than holding instructional time constant and allowing achievement to vary, it is better to hold achievement constant and allow instructional time to vary. That is, given enough time and appropriate intervention, most or all students can achieve mastery of the instructional objectives. Further, if a student is not allowed to achieve mastery of current instructional objectives, then he or she is certainly doomed to failure on later instructional objectives that are hierarchically built upon current instructional objectives.

Contributors to the mastery learning research stream typically measure the effectiveness of an instructional intervention by comparing the mean of the treatment (mastery learning) group to the mean and standard deviation of the control (conventional instruction) group on some final measure of performance. For example, a 1 sigma effect would mean that the average student in the treatment group was 1 SD above the average student in the control group on the final performance measure. This final performance measure may be a standardized achievement test but is usually an experimenter-generated local measure of performance on specific objectives.[2]

Retrospective. In a series of studies, Bloom (1984) reported two important findings about mastery learning and individualized instruction. First, under mastery learning conditions, students performed an average of 1 *SD* above traditionally instructed students, or at the 84th percentile (see Fig. 1.1). Second, under individual tutorial conditions, students performed an average of 2 *SDs* above traditionally instructed students, or at the 98th percentile (see Fig. 1.1). Bloom challenged researchers to develop mastery-based methods of achieving the 2-sigma effect in group teaching situations. These data, and the 2-sigma challenge, are the subject of some controversy (see especially Slavin, 1987; Kulik, Kulik, & Bangert-Drowns, 1990). The controversy centers on the question of whether such a large effect size can ever be consistently obtained in traditional instructional settings using standard achievement tests as criterion measures.

Slavin (1987) conducted a meta-analysis of 17 controlled evaluations of mastery learning programs. In 13 of those studies that looked at experimenter-made measures of summative performance rather than standard achievement tests, the effect size ranged from −0.11 to 0.90 sigma with a mean of 0.34 sigma. Slavin argued that Bloom's (1984) 2-sigma challenge is unrealistic and that his 1-sigma claim is based on studies that are too brief and too small. Although Slavin is seen

---

[2]There is little evidence of any mastery learning effect on standard achievement tests. This is a bone of contention to mastery learning detractors. It is not, however, damaging to the goal of developing instruction that is targeted to clear and specific objectives. There is good evidence that mastery learning can work in such cases.

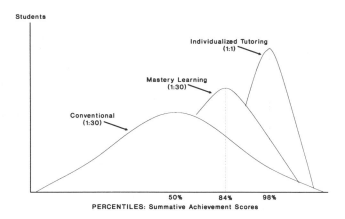

FIG. 1.1.   Distributions for different learning conditions (adapted from Bloom, 1984).

by mastery learning enthusiasts as a detractor (see, e.g., the emotional reply to Slavin, 1987, by Anderson & Burns, 1987), he actually believes a 0.33-sigma effect to be realizable in traditional instructional settings using standard achievement tests as criterion measures. Further, he pointed out that an effect of that magnitude would wipe outs the average achievement gap between lower- and middle-class children in just 3 years. He called for continued research to achieve the potential of mastery approaches in practical application.

Kulik et al. (1990) conducted a meta-analysis of 108 controlled evaluations of mastery learning programs. They looked at 36 evaluations of Bloom's LFM approach and 72 evaluations of Keller's PSI in college, high school, and upper elementary school settings. In these studies the effect size ranged from 0.22 to 1.58 sigma with an average of 0.52 sigma. Thus, the average student in the mastery learning condition performed at the 70th percentile on the summative evaluation, as compared to the 50th percentile for students in the control condition.

Finally, Shute (in press-b) reported the effect sizes from two evaluation studies conducted with intelligent tutoring systems (ITS): one teaching avionics troubleshooting—Sherlock (Lesgold, Lajoie, Bunzo, & Eggan, 1990), and one teaching scientific inquiry skills—Smithtown (Shute & Glaser, 1991). A 1-sigma effect size was computed for both tutors when two groups of learners were compared: learning the curriculum with and without the respective computer programs. These ITS evaluations are thus in the same league as the Bloom mastery learning data (i.e., 84th percentile).

Lessons Learned.   A review of mastery learning research shows that it is possible to use diagnostic tests and ongoing remediation during instruction to produce large enhancements in instructional effectiveness over traditional instruction. Apparently, however, the effect is limited to situations where the goal is to teach clear and specific objectives. Cronbach and Snow (1977) took strong issue with the claim that individual differences in achievement can be eliminated by varying instructional time. There is no convincing evidence that it is possible to eliminate or significantly reduce individual differences on standard achievement tests. Individual differences can, however, apparently be reduced significantly if achievement refers to specific performance objectives rather than general achievement.

Mastery enthusiasts say little about how to effectively diagnose student learning and say nothing about optimal remediation. This probably accounts for the large variability in the effect size. Overall, mastery approaches are poorly implemented in that teachers are not provided with necessary training, resources, or assistance (Slavin, 1987). For example, they are often provided with no training on how to create corrective instruction resulting from diagnostic information, and often the corrective instruction is just given too late. In some cases, remediation is provided as late as 4 weeks after diagnosis (Slavin, 1987). The mastery learning enthusiasts seem to have fallen prey to a pitfall pointed out by Cronbach and Snow, "What one cannot do is generalize about instructional techniques in the abstract" (Cronbach & Snow, 1977, p. 214). Thus, we see a great need to develop guidelines and principles to drive diagnosis and remediation.

Most mastery learning research has been done in the classroom under uncontrolled or partially controlled conditions (Block, 1974). For example, of several hundred studies under consideration for a meta-analysis, Slavin (1987) only deemed 17 to be rigorous enough for inclusion in his final set. Also, due to the bias for publishing positive results, there is no way to access information about mastery learning programs that failed to produce a treatment effect.

For several reasons it is difficult to implement mastery learning on a mass scale. Levin (1974) pointed out that in group settings, individual diagnostic information is costly, and even when it is obtained, knowledge of how to select individualized treatments is speculative.

APTITUDE-TREATMENT INTERACTION

The Approach. The goal of ATI research is to relate the selective effectiveness of various instructional treatments to measurable characteristics of individuals. The relationship can take the form of capitalization, remediation, or compensation (Cronbach & Snow, 1977). The treatment can capitalize on assets, preferences, or tendencies of the individual; compensate for weaknesses; or remediate shortcomings. Aptitude refers to any measurable characteristic of the individual that is propaedeutic to achievement in a given situation (Corno & Snow, 1986). Thus, aptitudes may include knowledge, skills, abilities, personality characteristics, attitudes, and so on.

Retrospective.   Opinions about ATI are polarized. Bracht (1969) reviewed 90 studies and concluded that ATI were found only as often in these studies as would be expected by chance. Glass (1970), commenting on Bracht's review of ATI studies, said: " 'There is no evidence for an interaction of curriculum treatments and personological variables.' I don't know of another statement that has been confirmed so many times by so many people" (p. 210).

Cronbach and Snow (1977), in the final chapter of their book on ATI, also commented on the Bracht review. In addition, they reviewed much of the same literature that Bracht did and more, although using a finer level of analysis:

> Aptitude × Treatment interactions exist. To assert the opposite is to assert that whichever educational procedures is best for Johnny is best for everyone else in Johnny's school. Even the most commonplace adaptation of instruction, such as choosing different books for more and less capable readers of a given age, rests on an assumption of ATI that it seems foolish to challenge (p. 492).

ATI involving general ability are far more common in the literature than ATI involving more specific abilities. A common finding is that when comparing fully elaborated treatments to student-directed treatments, highs (on general ability) profit from student-directed treatments, whereas lows are handicapped. Cronbach and Snow believe that highs "profit from the opportunity to process the information in their own way" (p. 500). This is consistent with the finding that curriculum preorganizers are useful for lows and sometimes detrimental to highs. There is some evidence that lows can be helped through the use of clarifying demonstrations or devices without damaging the performance of highs.

There are occasional interactions involving more specialized abilities such as spatial and mathematical abilities, and with other aptitudes such as prior learning, memory, and personality styles. Across studies looking for these effects, however, conflicting results are found more often than not. It is probable that there is fertile ground here for cultivation, but principles are not forthcoming as yet.

Lessons Learned.   ATI have been very difficult to find because of insufficient sample sizes, poor methodology, various uncontrolled conditions, and unanticipated interactions that occur across settings. Cronbach and Snow (1977) argued for several methodological rules of thumb in designing ATI research. Most studies of ATI are brief and artificial, pointing to a "need to collect data from instructional procedures that realistically progress through a body of material" (p. 509).

Cronbach and Snow believe that time should be held constant, allowing achievement to vary, rather than carrying each subject to criterion and allowing instructional time to vary. They specifically referred to both the mastery learning and the programmed instruction streams of research as often violating this rule.

Their argument rested strongly on the assumption that the end-user of instructional research is the traditional educational system. The recommendation is less critical for industrial or military training because the trainee becomes employable as soon as he or she reaches criterion on task performance.

ATI studies with random assignment to one of two treatments should use about 100 subjects per treatment. This rule of thumb can be relaxed somewhat for sufficiently powerful designs involving extreme groups or matched cases. Most investigators in the ATI tradition before 1977 used 40 or fewer subjects per treatment, and may have lacked the power to pick up even moderate effects.

Cronbach and Snow warned against oversimplification in research about ATI, arguing strongly for the measurement of multiple aptitudes, treatments, and outcomes. They also warned of the complexities of research in intact classes and naturalistic educational research.

Finally, Cronbach and Snow argued that the choice of treatment conditions should be principled, based on a detailed taxonomy of instructional situations, and on process analysis or other theoretical approaches to performance.

INTELLIGENT TUTORING SYSTEMS

The Approach.   The introduction of artificial intelligence technology to the field of computer-aided instruction (CAI) has prompted research and development efforts in an area known as intelligent computer-aided instruction (ICAI). We may conceive of computer-based training (CBT) systems as lying along a continuum that runs from CAI to ICAI. There are important differences between CAI systems and ICAI systems.

As we have discussed, a great deal of data indicates that under certain circumstances, diagnostically tailored instruction can be superior to untailored instruction. Thus, an important way in which CBT systems differ is in the degree to which their behavior is modified by an inferred "model of the student's current understanding of the subject matter" (VanLehn, 1986). The CBT system that is less intelligent by this definition may be conceived of as CAI. The system that is more intelligent may be conceived of as ICAI. Often, ICAI systems are referred to as intelligent tutoring systems (ITS; Sleeman & Brown, 1982). This term is particularly appropriate, as it brings to mind one-on-one tutoring.

With respect to individualization, it is important to note that virtually all traditional CAI systems are individualized in the sense that they are self-paced, and many are further individualized by virtue of branching routines that allow different students to receive different instruction. CAI systems with branching routines are, in fact, more individualized than those without branching routines. Thus, they are more intelligent by the current definition (although in a weak sense). In branched CAI the instructional developer must explicitly encode the actions generated by all possible branches, and there is a finite number of possible paths through these branches. As we move further away from the CAI to the ICAI end of the continuum, we begin to see a very different and more powerful approach to individualization. This more powerful approach was touched on by Wenger (1987) when he referred to explicit encoding of knowledge rather than encoding of decisions. An ITS (which term probably should be reserved for systems that are very far toward the ICA end of the continuum) uses a diverse set of knowledge bases and inference routines to "compose instructional interactions dynamically, making decisions by reference to the knowledge with which they have been provided" (Wenger, 1987, p. 5). The "intelligence" in these systems resides in cognitive diagnosis—the ability to analyze learners' solution histories dynamically, using principles rather than preprogrammed responses to decide what to do next and how to adapt instruction to different learners.

Retrospective.   Since the 1980s, many ITSs have been built incorporating various approaches to diagnostic student modeling and remediation. Far fewer systems have been formally evaluated, but of the subset of evaluated systems, some have approached the kind of instructional power produced by individualized human-taught instruction (e.g., Lesgold et al., 1990; Reiser, Anderson, & Farrell, 1985; Shute & Glaser, 1990).

Shute (in press-b) reviewed findings from four studies conducted with ITSs, some of the select few that have undergone empirical evaluation: (a) the LISP tutor, which teaches programming in LISP (Anderson, Farrell, & Sauers, 1984); (b) Smithtown, which teaches scientific inquiry skills in the context of microeconomics (Shute & Glaser, 1991); (c) Sherlock, which teaches avionics troubleshooting (Lesgold et al., 1992); and (d) the Pascal Tutor, which teaches programming in Pascal (Bonar, Cunningham, Beatty, & Weil, 1988; Shute, 1991a). The results of the evaluations were impressive. Learning efficiency (rate) with ITSs was accelerated in comparison to control conditions. Overall, students acquired the subject matter faster from various ITSs than from more traditional environments. For example, subjects working with the LISP tutor learned the knowledge and skills in one third to two thirds the time it took a control group to learn the same material (Anderson, Boyle, & Reiser, 1985). Subjects working with Smithtown learned the same material in half the time it took a classroom-instructed group (Shute & Glaser, 1990). Subjects working with Sherlock learned in 20 hours skills that were comparable to those possessed by technicians having almost 4 years experience (Nichols, Pokorny, Jones, Gott, & Alley, in preparation). And finally, subjects learning from the Pascal ITS acquired, in one third the time, equivalent knowledge and skills as learned through traditional instruction (Shute, in 1991b).

With regard to learning outcome, ITSs again performed well in comparison to control conditions. The LISP tutor group attained the same (or in one study, 43% better) criterion scores as a control group not using the tutor. Results from the

Smithtown analysis showed that subjects learned the same material as a classroom group, despite the fact that the tutor focused on the instruction of scientific inquiry skills, not the subject matter. The outcome data from subjects using Sherlock showed increases in scores comparable to an advanced group of subjects and significantly better than a control group. In all cases, individuals learned faster, and performed at least as well, with the ITSs as subjects learning from traditional environments. For a more thorough treatment of these evaluation studies, see Shute (1991b).

Lessons Learned.   A review of ITS research suggests that it is possible to use artificial intelligence to develop computer-based instructional systems that automatically generate and deliver tailored instruction. This automatically tailored instruction can (at least sometimes) produce large enhancements in instructional efficiency or effectiveness over nontailored instruction.

Although it is accurate to say that most of the evaluation studies published to date have shown positive effects, this is misleading. In studies of instructional interventions, there is a selection bias for publication of effective interventions. Also, controlled evaluations of ITSs are rare (Baker, 1990; Littman & Soloway, 1988), even though there are many published accounts of ITS design and development (see Wenger, 1987). A review of these accounts shows that ITSs are often designed haphazardly, the range of domains for which they have been built is somewhat narrow, and implementation of system components is often guided by "intuition" rather than theory (e.g., Koedinger & Anderson, 1990; Norman, 1989). If the current generation of ITSs were subjected to controlled evaluation, the results would probably be quite variable.

THE FUTURE OF AUTOMATED INSTRUCTION

Mastery learning researchers have tried to iteratively move learners toward mastery of task performance. ATI researchers have tried to match up instructional treatments with measurable characteristics of individuals. ITS researchers have tried to move learners toward a well-specified expert model of performance. There are success stories in each of these research streams. However, general and systematic principles of individualized instruction have not emerged. Studies in these areas are plagued by noisy data, methodological flaws, small samples, and various unpleasant constraints arising from the realities of educational environments. Donchin (1989) described some of the problems as follows:

> As my colleagues and I examined the literature on training and practice we became increasingly, and painfully, conscious of the fact that it is very difficult to integrate the studies we were reviewing. The theoretical acumen and the ingenuity of previous investigators was beyond reproach. A vast number of papers had been published within such domains as "learning theory," "training," "motor behavior"

and similar areas. However, it was quite evident that the diversity of paradigms and theoretical approaches within which the phenomena were studied, and the models tested, made it difficult to compare results across studies. The many contradictions which are frequent in any body of literature were difficult to resolve because much of the conflict could be attributed to the different settings, and paradigms, in which the phenomena were studied (pp. 4–5).

Many have argued that instructional research would benefit from a more systematic approach to pedagogy. We believe that progress can be enhanced by specifying instructional approaches clearly and in sufficient detail to allow others to apply, evaluate, and compare the approaches. The ensuing chapters in this volume outline a variety of approaches to automated instruction.

REFERENCES

Anderson, J. R. (1990). *Analysis of student performance with the LISP tutor. Diagnostic monitoring of skill and knowledge acquisition.* Hillsdale, NJ: Lawrence Erlbaum Associates.

Anderson, J. R., Boyle, C., & Reiser, B. (1985). Intelligent tutoring systems. *Science, 228,* 456–462.

Anderson, J. R., Farrell, R., & Sauers, R. (1984). Learning to program in LISP. *Cognitive Science, 8,* 87–129.

Anderson, L. W., & Burns, R. B. (1987). Values, evidence, and mastery learning. *Review of Educational Research, 57,* 215–223.

Baker, E. L. (1990). Technology assessment: Policy and methodological issues. In H. L. Burns, J. Parlett, & C. Luckhardt (Eds.), *Intelligent tutoring systems: Evolutions in design* (pp. 243–263). Hillsdale, NJ: Lawrence Erlbaum Associates.

Block, J. H. (1974). Mastery learning in the classroom: An overview of recent research. In J. H. Block (Ed.), *Schools, society, and mastery learning* (pp. 28–69). New York: Holt, Rinehart & Winston.

Bloom, B. S. (1956). *The taxonomy of educational objectives: Handbook 1: The Cognitive Domain.* New York: McKay.

Bloom, B. S. (1968). Learning for mastery. *Evaluation Comment, 1*(2).

Bloom, B. S. (1984). The 2-sigma problem: The search for methods of group instruction as effective as one-to-one tutoring. *Educational Researcher, 13*(6), 4–16.

Bonar, J., Cunningham, R., Beatty, P., & Weil, W. (1988). *Bridge: Intelligent tutoring system with intermediate representations* (Tech. Rep.) Pittsburgh, PA: Learning Research & Development Center, University of Pittsburgh.

Bracht, G. H. (1969). *The relationship of treatment tasks, personological variables and dependent variables to aptitude-treatment interactions.* Unpublished doctoral dissertation, University of Colorado, Denver.

Burton, R., & Brown, J. S. (1982). An investigation of computer coaching for informal learning activities. In D. Sleeman & J. S. Brown (Eds.), *Intelligent tutoring systems* (pp. 79–98). New York: Academic Press.

Carroll, J. (1963). A model of school learning. *Teachers College Record, 64,* 723–733.

Cohen, P. A., Kulik, J., & Kulik, C. C. (1982). Educational outcomes of tutoring: A meta-analysis of findings. *American Educational Research Journal, 19*(2), 237–248.

Corno, L., & Snow, R. E. (1985). Adapting teaching to individual differences among learners. In M. C. Wittrock (Ed.), *Handbook of research on teaching* (3rd ed., pp. 605–629). New York: Macmillian.

Cronbach, L. J., & Snow, R. E. (1977). *Aptitudes and instructional methods: A handbook for research on interactions.* New York: Irvington.

Donchin, E. (1989). The learning strategies project, *Acta Psychologica, 71,* 1–15.

Gamble, A., & Page, C. V. (1980). The use of artificial intelligence techniques in computer-assisted instruction: An overview. *International Journal of Man-Machine Studies, 12,* 259–282.

Glass, G. (1970). Discussion. In M. C. Wittrock & D. C. Wiley (Eds.), *The evaluation of instruction* (pp. 210–211). New York: Holt, Rinehart, & Winston.

Keller, F. S. (1968). "Goodbye, teacher . . ." *Journal of Applied Behavioral Analysis, 1,* 78–89.

Koedinger, K. R., & Anderson, J. R. (1990). *Theoretical and empirical motivations for the design of ANGLE: A new geometry learning environment.* Working notes: AAAI spring symposium series. Stanford University, Stanford, CA.

Kulik, C. L., Kulik, J., & Bangert-Drowns, R. (1990). Effectiveness of mastery learning programs: A meta-analysis. *Review of Educational Research, 60,* 265–299.

Lesgold, A., Lajoie, S. P., Bunzo, M., & Eggan, G. (1992). A coached practice environment for an electronics troubleshooting job. In J. Larkin, R. Chabey, & C. Cheftic (Eds.), *Computer assisted instruction and intelligent tutoring systems: Establishing communication and collaboration* (pp. 201–238). Hillsdale, NJ: Lawrence Erlbaum Associates.

Levin, H. M. (1974). The economic implications of mastery learning. In J. H. Block (Ed.), *Schools, society, and mastery learning* (pp. 73–88). New York: Holt, Rinehart & Winston.

Lewis, M. W., McArthur, D., Stasz, C., & Zmuidzinas, M. (1990). *Discovery-based tutoring in mathematics.* Working notes: AAAI spring symposium series. Stanford University, Stanford, CA.

Littman, D., & Soloway, E. (1988). Evaluating ITSs: The cognitive science perspective. In M. C. Polson & J. J. Richardson (Eds.), *Foundations of intelligent tutoring systems* (pp. 209–242). Hillsdale, NJ: Lawrence Erlbaum Associates.

Nichols, P., Pokorny, R., Jones, G., Gott, S. P., & Alley, W. E. (in preparation). *Evaluation of an avionics troubleshooting tutoring system* (Tech. Rep.) Armstrong Laboratory, Human Resources Directorate, Brooks AFB, TX.

Norman, D. A. (1989). *The psychology of everyday things.* New York: Basic Books.

O'Neil, H. F., & Baker, E. L. (1991). Issues in intelligent computer-assisted instruction: Evaluation and measurement. In T. B. Gutkin & S. L. Wise (Eds.), *The computer and the decision-making process* (pp. 199–224). Hillsdale, NJ: Lawrence Erlbaum Associates.

Shute, V. J. (1991a). Who is likely to acquire programming skills? *Journal of Educational Computing Research, 7*(1), 1–24.

Shute, V. J. (in press). A comparison of learning environments: All that glitters . . . In S. P. Lajoie & S. J. Derery (Eds.), *Computers as cognitive tools.* Hillsdale, NJ: Lawrence Erlbaum Associates.

Shute, V. J. (1991b). *Meta-evaluation of four intelligent tutoring systems: Promises and products* (AL-TP-1991-0040). Air Force Systems Command, Brooks Air Force Base, Texas.

Shute, V. J., & Glaser, R. (1990). Large-scale evaluation of an intelligent discovery world: Smithtown. *Interactive Learning Environments, 1,* 51–77.

Shute, V. J., & Glaser, R. (1991). An intelligent tutoring system for exploring principles of economics. In R. E. Snow & D. Wiley (Eds.), *Improving inquiry in social science: A volume in honor of Lee J. Cronbach.* Hillsdale, NJ: Lawrence Erlbaum Associates.

Skinner, B. F. (1957). *Verbal behavior.* Englewood Cliffs, NJ: Prentice-Hall.

Slavin, R. E. (1987). Mastery learning reconsidered. *Review of Educational Research, 57,* 175–213.

Sleeman, D. H., & Brown, J. S. (Eds.). (1982). *Intelligent tutoring systems.* London: Academic Press.

Stallings, J. A., & Stipek, D. (1985). Research on early childhood and elementary school teaching programs. In M. Wittrock (Ed.), *Research on teaching* (pp. 727–753). New York: Macmillan.

VanLehn, K. (1986). Student modeling in intelligent teaching systems. *Proceedings of the Research Planning Forum for Intelligent Tutoring Systems*. San Antonio, TX: Air Force Human Resources Laboratory.

Wenger, E. (1987). *Artificial intelligence and tutoring systems*. Los Altos, CA: Morgan Kaufman.

2 Aptitude-Treatment Interactions and Cognitive Skill Diagnosis

Valerie J. Shute
Armstrong Laboratory, Brooks Air Force Base, Texas

Individuals come to any new learning task with differing profiles of knowledge and skills. The "intelligence" in an intelligent tutoring system (ITS) resides in the ability to analyze solution histories dynamically, using principles, rather than preprogrammed responses, to decide what to do next (e.g., Clancey, 1986), and to adapt instruction to different learners (e.g., Sleeman & Brown, 1982; Wenger, 1987). Valid and reliable cognitive diagnoses, then, are essential to computer systems that adapt to their users' needs.

The standard approach to cognitive skill diagnosis represents *emerging* knowledge and skills of the learner. The computer responds to these updated observations with a modified curriculum, adjusted error by error, action by action, minute by minute. Instruction, therefore, is dependent on individual response histories. More sensitive approaches permit even greater tailoring of curriculum to learner characteristics by considering *incoming* as well as *emerging* knowledge and skills in the cognitive diagnosis. This enables the curriculum to adapt to both persistent and momentary performance information as well as the interaction.

One would think that increasing the personalization of instruction would enhance learning efficiency, improving both the rate and quality of cognitive skill acquisition. However, results cited in the literature on learning in relation to increased computer adaptivity are equivocal. In some cases, researchers have reported no advantage of error remediation in relation to learning outcome (e.g., Bunderson & Olsen, 1983; Sleeman, Kelly, Martinak, Ward, & Moore, 1989). In others, some advantage has been reported for more personalized remediation (e.g., Swan, 1983).

Cognitive diagnosis serves two main purposes: classification and explanation

(Snow, 1990). As explained previously, the result of cognitive diagnosis suggests uniquely appropriate curricular paths (classification); however, it also provides an interpretive theory about a learner's performance history (explanation). Snow (1990) has suggested using aptitude-treatment interaction (ATI) methodologies in order to exploit these two functions fully (for background, see Cronbach & Snow, 1977). ATI research provides information about initial states of learners that can be applied in macroadaptive instruction (e.g., selection of a learning environment for a particular student); then microadaptive instruction can be used as a response to particular actions (e.g., selection of the next small unit of instruction to be presented based on a specific response history). In other words, initial states are characterized by an aptitude profile.[1] Then microadaptive instructional systems can either focus on strengths, circumvent weaknesses, or highlight deficits to be remediated.

Obviously there is some cost associated with increasing a system's responsiveness, which raises two important practical questions: (a) How much, and what kind of, information about a learner is required to tailor instruction to his or her needs[2] so as to maximize chances for learning to occur? (b) What is the payoff of increasing a system's adaptability? Sleeman (1987) has argued that "if one takes seriously the findings of the ATI work of Cronbach and Snow (1977), it would appear that there is little likelihood of producing instruction that is uniquely individualized" (p. 242). The key word in this statement is "uniquely." An exhaustive characterization of a learner would probably not warrant the effort and expense in terms of increases in final outcome. However, the empirical question remains: How much is enough? Answers to these cost–benefit questions are discussed at the end of the chapter following a description of the macroadaptive approach and an examination of its theoretical and motivational bases.

Macroadaptive Approach

The approach to cognitive diagnosis taken in this chapter involves conducting a controlled experiment with the purpose of determining individual differences in learning and possible ATIs. Before the experiment, certain critical decisions have to be made. For instance, what aptitudes should be measured before the instruction, which treatment effects should be manipulated, what learning indicators should be recorded to measure learning progress, and what learning outcome and efficiency measures should be used?

The learning skills taxonomy developed by Kyllonen and Shute (1989) can assist in rendering principled decisions to some of these questions. This tax-

---

[1]I define *aptitude* in this chapter as the incoming knowledge and cognitive abilities possessed by individuals arriving at a new learning task. Personality variables, classified by some researchers as aptitudes, are not included in this definition.

[2]*Needs* are defined in this context as the individual differences measures (i.e., aptitudes) believed to impact learning outcome and efficiency.

onomy defines a four-dimensional space involving the subject matter, learning environment, desired knowledge outcome, and learner attributes. Interactions among these dimensions are believed to influence outcome performance. For example, no single type of learning environment (e.g., exploratory-discovery) is best for all persons. Rather, aptitude-treatment interactions occur in which certain learner characteristics are better suited to certain learning environments than to others in order to achieve optimal outcome performance (see Shute & Glaser, 1990). Similarly, some domains lend themselves more readily to certain kinds of knowledge outcomes than to others. For instance, nonquantitative fields (e.g., history) emphasize propositions, whereas quantitative fields (e.g., calculus) focus on procedures. And finally, knowledge outcomes covary with instructional method: Propositions are more commonly learned by rote and procedures are more commonly learned by practice.

So, to begin answering questions concerning the most appropriate aptitude, outcome, and efficiency measures to use, one must consider the effect(s) of possible combinations of the four dimensions comprising the taxonomy. Aptitudes to assess before instruction should be relevant to the subject matter, the desired knowledge outcome, and the type of learning environment in which instruction will take place.

Theoretical Basis for Macroadaptive Approach

The Learning Abilities Measurement Program (LAMP)[3] conducts basic research on the nature of human learning abilities. In the past, LAMP studies have examined relationships between aptitude measures and performance on simple learning tasks. Recently, large-scale studies have been conducted validating the computerized aptitude tests against more complex learning from intelligent tutoring systems (e.g., Shute, 1990, 1991). Major research now in progress examines whether learning can be predicted from basic cognitive process measures or aptitudes.

The theoretical model of learning underlying LAMP has been influenced by Anderson's ACT* model (see Anderson, 1983; Kyllonen & Christal, 1989). Basically, it posits three stages of learning (i.e., declarative knowledge, procedural skills, and automatic skills) and two sets of learning predictors: enablers (i.e., what one already knows and can transfer to new situations) and mediators (i.e., cognitive processes determining what one can acquire, such as working-memory capacity and information-processing speed). Relations among the learning stages, enablers, and mediators show how, as learning progresses, enablers become elaborated, and working-memory capacity and processing speed become functionally larger and faster, respectively (e.g., Chase & Simon, 1973; Chi, Glaser, & Rees, 1982; Siegler & Richards, 1982).

---

[3]LAMP is a project at the Armstrong Laboratory, Brooks Air Force Base, TX.

Justification and Motivation for This Approach

The justification for such a broad approach requires evidence that individuals do, in fact, perform better or worse under different learning conditions (or environments). As noted earlier, this is usually referred to as aptitude-treatment interaction research (Cronbach & Snow, 1977). ATI research was very popular in the 1960s and 1970s; then popularity waned. One of the major reasons contributing to the decline was that the older ATI research typically involved studies conducted in classroom environments. Data were confounded by many extraneous variables (e.g., personality of the teacher, instructional materials, classroom dynamics) making ATIs hard to find and difficult to interpret. A second factor contributing to the decline was the realization that we did not understand the processing requirements underlying performance on the various aptitude measures. This motivated process-oriented analyses, using elementary cognitive tasks as tests. A second generation of ATI research using theoretically derived aptitude measures and controlled learning environments is discussed.

Several factors motivated this approach to cognitive skill diagnosis. First, the learning skills taxonomy (with its four interactive dimensions) provided a framework for the systematic design and evaluation of intelligent tutoring systems. Second, after testing over 800 subjects on Smithtown,[4] it was clear that some individuals thrived in this type of guided-discovery environment, whereas others did not. This finding prompted the identification of characteristics of individuals who succeeded (and failed) in such a learning environment (see Shute & Glaser, 1990; Shute, Glaser, & Raghavan, 1989). Finally, findings reported in two recent studies reported no effect of different instructional treatments on learning outcome.

In the first, Sleeman et al. (1989) investigated the effects of different remediation techniques on high school students' learning of algebra. They concluded, "Three studies suggest that when initial instruction and remediation are primarily rule-based and procedural, remedial reteaching appears to be as effective as MBR (model-based remediation). From this it follows that classical CAI [computer-assisted instruction] would be as effective as an ITS" (p. 563).

In the other article, Anderson, Conrad, and Corbett (1989) reported results from various manipulations made to the LISP tutor environment. They concluded that "well-designed feedback can minimize the time and pain of learning, but has no effect on final instructional outcome" (p. 498).

There are at least two alternative explanations for both of these findings. The most obvious one is that the respective modifications were not distinct enough to impact learning outcome. A second explanation is that perhaps there was an effect of the manipulations (i.e., remediation and feedback), but to find it would require considering some additional variable(s).

---

[4]This is the name of a somewhat guided but mostly discovery environment for learning principles of microeconomics. The coach addresses specific scientific inquiry skills, such as changing one variable at a time while holding others constant. The coach does not address economic principles.

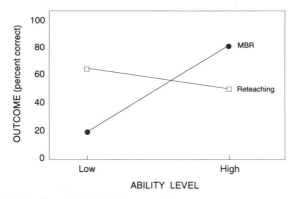

FIG. 2.1. Hypothetical depiction of Sleeman et al. (1989) data.

A hypothetical depiction of the Sleeman et al. (1989) data appears in Fig. 2.1, illustrating the second explanation. Although these data show no main effect between treatment condition on outcome measure (both about 50%) with aptitudes in the equation, we do see differential outcome effects due to treatment (or aptitude-treatment interaction). In this figure, high-aptitude individuals (possessing good reasoning and verbal skills, broad general knowledge, large working-memory capacities, and so on) benefit from the more elaborate explanations offered by the model-based remediation (MBR) approach. This approach addresses specific errors made during the solution process. On the other hand, low-aptitude individuals (possessing less of the same attributes) perform better in the reteaching condition. This approach simply demonstrates the relevant procedure without addressing the learner's error. There is some evidence for this proposition in the ATI literature. More elaborate explanations were found to help high-aptitude subjects, but less elaborate explanations were more effective for the low-aptitude subjects, "Elaboration that takes the form of systematic explanations places a burden of comprehension on the learner, which tends to help Highs" (Cronbach & Snow, 1977, p. 501).

Similarly, a hypothetical depiction of the Anderson et al. (1989) data appears in Fig. 2.2. One study they reported contrasted outcome (quiz) performance based on whether the student or the tutor controlled the feedback. The same logic applies here as with the previous illustration. Subjects with high aptitudes could, theoretically, benefit more by taking an active, independent approach during the learning process. They would have the necessary capabilities to direct the course of their own learning. But the low-aptitude subjects could perform better if the tutor guided them through the curriculum.[5] There is also some support for this

---

[5]Actually, John Anderson said that he did look for, but did not find, any ATI's in this data (see discussion section following this chapter). This was attributed to the restricted range of aptitude levels in the sample of university students used as subjects in the study.

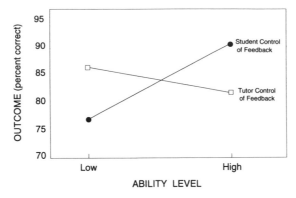

FIG. 2.2. Hypothetical depiction of Anderson et al. (1989) data.

premise in the ATI literature. Campbell (1964) contrasted two learning environments and found the "self-direction" condition was better for the high-aptitude group, whereas "programmed instruction" was better for the low-aptitude subjects. In addition, Cronbach and Snow (1977) reported that high-aptitude subjects profit from the opportunity to process the information in their own way, whereas low-ability subjects tend to be handicapped: "we see the Highs doing better when given greater freedom to proceed in their own manner, when thrown more upon their own resources. And we see regression slopes becoming flatter when more of the intellectual work is done for the learner" (p. 503).

These two graphs present alternative perspectives on the reported findings, but are hypothetical. To make the case more authentic requires empirical evidence from controlled research using a large, heterogeneous sample in order to allow the hypothesized ATIs to emerge. The following study was designed to provide such evidence.

Comparing Two Learning Environments

A study was conducted employing an intelligent tutoring system instructing basic principles of electricity (Ohm's and Kirchhoff's laws) as the complex learning task. Research questions examined in this experiment related to the influence of different learning environments on learning outcome and efficiency measures. Other research issues looked at the relationships among individuals' associative learning skills, learning environment, and learning outcome and efficiency measures.

I tested 282 individuals[6] (84% males, 16% females) participating in a 7-day (45-hour) study on the acquisition of basic principles of electricity. All subjects

---

[6]Approximately 320 subjects actually participated in the study, but only 282 completed all of the testing and learning activities reported in this chapter.

were high school graduates (or equivalent), with a mean age of 22 years. A restriction on this sample was that individuals could have no prior electronics training or formal instruction. Subjects were obtained from a temporary employment service and paid for their participation.

Experimental cognitive aptitude tasks were administered on Zenith 248 microcomputers (AT-compatible) with standard keyboards and EGA color video monitors. The intelligent tutoring system was administered on Xerox 1186 computers with standard keyboards and high resolution monochromatic displays on 19 in monitors. Software was written in InterLISP-D and LOOPS.

Subjects were tested in groups of 15–20 at Lackland Air Force Base, Texas, in the Complex Learning Assessment (CLASS) laboratory. They occupied individual testing carrels, and instructions, testing, and feedback were computer administered with proctors available to answer questions. On the morning of the first day, subjects were given a brief orientation to the entire study and then randomly assigned to one of two learning conditions. They were then administered half of the battery of cognitive ability tasks. On subsequent days, subjects were provided with instructions and practice problem solving involving electrical circuits delivered by the ITS. Upon completion of the tutor, subjects were given a criterion posttest battery and then completed the other half of cognitive ability tests.

Cognitive Ability Tasks

A comprehensive battery of computerized tests was administered to all subjects to assess their incoming knowledge and cognitive skills. A full discussion of this battery (Kyllonen et al., 1990) is beyond the scope of this chapter. The present focus is on just one of the cognitive process measures—associative learning (AL) skills. Because of the exploratory nature of this study, I wanted to investigate a fundamental learning ability. One such parameter involves the rate and quality of forming associations when learning something new. The notion that associative learning skills are general and important to knowledge and skills acquisition is certainly not new. Rather, the literature offers ample support for this proposition (e.g., Anderson, 1983; Kyllonen & Tirre, 1988; Malmi, Underwood, & Carroll, 1979; Underwood, 1975; Underwood, Boruch, & Malmi, 1978).

Three computerized tests were administered in each of the verbal, quantitative, and spatial domains for a total of nine tests on this measure. Examples of three AL tests are described here, one from each of the verbal, quantitative, and spatial domains (note matching test paradigm).

Verbal AL Test.   Subjects are required to learn eight pairs of words displayed in two rows at the top of the computer screen. The word pairs consist of an occupation directly above a piece of furniture (e.g., lawyer/table, carpenter/couch). The eight pairings remain the same throughout the test, although the pairs' positions vary with each new question. For example, while lawyer would always be paired with table, it may come either before or after carpenter/couch in the listing at the top of the screen. Questions appear one at a time at the bottom of the screen and consist of either a match or mismatch to the word pairs being learned. After the subject enters a response (typing "L" for like or "D" for different), another question is displayed. Subjects are asked to remember the word pairs as quickly and accurately as possible so that they will not have to keep looking up at the top of the screen to confirm a match. At the end of each set of questions (one set = 32 items), subjects are informed of their accuracy and latency on that set. There are 10 sets of items in the entire test (320 items), and for the first eight sets of items, word pairs remain on the screen. For the last two sets, word pairs do not appear on the screen and subjects are tested on how many pairs they successfully memorized during the preceding trials. Accuracy and latency data (milliseconds) are recorded. Odd–even reliability is .98.

Quantitative AL Test.   This test is identical to the verbal AL test just described, except that in this test, subjects are required to learn eight pairs of *numbers* located at the top of the screen, one row above the other (e.g., 41 over −2, 95 over 6, 89 over −9). The number pairings remain the same throughout the test while the pairs' positions may vary from question to question. Instructions, number of items, and goals are the same as presented above for the verbal AL test. Odd–even reliability is .96.

Spatial AL Test.   This test is the same as the verbal and quantitative AL tests, except that subjects must learn eight pairs of simple geometrical shapes located in two parallel rows at the top of the screen (e.g., arrow above L, triangle above +). Odd–even reliability is .96.

The other AL tests are similar, requiring connections to be established between verbal, quantitative, or spatial stimuli. Individual differences in associative learning skills have been shown to predict complex learning (see Kyllonen & Tirre, 1988). The complex learning task used as a criterion in the current study involved basic electricity content.

Complex Learning Task (Electricity ITS)

The electricity tutor was originally developed at the Learning Research and Development Center, University of Pittsburgh (Lesgold, Bonar, Ivill, & Bowen, 1989) and then modified at the Armstrong Laboratory. In particular, we created two learning environments, developed and coded a variety of learning indicators, established mastery criteria, refined principles, definitions and feedback, and modified the system's interface. Learning from the tutor resulted from working problems, reading definitions of concepts (hypertext structure), and exploring circuits (e.g., taking meter readings and changing values of components).

I created the two learning environments specifically to investigate possible ATIs in learning. To differentiate the two learning environments (rule-application and rule-induction), the ITS was manipulated by altering the nature of the feedback to the learner, all else being equal. After completing a problem, subjects in each group received feedback concerning whether their answer was correct. Moreover, the principle (Ohm's or Kirchhoff's laws) that was relevant to the problem was addressed in one of two ways. In the *rule-application* environment, feedback clearly stated the variables and their relationships for a given problem. This was communicated in the form of a rule such as, "The principle involved in this kind of problem is that current before a resistor is equal to the current after a resistor in a parallel net." Subjects then proceeded to apply the rule in the solution of related problems.

In the *rule-induction* environment, the tutor provided feedback that identified the relevant variables in the problem, but the learner had to induce the relationships among those variables. For instance, the computer might give the following feedback: "What you need to know to solve this type of problem is how current behaves, both before and after a resistor, in a parallel net." Subjects in the rule-induction condition, therefore, generated their own interpretation of the functional relationships among variables comprising the different rules. Subjects were randomly assigned to one of the two environments for the entire study.

The computer presented all problems (under both learning conditions) by showing different electrical circuits and asking questions about them. Figure 2.3 shows an example of the main screen. On the screen's left, a parallel circuit depicts various component values. The upper right of the screen shows the main options (e.g., look at definitions, take a measurement on the circuit). Problems were presented in the lower right quadrant of the screen with feedback given in the same window. A notebook in the lower left of the screen allowed students to store information from their explorations and manipulations. Finally, an on-line calculator was always available for computing solutions to more complex, quantitative problems.

Figure 2.4 shows an example of a definition. When the "View Definitions" option was selected, the screen cleared and a menu of items appeared. In the main definition window, bold-faced words implied connections between the immediate word and related concepts. Choosing a bold-faced word with the mouse resulted in that concept's appearance on the screen. In some cases, dynamic simulations, such as comparing current flow in series versus parallel circuits, were available to the learner.

The electricity curriculum consisted of 15 principles (see Table 2.1). Problems were generated by the computer based on those principles. Each problem was unique (i.e., generated "on the fly," not preprogrammed), based on the particular learner's response history. If a student needed more work on current flow in parallel circuits, for instance, the system would generate a problem satisfying specific constraints, such as, it must be a parallel circuit problem involving current, perhaps a more difficult quantitative solution required, and so forth.

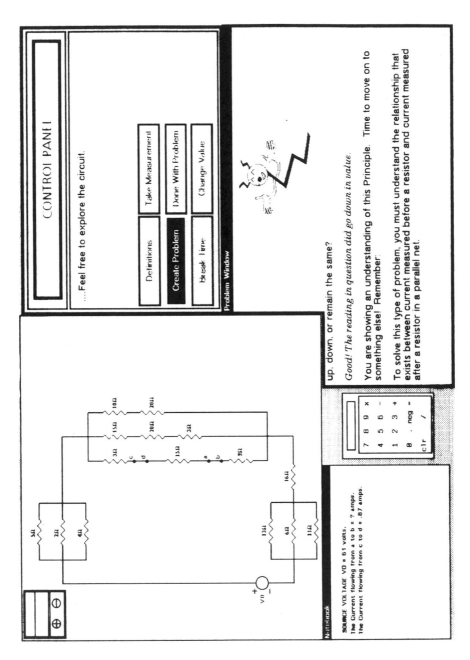

FIG. 2.3. Examples of electricity tutor screen.

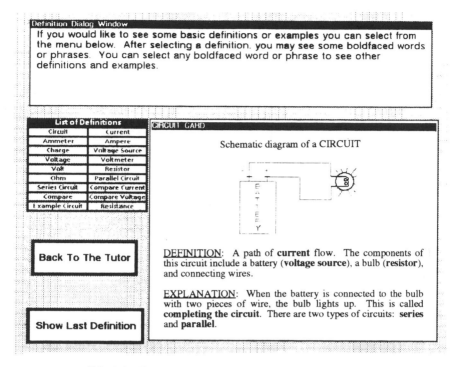

FIG. 2.4.   Example of electricity tutor on-line dictionary.

Problem types ranged from easy to difficult (Levels 1, 2, 3) and included qualitative problems (requiring responses of up, down, or stay the same), relative problems (requiring responses of higher, lower, or equal to), and quantitative ones (requiring calculations and numeric input). Learners "mastered" a principle once they had answered correctly three consecutive problems per principle.

Learning Outcome Measures

A four-part criterion test battery was developed measuring knowledge and skills acquired from the tutor. This battery was administered on-line after the student completed the tutor. The first two tests in the battery were also administered at the beginning of the experiment.

Part 1 of the criterion battery (pretest and posttest) assessed declarative knowledge understanding of different components and devices involved in basic electronics: ammeter, ampere, charge, circuit, current, ohm, parallel circuit, resistance, resistor, series circuit, volt, voltage, voltage source, voltmeter. Some example true/false questions included: A voltmeter is used to measure a voltage drop across two points in a circuit; there is a standard number of volts used in a parallel circuit; a resistor is designed to store electricity.

TABLE 2.1
Principles Underlying the Electricity Tutor

Kirchhoff's Laws

1.	The current at one point in an uninterrupted wire is equal to the current at another point in an uninterrupted piece of wire.
2.	The current is the same before and after a voltage source.
3.	The current is the same before and after a resistor.
4.	The current before a resistor is equal to the current after a resistor in a parallel net.
5.	The current in the branches of the parallel net sums to the current in the entire net.
6.	The current in a component is lower than the current for the entire net.
7.	Voltage drop is lower across any single component of a series net than across the whole net.
8.	Voltage drop is lower across any single component of a series net than across the whole net.
9.	Voltage drop is the same across parallel components.
10.	Voltage drop is the same across any component as across the whole parallel net.

Ohm's Laws

11.	Voltage is equal to the current multiplied by the resistance ($V = I \times R$).
12.	When the current goes up/down and the resistance stays the same, this implies that the voltage will go up/down.
13.	Current is equal to voltage divided by resistance ($I = V / R$).
14.	When the voltage goes up/down and the resistance stays the same, this implies that current will go up/down.
15.	Resistance is equal to voltage divided by current ($R = V / I$).

Part 2 of the battery tested qualitative understanding of Ohm's and Kirchhoff's laws. These questions did not require any computations to be performed. Instead, the subject needed to understand the important variable relationships corresponding to the different principles. An example test item can be seen in Fig. 2.5.

Part 3 assessed the degree to which procedural skills were acquired from the tutor. Subjects needed to *apply* Ohm's and Kirchhoff's laws in the solution of different problems. Because test items required computations in their solution, an on-screen calculator was provided. A typical problem presented a circuit, and the subject had to figure out what the reading was (at some point or points) for some component. An example question is shown in Fig. 2.6.

The last test in the criterion battery, Part 4, measured a subject's ability to *generalize knowledge and skills* beyond what was explicitly instructed by the tutor. The subject was required to generate or design circuits to do specific things. An example item from this test is included in Fig. 2.7.

In summary, the four tests measured different aspects of electronics knowledge and skill acquisition. Test 1 measured declarative knowledge understanding; test 2 assessed qualitative knowledge of variable relationships (mental model without procedural skills); test 3 measured quantitative understanding and ability to apply Ohm's law (procedural skills); and test 4 gauged transfer or generalization of skills (mental model with procedural skills).

Is the current from point a to b higher, lower, or equal to the current from point c to d?

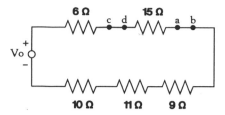

FIG. 2.5. Example item for posttest 2.

In this circuit, the voltage source is 11 volts and the voltage across a to b is 2.14 volts. What is the current flowing from b to c?

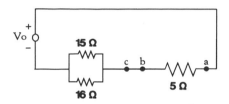

FIG. 2.6. Example item for posttest 3.

What are the resistor values for R_1 and R_2 that will yield a current from a to b of 2.5 amps and a voltage drop from c to d of 14 volts? The voltage source is 24 volts.

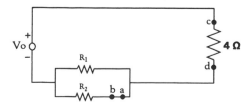

FIG. 2.7. Example item for posttest 4.

Learning Efficiency Measure

Another learning measure used in this study was defined as the total time spent completing the ITS curriculum. This "learning efficiency" measure involved both speed and accuracy because subjects could not proceed to the next principle until they had mastered the current one. Again, the mastery criterion was three consecutive correct responses per principle.

Research Questions

The research questions involving main effects included: (a) Is there an effect of learning environment on subsequent learning outcome? and (b) Is there an effect of learning environment on learning efficiency? I hypothesized that subjects in the rule-application environment would complete the tutor faster, but would not do as well on the posttests compared to subjects in the rule-induction environment. The basis for this belief was that the rule-application environment, by providing subjects explicitly with the relevant principle, was more straightforward and hence easier to get through. On the other hand, the more active participation required by the rule-induction environment was hypothesized to involve more of a time investment but to result in greater learning outcome (see Shute & Glaser, 1990).

The next question concerned the interaction between learning environment and aptitude affecting either learning outcome or learning efficiency. I hypothesized that high-ability subjects (i.e., those with above average associative learning skills) would benefit from the rule-induction environment because it provides more learner control (i.e., independence) compared to the rule-application environment. However, I hypothesized that lower-ability subjects would perform better on the outcome measures if they had learned from the rule-application environment because it provides more structure and support during the learning process than the rule induction environment.

RESULTS

A MANOVA was computed on the four posttest scores as dependent variables, the two pretest scores as covariates (to control statistically for incoming, related knowledge),[7] and environment as an independent variable (coded 0, 1 for rule-application, rule-induction, respectively). A composite AL score (i.e., the average of the nine standardized test scores) was included in the analysis as another independent variable along with the interaction between AL and environment.

Results showed the following. First, there was no main effect of learning

---

[7]Two MANOVAs were actually computed—with and without the pretest data as covariates. In both analyses, the F ratios and significance levels were the same.

TABLE 2.2
Summary Statistics of Posttest Scores, Time-on-Tutor, and Pretest Scores by Environment

Variable	Mean	SD	Minimum	Maximum
Rule-Application (N = 139)				
Posttest 1	73.7	12.1	44.3	96.7
Posttest 2	43.4	27.1	0.0	100.0
Posttest 3	60.8	28.0	0.0	100.0
Posttest 4	19.9	28.2	0.0	100.0
Time-on tutor (h)	11.25	4.2	5.2	25.6
Pretest 1	65.3	11.1	42.9	92.0
Pretest 2	22.7	22.1	0.0	88.3
Rule-Induction (N = 142)				
Posttest 1	74.1	13.5	40.9	98.1
Posttest 2	41.1	26.9	0.0	100.0
Posttest 3	57.2	22.6	0.0	100.0
Posttest 4	14.5	19.4	0.0	100.0
Time-on-tutor (h)	11.29	3.5	5.8	20.32
Pretest 1	64.7	11.1	42.3	92.3
Pretest 2	23.6	21.6	0.0	75.0

environment on learning outcome: $F_{(4,271)} = 1.58$. As can be seen in Table 2.2, the pretest and posttest data were remarkably similar between the two learning environments. Next, there was a significant main effect of AL on outcome: $F_{(4,271)} = 16.06$, $p < .001$. Individuals with high AL scores performed better than low AL subjects, overall, on the posttests. Furthermore, each of the four univariate F ratios was significant beyond the .001 level.

The nonsignificant effect of environment on learning outcome was unanticipated, suggesting that the feedback manipulations were simply too subtle to result in learning outcome differences. It is interesting to note that if I had not analyzed the effects of environment in relation to aptitude levels, I would have erroneously concluded that there was *no difference* between the two environments in terms of their effects on learning outcome. This is not unlike the conclusions reached by Sleeman et al. (1989) and Anderson et al. (1989), discussed earlier. But, in fact, there *was* a significant interaction between AL and environment on learning outcome: $F_{(4,271)} = 5.62$, $p < .001$. So, given this significant (albeit, general) interaction, the next step was to determine more precisely its nature—that is, its pattern across the four posttests.

An interaction term was computed by multiplying the composite AL score by environment (coded 0, 1). Multiple regression analyses were then computed regressing the four posttest scores, individually, on the following variables: AL, environment, AL × environment, Pretest 1, and Pretest 2. The pretest data were included in the equation to statistically control for incoming related knowledge, designed to correspond to the full MANOVA.

TABLE 2.3
Multiple Regression Solution Predicting Posttest 1 Scores (Multiple R = .75)

Variable	Sum of Squares	df	Unique R^2	F	Significance
AL	582.70	1	1.3%	7.97	.005
Environment	2.54	1	0.0%	0.03	.852
AL x Environment	298.73	1	0.7%	4.09	.044
Pretest 1	12,565.70	1	27.5%	171.95	.000
Pretest 2	257.57	1	0.6%	3.52	.062
Model	25,743.05	5	56.3%	70.45	.000
Residual	2,003.69	274	43.7%		

Results from these multiple regression analyses were as follows. Predicting Posttest 1 scores[8] (declarative knowledge acquisition), there were significant main effects of AL and pretest data on outcome, and no main effect of environment. However, of much more interest, a significant interaction appeared involving AL and environment for this outcome measure. These data may be seen in Table 2.3.

To illustrate this interaction, expected values were computed from the regression equation for all four groups of subjects: individuals one standard deviation above and below the mean AL in each of the two learning environments.[9] The results can be seen in the upper left part of Fig. 2.8. The subjects with higher associative learning skills performed better on this declarative knowledge test if they were in the rule-induction environment. However, subjects showing lesser associative learning skills performed better on Posttest 1 if they were in the rule-application environment.

Results from the regression analysis predicting Posttest 2 data (qualitative understanding) showed that the only significant independent variables were the pretest data. There was no main effect due to AL, environment, or the interaction between AL and environment. These data are summarized in Table 2.4. Although nonsignificant, a graph of the interaction data (expected values) is included in Fig. 2.8, upper right quadrant, to illustrate the trend of the interaction, AL by environment, across the four posttests.

Next, the regression analysis computed with Posttest 3 data (procedural skill acquisition) as the dependent variable yielded findings similar to Posttest 1 results, with an interesting twist. Similar to the regression solution predicting Posttest 1 scores, this analysis of Posttest 3 data produced significant main effects due to AL and pretest data, but not to environment. In addition, the

---

[8]The posttest data used in all analyses were the raw scores, as recommended in Cronbach & Snow (1977, pp. 514–515).

[9]Error bars are included in each of the four graphs in Fig. 2-8. These represent the standard error measures per group (i.e., square root of mean-square error divided by N).

TABLE 2.4
Multiple Regression Solution Predicting Posttest 2 Scores (Multiple R = .35)

Variable	Sum of Squares	df	Unique R^2	F	Significance
AL	362.24	1	0.2%	0.55	.457
Environment	651.44	1	0.3%	1.00	.319
AL x Environment	1,004.70	1	0.5%	1.54	.216
Pretest 1	6,537.73	1	3.2%	10.01	.002
Pretest 2	4,233.84	1	2.1%	6.48	.012
Model	24,518.45	5	12.1%	7.50	.000
Residual	179,101.19	274	97.9%		

interaction involving AL and environment predicting Posttest 3 data was also significant. This solution may be seen in Table 2.5. The "twist" was that for this outcome measure, high-AL subjects performed better in the *rule-application* environment than in the *rule-induction* environment. In addition, environment did not affect outcome performance for low-AL subjects. This finding can be compared to Posttest 1 results where high-AL subjects performed better in the *rule-induction* environment than in the *rule-application* environment and low AL subjects performed better in the rule-application environment than in the rule-induction environment. This interaction may be seen in Fig. 2.8, lower left quadrant.

The last finding from this regression analysis involved Posttest 4 data (generalization of skills) as the dependent variable. These results were comparable to those discussed with Posttest 3 data. That is, there were significant main effects due to AL and pretest data, and there was no main effect due to environment. The interaction between AL and environment on Posttest 4 data was also significant (see Table 2.6). Again, high-AL subjects performed significantly better on this more difficult test in the rule-application environment than the rule-induction environment. For lower-AL subjects, environment did not affect performance. This interaction can be seen in Fig. 2.8, lower right quadrant.

TABLE 2.5
Multiple Regression Solution Predicting Posttest 3 Scores (Multiple R = .69)

Variable	Sum of Squares	df	Unique R^2	F	Significance
AL	13,328.79	1	7.4%	38.89	.000
Environment	627.42	1	0.0%	1.83	.177
AL x Environment	1,415.65	1	0.8%	4.13	.043
Pretest 1	26,693.90	1	14.8%	77.88	.000
Pretest 2	2,517.41	1	1.4%	7.35	.007
Model	86,448.52	5	48.0%	50.44	.000
Residual	93,911.80	274	52.0%		

Posttest 1
% Correct

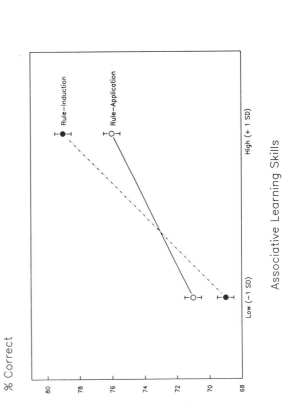

Associative Learning Skills

Posttest 2
% Correct

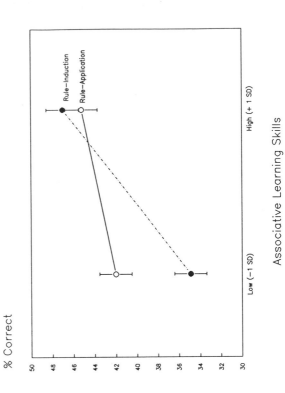

Associative Learning Skills

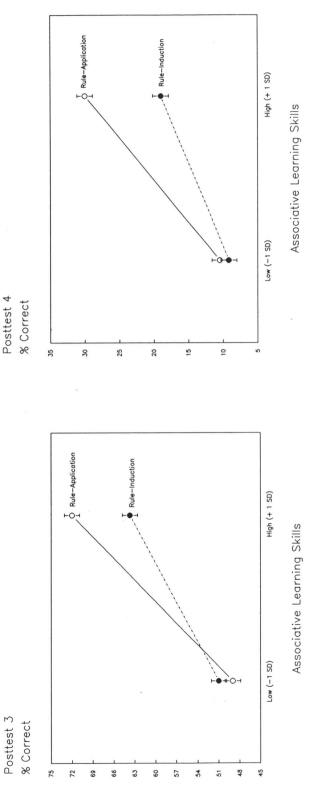

FIG. 2.8. Associative learning ability by environment interactions in relation to four outcome measures.

33

TABLE 2.6
Multiple Regression Solution Predicting Posttest 4 Scores (Multiple $R = .62$)

Variable	Sum of Squares	df	Unique R^2	F	Significance
AL	9,962.94	1	6.1%	27.05	.000
Environment	1,310.86	1	0.9%	3.75	.062
AL x Environment	1,412.56	1	1.0%	3.85	.050
Pretest 1	16,136.37	1	9.8%	43.81	.000
Pretest 2	5,201.54	1	3.2%	14.12	.000
Model	63,447.44	5	38.6%	34.45	.000
Residual	100,925.84	274	61.4%		

Post hoc comparisons were computed in order to establish some basis for the differential relations found between the aptitude-treatment interaction. These consisted of an overall posttest score and three orthogonal contrasts. Average was simply the sum of the four standardized outcome measures: $(Y_1 + Y_2 + Y_3 + Y_4)$. This represented a general outcome factor, independent of type of learning requirements inherent in the individual tests. The first contrast examined performance on Posttests 1 and 2 relative to 3 and 4: $(Y_3 + Y_4) - (Y_1 + Y_2)$. This new variable, *DecPro,* represented a declarative versus procedural distinction because Tests 1 and 2 required conceptual (declarative) understanding of the subject matter, whereas Tests 3 and 4 required procedural skills. The next orthogonal contrast, *MentMod,* compared outcome Measures 2 and 4 against 1 and 3: $(Y_2 + Y_4) - (Y_1 + Y_3)$. Posttests 2 and 4 required subjects to solve problems qualitatively; that is, they had to develop a mental model of how current, voltage and resistance interacted in the solution of a circuit problem. On the other hand, Tests 1 and 3 required a specific response to problems—a word/concept or a number (i.e., retrieval of facts or procedures in the solution process, not the more abstract creation of mental models). Finally, *Last* was defined as the remaining orthogonal contrast: $(Y_1 + Y_4) - (Y_2 + Y_3)$. It was not interpreted in terms of psychological meaning.

The orthogonal contrasts were analyzed with the same MANOVA design as described earlier, except that the *contrasts* (rather than the actual posttests) served as the dependent variables. Results from this MANOVA were as follows. The analysis was first computed for *Average,* and the interaction (AL by environment) was not significant ($F_{(1,274)} = 0.05$; $p = .82$). This was not surprising because combining the posttests obscured differentiating information. Results from the orthogonal contrasts, on the other hand, did reveal a significant aptitude by treatment interaction: $F_{(3,272)} = 7.47$, $p < .001$. The univariate F tests show clearly the basis for this finding. The only significant contrast was *DecPro.* The other contrasts were not significant: *DecPro* ($F_{(1,272)} = 20.07$, $p < .001$); *MentMod* ($F_{(1,272)} = 0.03$, $p = .87$); and *Last* ($F_{(1,272)} = 0.01$, $p = .93$).

Figure 2.9 depicts the AL by environment interaction in relation to the

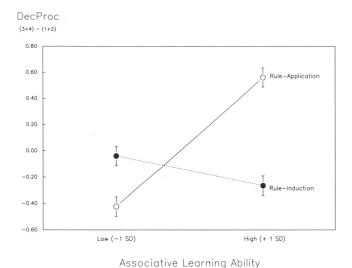

FIG. 2.9. Associative learning ability by environment interactions in relation to declarative/procedural outcome measure.

DecPro contrast.[10] Large positive *DecPro* values reflect higher scores on the more difficult, procedural tests in relation to the simpler declarative knowledge tests. Large negative values imply just the opposite (i.e., higher scores on the declarative than procedural tests). A *DecPro* value of zero indicates no difference between test scores. This figure shows that high-AL subjects acquired new procedural skills better (in relation to declarative knowledge acquisition) if they learned from the rule-application environment. High-AL subjects in the rule-induction environment were greatly impaired with regard to procedural skill acquisition. For low-AL subjects, the contrast between environments was not so great. Large negative *DecPro* values were associated with the rule-application environment, and there were no large positive *DecPro* values for the low-AL subjects. So, in regard to learning outcome, a significant ATI was found. Furthermore, the effects of the interaction differed by type of outcome (e.g., declarative vs. procedural skills).

Was learning efficiency influenced by ATIs? An ANOVA was computed on subjects' time to complete the tutor (dependent variable) by learning environment, aptitude, and the interaction between AL and environment (independent variables). The findings were similar to those reported above with outcome as the criterion. That is, there was no main effect of learning environment on this

---

[10]Expected values ($+1$, -1 standard deviation for high/low AL) were computed from the regression equation and plotted separately by environment. Standard error bars are included for each group.

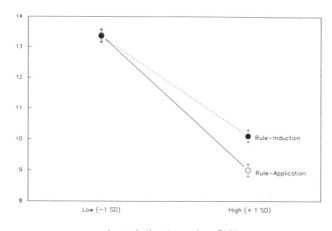

Hours on Tutor

FIG. 2.10. Associative learning ability by environment interactions in relation to time on tutor.

learning efficiency measure [$F_{(1,277)} = 0.01$]. There was a significant main effect due to AL [$F_{(1,277)} = 67.41, p < .001$). Finally, there was a marginally significant interaction between AL and environment $F_{(1,277)} = 3.73, p < .057$).

The same plotting convention was used as with the outcome data: expected values were plotted from the regression equation (regressing hours on AL, environment, and AL × environment) using plus and minus one standard deviation to represent high- and low-AL groups. Error bars are included for each group in the graph (see Fig. 2.10). First note that individuals in both learning environments took, on average, about the same amount of time to complete the curriculum (see Table 2.2). However, when AL was included in the analysis, the results showed that the rule-application environment was associated with more "efficient" behavior (i.e., it took less time to complete). This was true for the high-AL subjects but not for the low-AL subjects.

DISCUSSION

Three studies involving learning environment manipulations were discussed in this chapter. None of the three showed main effects of environment on outcome performance for different domains. First, Sleeman et al. (1989) reported no main effects on high school students' learning of algebra when they compared two types of mediation techniques (i.e., model-based remediation versus reteaching the subject matter). Second, Anderson et al. (1989) reported no main effects of student- versus tutor-controlled feedback on an outcome quiz measuring acquisition of LISP procedures. Third, in the study reported in this chapter, no main effects were found between the inductive versus more applied learning environments in terms of acquiring basic principles of electricity. However, when associative learning data were examined in relation to learning electricity principles, then learning environments did appear to be differentially effective.

In the focal study, I created two different learning environments (i.e., rule-application and rule-induction) to systematically examine possible aptitude-treatment interactions. Four outcome measures were developed to assess declarative knowledge (Tests 1 and 2) and procedural skill (Tests 3 and 4) acquisition. The four main results were as follows:

Declarative Knowledge Acquisition:
1. High-ability subjects learned more if they had been assigned to the rule-induction environment, and
2. Low-ability subjects learned more if they had been assigned to the rule-application environment.

Procedural Skill Acquisition:
3. High-ability subjects developed more skill if they had been assigned to the rule-application environment, and
4. Low-ability subjects performed poorly on the procedural skills tests, regardless of learning environment.

To understand these findings, consider the cognitive activities invoked by each environment in conjunction with the learning outcome being assessed and the cognitive abilities of the learner. For example, the rule-induction environment invoked declarative representations. Learners had to first understand the concepts involved in a given problem, then formulate a rule by connecting relevant concepts together in a meaningful way. To illustrate, an early, relatively simple principle to be learned was: The current is the same before and after a resistor. In the inductive environment, learners would receive a problem involving this principle. They had to determine the relevant variables embedded in the problem (i.e., current and resistance), then induce the functional relationships—what happens to current after it crosses a resistor (i.e., increases, decreases, or stays the same). Finally, they had to verify whether this relationship held up in related problems involving current and resistors. Cognitive resources would thus be wrapped up in elaborative processing and testing.

High-ability subjects in the inductive environment performed well on the declarative knowledge tests (Finding 1). A possible explanation is that there was a good match among learning environment, outcome measure, and cognitive ability: (a) the rule-induction environment supported declarative representations, (b) the outcome tests required accessing declarative representations, and (c) the high-AL subjects possessed relevant cognitive skills.

Another good match accounted for Finding 3. The rule-application environment simply informed learners of the appropriate rule underlying each problem. For related problems, learners promptly applied the rule during the solution process. The cognitive activity supported by this environment was the proceduralization of skills. Subjects with good associative learning skills performed well on the procedural skills tests in the applied environment because (a) the application environment supported proceduralization, (b) the outcome tests required the application of rules and procedures in the solution of problems, and (c) the high-AL subjects possessed good cognitive abilities.

Low-ability individuals acquired more declarative knowledge from the tutor if they were in the rule-application environment (Finding 2) as opposed to the induction environment. This was probably due to its straightforward instructional approach (i.e., the explication of rules). Furthermore, these low-ability subjects' deficient skills were not as burdened as they would have been in the induction environment. Because the computer provided the relevant rules explicitly (and repeatedly), this should have enabled memory for the associated principle, thus enhancing performance on the declarative knowledge tests. When the outcome being measured was procedural, however, neither learning environment enhanced outcome performance for these low-ability subjects. They scored equally poorly (Finding 4).

What are the implications of mismatching conditions? One mismatch between environment, outcome, and subject abilities included high-AL subjects assigned to the rule-application environment and tested on their declarative knowledge acquisition. These subjects performed poorly on declarative knowledge tests compared to high-AL subjects in the inductive environment. This may be explained by ACT* (see Anderson, 1983). That is, when learning a new cognitive skill, initial learning is declarative. With practice, the skill can be executed progressively faster. The cost of this speed-up is the gradual inability to describe the underlying procedures. In other words, as a skill becomes more automatic, the ability to talk about constituent procedures decreases. Because the applied environment fostered proceduralization, and the outcome measured in the mismatch condition was declarative, high-AL subjects may have lost access to the original declarative representation during the process of practicing and proceduralizing new skills.

One other mismatch with negative consequences involved high-AL subjects in the rule-induction environment being tested on procedural skill acquisition. Their procedural skills were significantly worse compared to high-AL individuals from the rule-application environment. The disadvantage of the rule-induction environment in relation to the complex procedural tests was that it did not provide time for necessary practice. Instead, it continued to demand and use cognitive resources in estimating variable relationships. If cognitive resource demands are continually kept high and learners never have the opportunity to practice certain skills, they will inevitably fail on the complex tasks that require high levels of proficiency (see Ackerman, 1988). So the more demanding rule-induction environment simply does not "pay off," except if the outcome measures declarative knowledge acquisition. The rule-application environment, in contrast, does not "waste" cognitive resources in the induction of variable relationships. By providing these relationships to subjects explicitly in the form of specific feedback, learners can proceed immediately to apply them across various circuits. In order to solve the more complex procedural skills tests, a learner must have had sufficient and consistent practice across a variety of circuit types (for more on practice effects, see Regian & Schneider, 1990; Schneider & Shiffrin, 1977).

Relating these findings back to cognitive diagnosis, the question posed earlier concerned which aptitudes should be diagnosed, and when. In the present study, a composite measure of associative learning skill was found to be an informative predictor of various learning outcome measures. Any or all of these tests could be administered prior to ITS instruction. But the decision about what aptitudes to measure should depend on the subject matter being instructed as well as the desired knowledge outcome. For example, suppose you wanted to teach 12th-century English history, and you wanted your students to walk away with declarative (propositional) knowledge. An individual's verbal skills, associative learning skills, and/or general knowledge represent reasonable and relevant aptitudes to assess prior to instruction. As different ITS are tested across a variety of domains, more precise information about important cognitive correlates should be forthcoming. At the Armstrong Laboratory, we have begun this mapping process between cognitive factors and knowledge and skill acquisition in a variety of areas, including logic gates, microeconomics, Pascal programming, principles of electricity, and flight engineering.

In terms of macroadaptation, the pertinent question becomes: Does preliminary aptitude testing increase tutor effectiveness? Although the range of applicability remains an empirical question, results from this study suggest that it potentially can increase performance (i.e., instruction and consequently learning). For instance, consider the following decision rules determining the optimal environment for persons based on their AL score (see Fig. 2.9).

When outcome = *declarative knowledge* (posttests 1 and 2)—If high AL (greater than or equal to the mean AL), then rule-induction environment, else rule-application environment (for low AL).

When outcome = *proceduralization of skills* (posttests 3 and 4)—If high or low AL, then rule-application environment since that environment is better for the high AL subjects and does not effect outcome for low-AL subjects.

Also related to tutor and learner improvements, a pragmatic concern involves the payoff of this proposed approach. There are two parts to this question. The first part concerns the cost of employing the macroadaptive method (i.e., preliminary aptitude testing and global adjustment of environment based on the results). The second part addresses the impact on learning.

The cost of prior testing is minimal. The average time to finish the associative learning tests ranges from 2 to 10 min (mean completion time per test = 4.8 min). In addition, the odd–even reliabilities of these tests are high, ranging from .82 to .98 (mean reliability of all nine tests > .90). The cost associated with altering the tutor's learning environment is also very small. To illustrate, in the electricity tutor discussed in this chapter, simple modifications were made to the feedback, with all else equal. At most, it required 2 hr to rewrite the feedback from the explicated form (e.g., "The principle involved in this kind of problem is that current before a resistor is equal to the current after a resistor in a parallel net") to the more inductive form (e.g., "What you need to know to solve this type of problem is how current behaves, both before and after a resistor, in a parallel net"). The variables remained the same, but the structure of the sentences was altered. This resulted in a single computer program with a yes/no "environment flag" denoting learning environment. In this study, when the program was initialized, the flag was set to either rule-application (environment flag = yes) or rule-induction (environment flag = no). Given the exploratory nature of this study, assignment to learning environment was random. However, the computer could just as easily set the flag itself based on the results from preliminary aptitude testing (i.e., the action taken in response to the evaluation of a decision rule).

To answer the second part of the question concerning the benefit(s) of such an approach, consider the amount of variance explained by these independent variables: AL, environment, AL × environment, Pretest 1 and Pretest 2. These variables accounted for 56% of Posttest 1 outcome variance (declarative knowledge acquisition), 12% of Posttest 2 variance (qualitative understanding), and 48% and 39% of the outcome variance, respectively, for Posttests 3 and 4 (proceduralization and generalization of skills). Also, the AL by environment interaction accounted for unique, significant variance underlying Posttests 1, 3, and 4 (see Tables 2.3, 2.5, and 2.6). These findings suggest that tutor improvements are possible using the appropriate decision rules. Additional analyses are planned that will investigate the relationship(s) among other cognitive process measures (e.g., working-memory capacity, information-processing speed), learning environment, and learning outcome and efficiency measures. This may lead to even more complex and informative decision rules.

The implications of these findings for ITS design are as follows. To teach procedural skills, use a more structured, rule-application environment, allowing for sufficient practice on the skills being instructed. In the present study, high-AL subjects were shown to perform better in this environment, whereas low-AL subjects were not affected by environment. But to teach declarative or conceptual knowledge, assign high-AL subjects to a more self-directed, inductive environment and low-AL subjects to a more tutor-directed, applied environment. The present findings thus go beyond what Anderson et al. (1989) found, that "well-designed feedback can minimize the time and pain of learning but has no effect on final instructional outcome" (p. 498). In fact, feedback may affect final outcome performance, but it depends on learner traits as well as the outcome measures.

A number of empirical research questions remain. What are the characteristics of learners who perform better in what types of learning environments? Are certain domains better suited for specific instructional methods? At what point should feedback be provided, what should it say, how is it best presented, and what is the relationship of feedback to learner characteristics? How much learner control should be allowed? What other learner attributes influence outcome performance (e.g., motivation, interests, activity level, independence). Do the same aptitudes predict learning outcome and efficiency across various subject matters? What treatment effects should be manipulated and how?

ATI research, conducted with ITS, can help answer some of these questions. Furthermore, the learning skills taxonomy (Kyllonen & Shute, 1989) provides a framework for conducting systematic and controlled ATI studies that was not possible prior to the arrival of ITSs. Instead of continuing to add to the growing pool of ITSs, the field can profit from controlled research altering, systematically, the design of existing ones and evaluating the results of those changes in accordance with a principled approach. Results from this study showed that different learning environments are differentially effective for learners; however, treatment conditions mostly affected the performance of high ability subjects. Research is needed to determine what kinds of environments promote learning for low-ability persons, precisely the population that needs help the most.

REFERENCES

Ackerman, P. L. (1988). Determinants of individual differences during skill acquisition: Cognitive abilities and information processing. *Journal of Experimental Psychology: General, 117,* 288–318.

Anderson, J. R. (1983). *The architecture of cognition.* Cambridge, MA: Harvard University Press.

Anderson, J. R., Conrad, F. G., & Corbett, A. T. (1989). Skill acquisition and the LISP tutor. *Cognitive Science, 13*(4), 467–505.

Bunderson, V. C., & Olsen, J. B. (1983). *Mental errors in arithmetic skills: Their diagnosis in precollege students* (Final project report, NSF SED 80-125000). Provo, UT: WICAT Education Institution.

Campbell, V. N. (1964). Self-direction and programmed instruction for five different types of learning objectives. *Psychology in the Schools, 1,* 348–359.

Chase, W. G., & Simon, H. A. (1973). The mind's eye in chess. In W. G. Chase (Ed.), *Visual information processing* (pp. 215–281). New York: Academic Press.

Chi, M. T. H., Glaser, R., & Rees, E. (1982). Expertise in problem solving. In R. Sternberg (Ed.), *Advances in the psychology of human intelligence* (Vol. 1, pp. 7–75). Hillsdale, NJ: Lawrence Erlbaum Associates.

Clancey, W. J. (1986). *Intelligent tutoring systems: A tutorial survey* (Report No. KSL-86-58). Stanford, CA: Stanford University.

Cronbach, L. J., & Snow, R. E. (1977). *Aptitudes and instructional methods: A handbook for research on interactions.* New York: Irvington.

Kyllonen, P. C., & Christal, R. E. (1990). Cognitive modeling of learning abilities: A status report of LAMP. In R. Dillon & J. W. Pellegrino (Eds.), *Testing: Theoretical and applied issues* (pp. 112–137). San Francisco: Freeman.

Kyllonen, P. C., & Shute, V. J. (1989). A taxonomy of learning skills. In P. L. Ackerman, R. J. Sternberg, & R. Glaser (Eds.), *Learning and individual differences* (pp. 117–163). New York: Freeman.

Kyllonen, P. C., & Tirre, W. C. (1988). Individual differences in associative learning and forgetting. *Intelligence, 12,* 393–421.

Kyllonen, P. C., Woltz, D. J., Christal, R. E., Shute, V. J., Tirre, W. C., & Chaiken, S. (1990). *CAM-4: Computerized battery of cognitive ability tests.* Unpublished computer program, Brooks Air Force Base, TX.

Lesgold, A. M., Bonar, J., Ivill, J., & Bowen, A. (1989). An intelligent tutoring system for electronics troubleshooting: DC-circuit understanding. In L. Resnick (Ed.), *Knowing and learning: Issues for the cognitive psychology of instruction* (pp. 29–53). Hillsdale, NJ: Lawrence Erlbaum Associates.

Malmi, R. A., Underwood, B. J., & Carroll, J. B. (1979). The interrelationships among some associative learning tasks. *Bulletin of the Psychonomic Society, 13,* 121–123.

Regian, J. W., & Schneider, W. (1990). Assessment procedures for predicting and optimizing skill acquisition. In N. Fredericksen, R. Glasser, A. Lesgold, & M. Shafto (Eds.), *Diagnostic monitoring of skill and knowledge acquisition* (pp. 297–323). Hillsdale, NJ: Lawrence Erlbaum Associates.

Schneider, W., & Shiffrin, R. M. (1977). Controlled and automatic human information processing: Detection, search, and attention. *Psychological Review, 84,* 1–66.

Shute, V. J. (1990). *A comparison of rule-induction and rule-application learning environments: Which is better for whom and why?* Paper presented at the American Educational Research Association (AERA), Boston, MA.

Shute, V. J. (1991). Who is likely to acquire programming skills? *Journal of Educational Computing Research, 7*(1), 1–24.

Shute, V. J., & Glaser, R. (1990). A large-scale evaluation of an intelligent discovery world: Smithtown. *Interactive Learning Environments, 1*(1), 51–77.

Shute, V. J., Glaser, R., & Raghavan, K. (1989). Inference and discovery in an exploratory laboratory. In P. L. Ackerman, R. J. Sternberg, & R. Glaser (Eds.), *Learning and individual differences* (pp. 279–326). San Francisco: Freeman.

Siegler, R. S., & Richards, D. D. (1982). The development of intelligence. In R. J. Sternberg (Ed.), *Handbook of human intelligence* (pp. 897–971). Cambridge, England: Cambridge University Press.

Sleeman, D. (1987). PIXIE: A shell for developing intelligent tutoring systems. In R. W. Lawler & M. Yazdani (Eds.), *Artificial intelligence and education* (vol. 1, pp. 239–265). Norwood, NJ: Ablex.

Sleeman, D., & Brown, J. S. (1982). *Intelligent tutoring systems.* London: Academic Press.

Sleeman, D., Kelly, A. E., Martinak, R., Ward, R. D., & Moore, J. L. (1989). Studies of diagnosis and remediation with high school algebra students. *Cognitive Science, 13*(4), 551–568.

Snow, R. E. (1990). Toward assessment of cognitive and conative structures in learning. *Educational Researcher, 18*(9), 8–14.

Swan, M. B. (1983). *Teaching decimal place value. A comparative study of conflict and positively-only approaches* (Research Report No. 31). Nottingham, England: University of Nottingham, Sheel Center for Mathematical Education.

Underwood, B. J. (1975). Individual differences as a crucible in theory construction. *American Psychologist, 30,* 128–134.

Underwood, B. J., Boruch, R. F., & Malmi, R. A. (1978). Composition of episodic memory. *Journal of Experimental Psychology: General, 107,* 393–419.

Wenger, E. (1987). *Artificial intelligence and tutoring systems*. Los Altos, CA: Morgan Kaufmann Publishers.

TRANSCRIPTION OF DISCUSSION

John Anderson: That was very nice data. In our study that you mentioned, we didn't find aptitude-treatment interactions, but our students all have Math SAT scores around 600–800 (so no aptitude variance). Although we have not been able to identify such interactions, for a long time we've had a suspicion that there was a trade-off going on with respect to learning. Some situations call for students to work out things themselves. And there is a whole lot of research suggesting that better memory results when you generate answers yourself rather than being told things. On the other hand, if you can't generate the answers yourself, then obviously you have to be told. We have been struggling with ways to do this. We think this happens on an item-by-item basis. Even within a particular student, there are going to be problems that the student can't actually solve, and other points of difficulty that they can't control. In that direction, we've been trying to adapt instruction on a problem-by-problem basis. This might be a reasonable way of organizing your results. That is, when it's the case that students are having difficulty, then a more direct approach helps. But, in general, leaving problem solution more in the students' hands is positive. In the first study, you analyzed different learning outcome measures. In the case where the questions were easy (the declarative questions), high-aptitude students were doing better in a more discovery-based environment. But then, when the questions were getting presumably more difficult, even for the high-ability students, that was the point in which more directed instruction was needed.

Val Shute: That's a pretty good summary. What I envision is a kind of *interplay* between macro- and microadaptation. I think that the problem-by-problem adaptation of instruction that you mentioned is a good idea. This takes place during the learning process where the computer deals with each problem-solving episode individually. That's what I think of as "microadaptation." But the nature of these low-level computer responses is a function of "macroadaption." Suppose you had information about a student, like she had a high aptitude. And you also had a specific learning goal in mind, like the student should be able to effortlessly apply Ohm's law in solving circuit problems. The results from my research suggest that she should be placed in a more applied learning environment to achieve the goal state. This environment would provide her with the principles and the time to practice solving circuit problems rather than making her spend time inducing principles first. Although these were exploratory studies, it seems that both micro- and macroadaption may be important in terms of optimizing learning.

Dan Fisk: Can you tell me a little bit more about what the associative learning tasks are and how they relate to a measure I might be familiar with?

Val Shute: These computerized tests measure how quickly a person can form associations between different things, like words, numbers, or geometric shapes. For example, one of the verbal associative learning tests showed subjects eight pairs of words at the top of the screen that they had to remember. The pairings between the words always stayed the same and always remained at the top of the screen, but for each new test item, the pairs appeared in random order. Subjects had to answer true/false questions presented at the bottom of the screen, like: lawyer/bed? For subjects to answer the questions quickly and accurately, they needed to memorize the top pairs so they wouldn't have to keep looking up and searching through the list.

Dan Fisk: And how they relate to other measures?

Val Shute: The associative learning tests were all pretty highly correlated with one another (from .3 to .7) and the odd–even reliabilities of these tests were all above .95. The relation to the other cognitive factors showed these tests correlated most highly with working memory (.6), general knowledge (.5), and inductive reasoning skills (.5).

Jim Pellegrino: Were your primary dimensions operating in your analyses of cognitive abilities the abilities themselves or the content domain?

Val Shute: I've done some analyses that show the data cluster more on the process than the content dimension. For example, when I computed a factor analysis on all of the test data, three factors emerged. But the factors weren't verbal, quantitative, and spatial. Instead, they were (a) working memory and associative learning skills, (b) general knowledge and inductive reasoning skills, and (c) processing speed. Within each factor, all content domains were mixed up. This factor analysis accounted for a whole bunch of the variance (75%).

Bill Johnson: As I got my presentation material together, I asked myself what a human tutor would do at any given point in an instructional scenario. When I think about aptitude, a human tutor knows the general characteristics about the population that he or she is training. We know that they have X number of years of school, it is an environment where they have 2 or 3 years of on-the-job experience, and they understand some of the prerequisites coming in. Therefore, the human tutor can predict some of the aptitude. Now you use a pretest battery of tests to understand what some of the aptitudes are. I guess my question is: What does an intelligent tutor system do at the very beginning? I know that Doug Towne's system asks a student what his or her skill level is. That's a good idea, but what are some other ways early on what would help assess what the student's aptitude is, make adjustments, and then decide what kind of tutoring to provide?

Val Shute: That's a really good question. I think that the answer depends on what you want to teach and what you want your students to walk away with. That information would constrain the decision about what to assess. For example, if you wanted to teach conceptual understanding of Ohm's law, then the computer could administer a 20- to 30-minute test measuring verbal aptitude, like word knowledge or associative learning skills. Results from that testing would inform the tutor about which environment would be best. By using tutors that teach different domains by different instructional methods, I'd like to be able to figure out the best combinations among domain, learning environment, and desired knowledge outcome. I suspect that some learning environments may be better for certain domains with specific knowledge outcomes in mind. So more empirical studies can begin filling in the missing pieces of this puzzle, and we might eventually be able to really constrain decisions about how to teach a particular person. Right now I'm just limited to talking about teaching electricity and Pascal programming and have only tested two contrasting environments (inductive and applied).

John Anderson: In the university environment, most people actually walk in with lots of good measures. Is that true in other environments too?

Val Shute: If by "good measures" you mean "high aptitudes," then I guess other environments are comparable. Sometimes I test Air Force recruits. These people are selected on the basis of their ASVAB scores, so there is a selection criterion, but not as high as, say, Carnegie-Mellon students. The subject populations I use in my large-scale studies are not university students or Air Force recruits. They come from temporary employment agencies. So my subjects are students, housewives, unemployed carpenters, and "others." These people are very heterogeneous, showing a range on all the aptitude measures. And there are lots of individual differences on the outcome measures as well.

Alan Lesgold: I have two questions. It seems to me that calling this an "aptitude issue" is a peculiar convenience. I think, although I could be mistaken, the model you are heading toward is sort of a Swellard-like model, that says that people are lacking certain capabilities. There is too much stuff to do in the *middle* of problem solving, and if you give them one more thing to do, we simply overburden them. We might be better off figuring out for them what information they need. And then giving them that information rather than giving them the extra burden of trying to figure out what information to go after, and when to try to figure something out on their own. If that's the case, then the question arises: "What is the utility of the aptitude approach?" The aptitude approach says that, for some reason, we think we would like to measure enduring characteristics of these folks and then use an instructional strategy that is tailored to those enduring characteristics. The alternative would be to try to find ways to assess information about people while they are in the middle of doing complex activities, when they're being swamped by the burdens that are being placed on them by the instructional approach, and essentially microadapting. You made a strong case for adapting and I'm inclined to believe it. The reason I would raise the possibility of microadapting is that there is just a chance that this ability to, this sort of "learning to learn" capability that is involved in inductive learning, might be part of (somewhere in the back of your mind) what you think you are teaching. In particular, what about teaching Air Force jobs, where you hope that if they suddenly need to do a different job, they can pick it up fairly quickly without too much formal instruction. When you choose to go the route of *macroadapting,* saying that we are going to give you the rules and be as efficient as possible, are you costing people anything? I don't know the answer to that. You showed us that adaptation is important, but have you showed us that macroadaptation is preferable to some more micro-oriented or some more domain-centered adaptation?

Doug Towne: Of course, they don't have to be mutually exclusive either.

Val Shute: I view micro- and macroadaptation as complementary approaches, hand-in-glove, rather than being mutually exclusive. Now, with macroadaptation, I have seen a lot of instances where people placed in an inductive environment (like Smithtown) either thrive and do well, or just flounder around and do poorly. For some people, garden paths are fruitful, more fruitful than, say, the straight and narrow. For example, when I get new software, I rarely open the manual, but I learn a lot just by trial and error. But other people do better in a directed environment. If we just default to using inductive kinds of environments, then that would only benefit some folks, and impede learning for others. Also, by using this macro- and microadaptive approach, if we select a learning environment at the outset based on aptitude data but the learning-in-progress data indicate that it's not being effective, well, nothing is written in stone. In other words, there's no reason why the learning environment couldn't be switched midstream, why the computer couldn't make another "macro" decision rule later on based on new information. So microadaptation is always going on, and macroadaptation can occur at the outset of learning, and possibly during the course of learning. So there's a constant interplay between micro- and macroadaptive responses.

Walt Schneider: I'm kind of concerned that after 30 years of searching for aptitude-treatment interactions, so many studies were below the level of statistical chance. So going after it now, anew, should be at least somewhat concerning. In the cases that you've illustrated, for example, one out of the four cases looks like an interaction. You have not just one test, there were a number of aptitudes you compared to a number of treatments, so how do you do the post hoc verification, whether there is anything there, is iffy at best. In order to have a chance at being able to impact an instructional domain, first you have to be able to have an a priori specification of an aptitude-treatment interaction. Then you have to be able to design a number of tutor systems that do all of those treatments so you have now increased your costs, perhaps significantly. The trick is coming up with an a priori interaction. I totally agree that, particularly in the military environment, you have lots of aptitude measures that just come in for free. Recruits come in and the first thing you do is test them. If there is something there, you need to be able to show when that treatment will be true and when it will be generalizable, so that it can impact the next person's tutor. In each case that you deal with, you need to figure out how to specify the decision rules. What is your reason for optimism?

Val Shute: My reasons for optimism are because the older ATI studies, hundreds of which are reviewed in Cronbach and Snow's 1977 book, are filled with confounded, noisy data. Those studies used different classrooms, different teachers with different personalities, different instructional materials that weren't controlled, and so on. A whole lot of noise entered into the equation so I'm not surprised that there were so few significant ATIs reported. But with ITSs, you can control these variables. I guess my optimism is partly innate, but also springs from having been successful in finding several significant aptitude-treatment interactions. And actually my tests were very conservative. I may have given the wrong impression that I just tested a bunch of interactions until I found some that were significant. That's not what I did. What I *did* was first compute a MANOVA and found that the overall aptitude by environment interaction was significant for all outcome measures considered simultaneously. That permitted me to then zoom in on the data, and I chose to start with a really basic ability: associative learning skill. So the MANOVA told me that, yes, there is something there, in general. This macro/microadaptive approach does provide a systematic way of fitting learning environments to individuals to optimize learning, which is the name of the game in ITS design.

Dan Fisk: But your optimism for generalizing these findings still has to be somewhat task specific.

Val Shute: Yes, absolutely. I am limited to only speaking about teaching different aspects of electricity, like conceptual knowledge or procedural skills. But the approach provides a framework for conducting additional studies, those that can systematically permute various things like learning environment and domain. Then I can collect more data and start making generalizations. I've just completed another large-scale study with a tutor that teaches flight engineering skills. I developed alternative learning environments, and have found some tantalizing ATIs involving working-memory capacity and general knowledge by different learning environments. But that's a story for another time.

3 Possibilities for Assessment Using Computer-Based Apprenticeship Environments

Alan Lesgold
Gary Eggan
Sandra Katz
Govinda Rao
University of Pittsburgh

Over the past decade or so, two distinct strands of work have produced promising results for the technical training world. On the technology side, there has been a significant advance in our ability to build intelligent instructional systems, systems that interact with students based on a pedagogical strategy that is applied to a model of the knowledge being taught and the current knowledge of the student. Although there are real questions arising concerning the utility and tractability of student modeling in intelligent computer-based instruction, there is no question that current systems can do much more effective training than was possible in the past. In particular, the emergence of multiple levels of simulator technology, from full-fidelity cockpit simulators to partial simulations of simpler mechanical and electronic devices, has been an important contribution to efficient training of complex skills.

A second strand of work has focused on how learning takes place in the absence of formal schooling. Apprenticeships, both formal and informal, have been the object of much of this strand's efforts, and it is now clear that "learning by doing" deserves to play a larger role in organized training efforts. When people have real tasks to accomplish, motivation is less of a problem than when they simply have exercises to practice. Equally important, when knowledge is anchored in experience, then it becomes more than sentences to be memorized: The sentences have meaning for the trainee because they are rooted in his or her personal experience. A third reason for apprenticeships is that the social structure of multiperson work affords opportunities for supporting complex skills while they become more automated. In the delicate period during which a trainee knows more or less what to do in a problem situation but is unable to keep track of his efforts because each requires focused attention to be carried out successfully, coworkers and "masters" become supportive external memories that share the attentional load while still affording opportunities for practice. Perhaps most important, apprenticeship affords opportunities for the master or coach to provide knowledge in the context of its use, so that the trainee learns both what to do and when to do it.

In the informal social structure of a master working with apprentices, performance assessment is not really a problem. The apprentice's work is readily observable, as is the amount of support it requires from others. In some cultures, including certain American Indian tribes, the apprentice himself will publicly announce when he is able to carry out certain tasks on his own, verifying the observations of his co-workers. In our high-technology society, where performance and performance capability are often rewarded highly, assessment needs to be done more formally, especially in public institutions that have a responsibility to treat all employees equally and to be accountable for this.

We decided that it would be useful to blend intelligent simulation and training technology with apprenticeship, hopefully to get the best of both. The realistic work of the apprentice can be emulated by presenting the trainee with tasks he would like to be able to perform, using simulator technology. Further, the support and coaching that a human master might supply to an apprentice can be provided via intelligent systems, we believe, producing a system with most of the good properties of human apprenticeships. On the assessment side, such a system can record both the performance of the trainee and the assistance that was needed to support that performance. Thus, it can make available exactly the information that a master would have for evaluating an apprentice's progress, but this performance trace is explicit and replayable. By applying policy-capturing techniques to expert ratings of such performance traces (Nichols, Pokorny, Jones, Gott, & Alley, in press), we can achieve replicable and auditable assessments of competence, on which employment decisions can be made.

As a byproduct of this approach, an additional form of learning is supported. Very often, we learn from analyzing what we have done, how well it worked, and what other, better, approaches there might have been. Once a training system is recording the details of a trainee's performance and also knows enough to demonstrate expert performance, then it has, in principle, all of the knowledge needed to support reflective opportunities for a trainee, in which he might replay and study his performance and compare it to that of an expert. Thus, performance assessment, as we envision it, also supports better learning.

THE SHERLOCK TROUBLESHOOTING TUTORS

To test our ideas, we have developed intelligent coached practice environments for the F-15 Manual Avionics Test Station job. This job involves the use of test stations to diagnose failures of certain navigational electronic equipment from the

F-15 aircraft. A test station is a large switching system like a telephone exchange that permits tests to be carried out on an aircraft component. A test, in electronics troubleshooting, involves applying some type of current to certain pins of the unit under test (UUT) and making a measurement of the output from certain other pins. By setting switches, an airman configures the test station to supply the appropriate current to the right UUT pins, to set a measurement device (e.g., a multimeter or an oscilloscope) appropriately, and to connect the measurement device to the right output pins of the UUT. Sometimes a load is added to the test circuit as well. Because the switching is done manually by the airman, the test station for which we did our work is called a manual test station. On other systems, a computer running a diagnostic program generates the signals that effect switching. These are called automatic test stations.

Airmen do not find it difficult, after basic electronics training, to test aircraft components. Either the work is done by a computer program, or, in the case of the manual test station, there are printed Technical Orders that tell the airman which switches to set to which values. On the other hand, when the test station itself breaks, the airman has a real problem to solve. In principle, he[1] could use printed confidence testing procedures to isolate a test station failure, but these take far too long to run. Instead, he must consider what the test station was trying to do when it failed, develop a mental representation of the circuitry involved in the failed function, and develop a plan for testing that functional circuit. If he can do this, the problem is reduced to finding the fault in a system of perhaps a dozen printed circuit boards, where each board has only a small part of its circuitry involved. If he cannot do this, he finds himself searching for the fault in a system with tens of thousands of parts.

A coached practice environment must provide a simulation of the work environment in which complex problem solving takes place, in this case of the test station as a circuit that can itself be tested with external measurement devices.[2] The simulation must be rich enough to afford opportunities for nontrivial practice, that is, practice of problems beyond the current capability of the trainee. In addition, tools should be provided to optimize learning. Such tools can include coaching of student problem-solving performance, assessment (modeling) of student strengths and weaknesses, and problem assignment driven by such assessments. Other possibilities exist, too, such as informational lessons to fill specific knowledge gaps (for example, a refresher on how to use an oscilloscope might be added to an electronics troubleshooting practice environment).

---

[1]We use the pronoun *he* for simplicity. A significant minority of trainees were female.

[2]Actually, the test station's own internal measurement devices are sometimes usable for testing parts of the test station itself. For example, the oscilloscope has leads that can be applied to test points on other parts of the station.

Sherlock I

The Sherlock family of coached practice environments is a concrete realization of this design idea. So far, there is a tested first-generation system, Sherlock I, and a second-generation system that is about to be completed, Sherlock II.[3] Sherlock I[4] was our first effort to field an intelligent coached practice environment. Like any first effort, it involved a number of compromises, largely driven by equipment limitations and by the need for our clients, the Air Force, to get an early sense of whether the concept of an intelligent coached practice environment was worth pursuing. Sherlock I runs on Xerox AI workstations and is written in Loops, an object-oriented programming language layered on top of InterLISP-D. The choice of languages was dictated by equipment available at the time we began the project, but the use of an object-oriented approach is central to the design philosophy as it has developed.

Sherlock I provided a partial device simulation that was rather limited, but it proved to be a powerful training approach. The front panels of the test station were fully simulated, so that their displays changed as switches were "flipped" (via the mouse) or their knobs were turned. For example, one could rescale the oscilloscope or set the digital multimeter to measure voltage instead of resistance. One could also "open up" the test station and make measurements on its internal circuits with an oscilloscope or "handheld" multimeter. The interface for these simulated measurements was a library of schematic diagrams that reproduced sections of the real device schematics. One pointed to pin numbers and other connection points to indicate where a simulated meter probe should be placed. Appropriate values were retrieved from a table of relevant test values.

This led to some problems that were relatively minor with respect to training effect but important for user acceptance. Measurement values were placed in the

---

[3]Sherlock II is being developed by a team that has included (either currently or in the recent past) Marilyn Bunzo, Richard Eastman, Gary Eggan, Maria Gordin, Linda Greenberg, Edward Hughes, Sandra Katz, Susanne Lajoie, Alan Lesgold, Thomas McGinnis, Rudi Prabowo, and Govinda Rao, and Rose Rosenfeld. It is funded by the Air Force through subcontracts from Advanced Technology, Inc., Hay Systems, and Metrica, Inc. Dr. Sherrie Gott and her colleagues at the Air Force Human Resources Laboratory (AFHRL) are active colleagues in this effort.

[4]Sherlock I was done as part of subcontracts with HumRRO and Universal Energy Systems, who were prime contractors with the Air Force Human Resources Laboratory. Early investments in the possibility of intelligent instructional systems and in cognitive research to support them were made by the Office of Naval Research, notably Henry Halff, Susan Chipman, Marshall Farr, and Michael Shafto. The system designers and developers were Alan Lesgold, Susanne Lajoie, Marilyn Bunzo, and Gary Eggan. Joining us in the effort at one point or another were Jaya Bajpayee, Jeffrey Bonar, Lloyd Bond, James Collins, Keith Curran, Richard Eastman, Drew Gitomer, Robert Glaser, Bruce Glymour, Linda Greenberg, Denise Lensky, Debra Logan, Maria Magone, Tom McGinnis, Valerie Shalin, Cassandra Stanley, Arlene Weiner, Richard Wolf, and Laurie Yengo. Equally important were Sherrie Gott and others at the Air Force Human Resources Laboratory, Dennis Collins and other Air Force subject matter experts who helped us when we needed it most, and the officers and personnel of the 1st and 33rd Tactical Fighter Wings, at Langley and Eglin Air Force Bases.

tables for a given fault isolation problem only if they were relevant to problem solution, that is, on the functional circuit path for the particular function the test station had failed. As a result, a novice trainee who attempted to measure something irrelevant would be told that the measurement was not relevant. Of course, there are borderline calls, and a few airmen who were already rather expert found values that they could argue were relevant but that were still not available. This is an inevitable problem with "canned" feedback, whether from a device simulation or a coach.

Student modeling also had limitations. For each problem, Sherlock I contained an and/or goal-structure tree. The top-level goal, solving that problem, might be satisfied, in whole or in part, through several different approaches. Any given goal in the tree, more generally, could be satisfied by one of possibly several approaches (the "or" aspect of the tree), each of which might contain several subgoals (the "and" aspect of the tree). If a given goal in the tree was one held by experts, then it could be satisfied by at least one approach called an expert move. On occasion, there were multiple expert ways of satisfying the goals. This was handled via the "or" possibility in the and/or graph, combined with a slot in each subgoal object that marked whether it was an expert approach or not. Additional alternatives, if any, represented likely approaches to the sub-problem by nonexperts and were so marked. For example, if a goal was to isolate a fault to a linear sequence of components, then the expert move might be "space splitting," testing near the middle of the circuit path to isolate the fault to one half or the other. A novice approach might be to start testing at one end of the path and test until the fault was found.

A student's performance could then be characterized in terms of how good his moves were at each subgoal node of the goal structure that his performance "touched." We used only three performance ratings: Good, OK, and Bad, re-flecting expert, acceptable nonexpert, and wrong moves, respectively. We hand coded, for each node of the goal tree for each separate problem, a list of knowledge components we thought were needed to attain the given goal. Table 3.1 gives two examples of the assignment of knowledge components to perfor-mance subgoals. For each student, we maintained a student competence model, which was simply a rating of competence for each knowledge component on our list. We used four rating categories for knowledge components: Unlearned, Per-haps, Probably, and Strong.

These categories corresponded roughly to the stages of Anderson's (1983) ACT model. The notion is that when a piece of knowledge is first manifested, it may be due to a fluke (right action; wrong situation representation). Thus, multiple correct performances were needed to move to the probably level. Fur-ther, the move to strong was assumed to require extended practice, so it was made conservatively. When the student began a problem, a predicted perfor-mance model would be generated by estimating how well the student might do on each subgoal of the goal tree. The estimate for a given node was essentially an

TABLE 3.1
Examples of Mapping From Task Subgoals to Curriculum Knowledge Components

---

Subgoal: Test A1A3A1 Circuit Card Option A

Choose correct test equipment and set up properly
Use digital multimeter correctly for continuity test
Select correct test points
Know direction of signal flow
Interpret test results

Subgoal: Plan Test for RAG Drawer

Space splitting
Hypothetical reasoning
TO search and analysis
Understanding how to go from schematics to circuit card
Trace signal through drawer
Know direction of signal flow
Functional chunking of circuit diagram

---

average of the ratings of the student on the knowledge components listed for that node. After the student completed the problem, the actual performance was compared node by node with the expected performance, and the ratings for knowledge components associated with a node were adjusted to reflect the student's actual performance.

Hints were also associated with the alternatives at any node in the goal tree. Further, the expected performance model was used to tailor advice. If a student was expected to do well at a given node, he was given advice sparingly; if not, he was given richer advice. By repeatedly asking for help at the same point in the problem, a student could eventually access all available advice, but the variable inertia in providing detailed "here's what to do" information was designed to force students to think on their own when the expected performance model predicted that this could be successful. This approach worked so well that it was unusual for students to ask for more than one or two hints at a given point.

Evaluation of Sherlock I.   Overall, Sherlock I was excessively rigid but remarkably successful. Because the goal structures for each problem were hand coded and many hints were specific statements written in advance, the system was not very extensible, and the interaction between trainee and machine was somewhat rigid. However, the bottom line is that 20–25 hr of Sherlock I practice time produced average improvements that were, in many respects, equivalent to the effects of 4 years on the job.

Given the focus of this volume, we expand on the evaluation approach a bit. The goal of Sherlock I was to train the ability to diagnose test station faults, the hardest part of the F-15 manual test station job. We[5] used simulated test station diagnosis problems in the field evaluation (see Nichols et al., in press, or Gott, 1989, for details). Virtually all of the job incumbents at two Air Force bases participated in the evaluation, a total of 32 airmen in their first 4-year term and 13 at more advanced levels. The 32 first-termers were split into an experimental and a control group of 16 each. This was done by matching pairs on their ASVAB electronics subscores. As an accident of this matching, the experimental group had a mean experience of 28 months in the Air Force, while the control group had a mean of 37 months. This difference was not significant and was due to high variance in experience levels. The advanced group had about 6 more years of experience, a mean of 114 months. The simulated test station diagnosis problems were presented verbally. An example problem is the following:

> While running a Video Control Panel unit, Test Step 3.e fails. The panel lamps do not illuminate. All previous test steps have passed.

In such a situation, the unit being tested is usually defective, but as the problem-solving situation unfolds in this particular case, it turns out that a relay card in the test station is bad. This type of problem is one that is extremely difficult for novice technicians. In the evaluation study, the technician would hear the problem statement and then be asked two questions: What would you do next? and Why would you do that? He would then be told the result of his action and the cycle of questioning would repeat until the problem was solved or an impasse was reached. Verbal protocols of these problem-solving interviews were then given to two Air Force experts who scored them blind to the condition assignments of the subjects. Using policy capturing techniques, scoring scales were derived from expert rankings of the problem-solving performances (discussed later).

Figure 3.1 shows the results. Given group standard deviations ranging from 12 to 29, the results show that the experimental and control group pretest means and the control group posttest mean are at one level and the experimental posttest mean and the advanced group mean are at a second, much higher, level. The data were also considered from a second viewpoint, the amount of on-the-job experience needed to produce gains equivalent to those produced by the Sherlock experience of 20–25 hr of coached practice. The pretest data was used to gener-

---

[5]The pronoun *we* is convenient but inaccurate. The Air Force Human Resources Laboratory carried out the evaluation study with our support. Official reporting of their results will appear in Nichols et al. (in press). The summary we provide is not endorsed by the Air Force. While we have attempted to accurately convey our best understanding of the results, the official Air Force position on the methods employed and results obtained may deviate from our interpretation. We did conduct additional evaluations on our own, which are reported in Lajoie and Lesgold (1989). Those results are consistent with the present discussion as well.

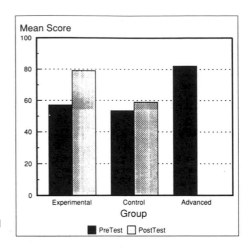

FIG. 3.1. Results of Sherlock I evaluation by the Air Force.

ate a regression coefficient for predicting months of Air Force job experience from scores on these tests. Using the scale created by this regression, the gain shown by the experimental group from pretest to posttest is equivalent to about 4 years of job experience, using conservative estimates.[6] A follow-up testing 6 months after training showed retention of over 90% of the gains made from pre- to posttesting. Overall, then, Sherlock was very successful, in terms of producing the ability to do the specific job of manual F-15 test station diagnosis, which does not readily happen from on-the-job experience or from the training now available prior to reporting for work.

Areas for Improvement.   In spite of the great success of Sherlock I, we were concerned that it was not an adequate model for coached practice. There were a few problems. First, the more capable trainees did not seem as impressed with Sherlock as the real novices. Second, a few trainees among the 16 did not learn very much, although all improved and the overall level of performance rose dramatically. Third, we could not convince ourselves that airmen could transfer what they learned about the F-15 manual test station to other electronics troubleshooting, since coaching focused on what to do, procedural knowledge, rather than why it should be done that way, conceptual knowledge. Finally, we were concerned that because of the substantial amount of explicitly written out hints and the hand coding of each problem's goal structure tree, we had not really provided a technology that could be readily acquired by others.

---

[6]There is considerable variance in this estimate, of course. However, it is consistent with the pre-to-post changes and with the fact that the performance of the experimental group approached that of the advanced sample. In essence, it takes a long time on the job to become able to efficiently diagnose test station failures, and the Sherlock effect was to produce much of that expertise.

These problems derive from two basic characteristics of Sherlock I: its lack of intelligence, and its compression of all learning activity into the midst of problem solving. The lack of intelligence arises primarily in two areas, device modeling and expert performance modeling. Given smarter device modeling capability, a trainee could make any measurement he wished, whether or not the instructional designer anticipated it. More important, new circuits could more readily be configured. The Smalltalk inheritance hierarchy of object classes (declarative knowledge) and their associated methods (procedural knowledge) is exactly the right way to deal with device modeling. Each kind of constraint among the ports to a component (i.e., its inputs and outputs) can be specified generically and specialized only to the extent needed. Further, by having generic methods for faulting components, it would be possible to provide substantial and systematic authoring aids for trainers who wanted to change the Sherlock problem mix, add circuits, correct for changes in the circuitry (field change orders from the manufacturer), and so on.

Similarly, through proper use of inheritance hierarchies of intelligent methods for developing a troubleshooting plan and carrying it out, it becomes possible to provide advice in contexts that the designer may not have fully planned for. That is, no matter what bizarre sequence of actions a trainee takes, it could still be possible to provide an expert overview of what is known so far and how an expert might next proceed. Also, if the expert knowledge is organized appropriately, the advice that is generated can provide a better basis for transfer, by choosing appropriate levels of abstraction to which hinting should be elevated while still retaining the capability for situating all coaching in specific situations.

We are currently working on improved approaches to task analysis that will interact with expert models that are based in inheritance hierarchies of intelligent procedures. The basic idea is that a family of jobs over which transfer was desired would be analyzed together. Expert procedures would be compared over jobs. Procedures sharing substantial content would be redefined in terms of generic methods and more specific methods that specialize the generic approaches to the various particular job environments. Once the inheritance hierarchy for a collection of jobs is organized to reflect the levels of abstraction at which expertise is shared across jobs for particular bits of expertise, then such an "expert model" is also organized perfectly with respect to training for transfer. For any given aspect of job performance, it is then possible both to provide advice tailored to the specific problem situation that prompts the advice request and to provide indications about the level of abstraction at which experts consider the situation in question.

This represents a significant contrast with current approaches to training for transfer, where "theory" and "practice" are often completely separated. The situated learning approach that we have favored fosters conceptual abstraction via coaching and commenting upon specific problem situations. This leaves open the question of how far to abstract. With the "task analysis for transfer" approach we have begun to pursue, transfer requirements determine how far to abstract, and inheritance hierarchies of expert knowledge directly represent not only the expertise but also the transfer analysis. We expect to write more extensively on this topic in future papers.

The other problem we perceive in Sherlock I is that it teaches only in the context of solving problems. Although it is good to situate learning opportunities in the context of valued tasks in the world, there is substantial evidence that some aspects of learning cannot occur very well while one is solving a difficult problem (Owen & Sweller, 1985; Sweller, 1988; Sweller & Cooper, 1985). Basically, when one is using all available cognitive resources to address a problem, no resources are available for cognitive activities that might optimize learning but that do not directly aid in immediate problem solution. This poses a dilemma. On the one hand, learning appears to proceed better when it is grounded in specific problem situations that one faces in meaningful work environments. On the other hand, abstraction, given current ideas about induction, requires explicit information-processing activity that goes beyond what is needed to solve the problem at hand.

We believe we know how to resolve this problem. The approach taken in Sherlock II is to separate learning activity around a problem into two parts. First, the trainee solves the problem, getting advice as required. Because most learning-by-induction procedures involve comparing alternative interpretations and courses of action, the problem-solving process is followed by a period we call reflective followup. Here, the trainee can replay his solution while looking at a diagram of the relevant circuitry (see Fig. 3.2). By clicking with the mouse on a component in the diagram, the trainee can get an explanation of its current status (has it been proven good or bad by the tests already carried out?) and can also have access to information about how Sherlock (i.e., the expert model) would solve the problem. All of the activities that promote learning from experience are thus supported via situated problem-solving experience, but they are not interfered with by the actual need to complete the problem solution.

Sherlock II

We can now recapitulate the changes embodied in Sherlock II. It has deeper intelligence, greater extensibility, a new interface, the additional training approach of reflective follow-up, and a new student modeling approach (which is germane to the assessment concern of this book). It also runs on different hardware. The hardware difference is the easiest to deal with. Sherlock II runs on an 80386 machine, requires around 8 MB (depending on the version used and research requirements for data collection), about 20 MB of hard disk, a processor speed of 20 MHz or higher, a videodisc player and interface, and a GENLOCK card to mix the video and computer graphics images.

The deeper intelligence is, as we indicated earlier, mainly in the expert model-

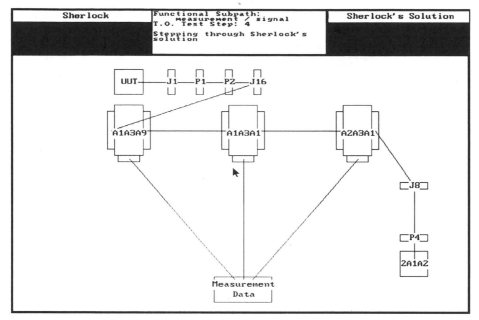

FIG. 3.2.   Example of circuit path display.

ing capability and in the device modeling capability. In addition, some intelligence is required to generate coaching advice from the data structures that embody the device and expert models. Greater extensibility is supplied via a variety of still relatively ad hoc automatic programming tools to help users develop new problems involving different circuit faults, different circuits, and even circuits with different components.

The interface is quite different. In Sherlock I, students carried out tests by pointing, with the computer mouse, at schematic diagrams to indicate where they wanted to place the "probes" of simulated meters. In Sherlock II they point to video images of real test points such as extender boards. When a component could not be filmed (some are buried in places not permitting good camera angles, and the Air Force could not afford the equipment downtime to "dissect" down to them), graphics of its test points are substituted for the video image. Another interface improvement is clutter control. In Sherlock II, there are only four basic windows, for video, coaching advice, action menus, and current status information. These are tiled, with most of the screen reserved for video. The action menus, which are hierarchical, expand as necessary when the mouse enters the small menu tile, and the coaching window similarly expands when its tile is entered. Because people tend to point at what they are looking at, this scheme is very natural, and it avoids the problem of clutter that arises when multiple overlapping windows are used.

The reflective follow-up idea was discussed earlier. After each problem is completed, students can see a summary evaluation of their performance on a number of dimensions (the summarization process is based on the fuzzy variable scheme discussed later), a replay of their own actions, and a presentation of an expert solution. At any step in replaying their own solution, trainees can ask what Sherlock would have done instead of their last move. In some cases, this question is ambiguous. If Sherlock would have tested a different component, then it is unclear whether the student wants to know this or instead to know how Sherlock would have tested the component on which the student was focusing. Such ambiguities are resolved via pop-up menus.

A major concern of the reflective follow-up is the representation of the problem situation. An important representation is that of the functional circuit, the part of the system actively involved in the function that has failed. This representation is better presented graphically because the effects of many measurements are to implicate or rule out parts of the functional circuit that are "upstream" or "downstream" from the point of measurement. In Sherlock II, especially during the reflective follow-up, certain information, such as the effect of a given expert test, is provided via graphical circuit displays in which components and paths are colored to indicate that they are ruled out as the locus of the fault (green), carrying a faulty signal (red inputs and outputs), or uncertain (yellow). An example is shown in Fig. 3.2, though the color coding is not captured by the black-and-white rendering.[7] If, for example, the inputs to A2A3A1 in the example were verified to be good, and the outputs were verified to be bad, then, under the single-fault assumption of Sherlock, components "before" A2A3A1 (including the UUT, the Test Package, A1A3A9, and A1A3A1) would be colored green, as would units "after" A2A3A1 (i.e., 2A1A2). The path out of A2A3A1 would be colored red, and A2A3A1 itself and the "Measurement Data" box would be colored yellow.

Sherlock II development was almost complete as we wrote this chapter. The area on which the most adjustment remained to be made was the student modeling scheme, which will be adjusted in response to preliminary field test results. In the next section of this chapter, we describe this scheme.

THE RULE-DRIVEN FUZZY VARIABLE MODELING SCHEME

The basic student modeling scheme we have designed for Sherlock II consists of a hierarchy of student modeling variables, each of which is an indicator about

---

[7]As a technical aside, we note that the circuit displays, along with the student model structures, make heavy use of the directed graph tools available with Smalltalk V/286. In many respects, the directed graph of objects is our equivalent of the list data structure in Lisp, but it is more powerful, since it contains graph structures of objects or schemata rather than merely graph structures of names.

some characteristic of student capability. The lowest-level variables, which we call local variables, have a very close relationship with the expert model and with actual trainee problem-solving behavior, so they are close to an overlay of competence estimates on the expert model (an approach often called model tracing). The higher-level variables represent abstractions over groups of competences and thus correspond to an overlay on a curriculum model (see Lesgold, 1988, for a discussion of this distinction). Our approach is also distinguished by the use of fuzzy variables, rather than scalar quantities, as modeling variables.

What Is a Fuzzy Variable?

A fuzzy variable can be thought of as a distribution over the set of possible levels of competence or knowledge a trainee might have in a particular skill. We have five such knowledge states for each student modeling variable: no knowledge, limited knowledge, unautomated knowledge, partially automated knowledge, and fully developed knowledge. Initially, if we know absolutely nothing about a trainee, we might assume that each of the five states has equal (20%) probability, as shown in the top part of Fig. 3.3. If we have some prior knowledge, we can bias the distribution, of course. For example, if we know that the fuzzy variable indexes a particularly hard skill, we might specify the distribution as (20%, 60%, 20%, 0%, 0%). This would indicate that we are 60% certain that the knowledge indexed by this particular variable is limited in this particular student, but it might be nonexistent, and it might even have reached the level of being established but not automated. The distribution of fuzzy variable i can be denoted by the vector F_i, with the jth probability category of F_i being denoted by F_{ij}. So, if the top of Fig. 3.3 represents F_i, then $F_{i2} = 0.60$.

An updating procedure for such a fuzzy variable can be specified by two pieces of information, a range and a change percentage (which can be positive or negative). The range indicates what part of the fuzzy distribution, in terms of expertise levels, we should focus on, and the change percentage indicates the magnitude of change we want to make within that focus. For example, if a trainee demonstrates incomplete knowledge of the troubleshooting procedure for a component i, then the update rule might specify a -10% change for (0%, 30%, 100%, 100%, 100%), which means downgrade the top three categories by 10% (1.00×-0.10) and the limited knowledge category by 3% (0.30×-0.10). The result, illustrated in the bottom part of Fig. 3.3, would be a new F_i computed as follows:

$$F_{i1} \leftarrow F_{i1} + 0.10 \times 0.30 \times F_{i2}$$
$$F_{i2} \leftarrow F_{i2} + 0.10 \times 1.00 \times F_{i3} - 0.10 \times 0.30 \times F_{i2}$$
$$F_{i3} \leftarrow F_{i3} + 0.10 \times 1.00 \times F_{i4} - 0.10 \times 1.00 \times F_{i3}$$
$$F_{i4} \leftarrow F_{i4} + 0.10 \times 1.00 \times F_{i5} - 0.10 \times 1.00 \times F_{i4}$$
$$F_{i5} \leftarrow F_{i5} \qquad\qquad\qquad - 0.10 \times 1.00 \times F_{i5}$$

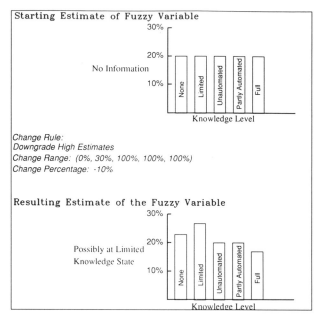

FIG. 3.3.   Fuzzy variable updating.

Note this formulation automatically preserves the fuzzy variable as a distribution summing to 1.

An Overview of the Approach

In developing our approach to student modeling, we borrowed heavily from work by Sharon Derry at Florida State University, her colleagues Lois Hawkes and Abraham Kandel, and their students (e.g., Hawkes, Derry, & Kandel, 1991). Derry has been working on student modeling schemes that represent student capability on a number of dimensions using fuzzy variables. The Sherlock II student model consists similarly of a number of fuzzy variables. Corresponding to each type of circuit subpath[8] there is a student modeling variable. Correspond-

---

[8]The basic model of a test involves a stimulus, or source of electrical energy, being connected to the component being tested, with a measurement device also being connected to that component. The test station, when it fails to do a test correctly, can be represented partially in terms of the signal paths it was supposed to have created, a stimulus signal path from a power supply or signal generator to the component being tested, and a measurement signal path from the component being tested to a measurement device. The other part of the representation involves the circuitry that does the switching to create these signal paths; we call this circuitry the data paths or control paths. Because switching control is slightly different on the stimulus side than on the measurement side, our core representations of functional test circuits are divided into four subpaths: stimulus signal, measurement signal, stimulus data, and measurement data.

TABLE 3.2
Student Modeling Variables Currently Being Used

Global testing ability variables
Circuit variables
Circuit strategy variables by path type
Circuit tactical variables by path type
Component variables: strategic
Component variables: tactical
Overall score on testing component (strategic plus tactical ability)
Test equipment usage skills
Other test-taking skills
        Overall ability to interpret test results
                Circuit-level ability to interpret test results
                Component-level ability to interpret test results
        Ability to read schematics
Domain knowledge
        System understanding
        TO understanding
Dispositions
        Swapping vs. testing
        Testing for the appropriate signal type
        Thrashing
        History-taking
        Overall systematicity and completeness
        Attention to safety preconditions
        Redundant testing
        Attention to probability of failure
        Independence and self-confidence
        Accepting help

ing to each replaceable circuit path component (printed circuit card, switch, etc.), there is another student modeling variable. Additional fuzzy variables index general component testing skills, such as ability to interpret test results, and prerequisite domain knowledge and skills, such as ability to use a particular type of test equipment (e.g., an oscilloscope). Finally, there is a set of performance variables that include dispositions such as systematicity, tendency to ask for help, and certain indicators of general confidence.

A list of the main types of student modeling variables is given in Table 3.2. The student's knowledge is represented in an object-oriented language. Thus, circuit subpaths and components are represented in a circuit path model by instances of objects. Each instance is associated with a class. The student modeling variable for any object is associated with that object's class, so that information can be aggregated across different circuits and different problems in which that object is represented. Classes are part of an inheritance hierarchy, and a class's student modeling variable may be represented at one or another level of the class hierarchy depending on the similarity of objects at the various hierarchy levels. For example, we might have one general variable to represent how well the trainee can test relay cards, but there are one or two special types of relay cards for which we might keep a separate special student modeling variable (e.g., cards that contain circuitry for more than one type of function, such as switching control logic and signal transmission). An object knows that to access its student modeling variable, it should check its own class for the value and, if none is found, then check its parent class recursively. Similarly, updating of a student variable occurs for the most specific version of the variable that is available but then for all higher-level versions of that variable as well.

Several student modeling variables are defined to capture general properties of student performance, such as the following, which are specified as performance objectives for ease of exposition.

1. Swapping versus testing. The student does not swap a component until he has established that it is defective.
2. Redundant testing. The student does not work on any type of subpath more than once. For example, he fully isolates the fault to a particular place in the signal path before beginning to test in the associated data path and does not have to return to signal path testing thereafter.
3. Accepting help. The student tends to ask for help when he needs it (i.e., when he is expected to have trouble with a subpath or component and actually is having trouble).
4. Independence and self-confidence. The student tends not to ask for help when he does not need it (i.e., when the component or path models of relevance show high [expertlike] levels of competence).
5. Systematicity. The student restricts his search for the fault to the relevant circuit path for the test station function that is failing. Within a component, the student's tests are systematic, achieving relevant, though not necessarily expert, goals.

Anchoring of Student Model Variables

The overall scheme for our student modeling is summarized in Fig. 3.4. The model consists of a collection of fuzzy variables. A subset of those variables, which we call local variables, are computed or updated via rules whose conditions are observable properties of trainee troubleshooting performance and whose actions are incremental changes in the relevant fuzzy variable. These rules generally map onto specific test station component objects and are derived from the cognitive task analysis of the job being trained. For example, in testing a system component, an expert would satisfy the overall goal of verifying that component with a small number of tests, while a less-expert person might make more tests. So, that component will have associated with it a student modeling variable indexing efficiency of testing it. A rule would update that variable after the trainee tests the given component, upgrading the assessment of the trainee if he tested efficiently and downgrading the assessment if he did not. Other rules would update other local variables to take account of correct meter usage, relevance (as opposed to efficiency) of tests of the component, and so on. So, as Fig.

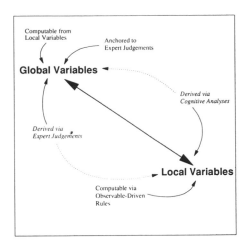

FIG. 3.4 Multilevel assessment scheme.

3.4 indicates, the local variables are computable from functions driven by ob-
servables, and these functions are linked to an analysis of expertise. In a secondary way (indicated by the dashed lines), the local variables reflect expert judgments of what properties of local performance are important to measure.

Another subset of the modeling variables is cumulations, fuzzy combinations,
of the local variables, which we call global variables. These are computable as
weighted combinations of local variables. However, because there are so many
potentially sensible cumulations, we think it important to anchor global variables
in expert evaluations of trainee performance. For example, a global variable
might index good strategy in troubleshooting signal paths between the device
being tested and the measurement device (measurement signal paths). An expert
could certainly look at a trainee's overall performance and judge whether his
measurement signal path strategy was good or not. This judgment would anchor
a fuzzy variable that might be a combination of local variables indexing a variety
of more specific details of performance.

Fuzzy Variable Upgrading and Downgrading Conditions

At the end of each problem, every circuit subpath's object instance is asked to
update student modeling variables. The subpath, in turn, asks each of its component objects to update student modeling variables. Each object needs to update its
own student model and also to update any generic models of relevance (e.g., if a
student asked for help with a component, then that component's object must
decide if the help was really needed or not).

While the actual rules for student model updating will be tuned with experience, we are beginning with rules more or less like those shown below and in

TABLE 3.3
Upgrading Conditions for One Fuzzy Variable

Example of a Sherlock Fuzzy Variable and Its Upgrading and Downgrading Conditions

---

HANDHELD METER USAGE

Description: measure of knowledge about when to use the handheld meter; tactical ability is assumed

Initial distribution: journeyman

Upgrading conditions:

1. Uses handheld meter appropriately to measure resistance, i.e., when there is no power, without help from Sherlock (+++).

2. Uses handheld meter appropriately to measure DC voltage, i.e., DC power is on, without help from Sherlock (+++).

3. Uses handheld meter appropriately to measure AC voltage, i.e., AC power is on (+++).

Downgrading conditions:

1. Uses handheld meter to measure resistance when power is on (e.g., shorting in the data area) (−).

2. Uses handheld meter to measure voltage when there is none (−−).

3. Uses handheld meter to measure DC voltage when it is AC (−−).

4. Uses handheld meter to measure AC voltage when it is DC (−).

Table 3.3. For these examples, we use an arbitrary convention, where $+++$ means to upgrade a variable by a relatively large amount, $++$ means a smaller upgrade, $---$ means a large downgrade, $--$ means a smaller downgrade, and so on. In each case, we speak of an update amount and an update range, referring to the immediately preceding discussion of fuzzy variables. The amounts are particularly uncertain because they depend partly on the number of opportunities for updating that different variables have. For example, one local variable might be updated 10 times during a single problem solution, whereas another may only have one update opportunity. If the same update amount is used for both, then the first will reach the expert level way ahead of the second. We must scale updates to reflect these opportunity differences.

1. Expertise detection. If the ratio of the expert score for the component to the trainee's actual score is 0.9 or higher, then update the object's student modeling variable by $+++$ on (100%, 100%, 60%, 30%, 0).

2. Incompetence detection. If the ratio of the expert score to the trainee's score is less than 0.6, then update the object's student modeling variable by $---$ on (0, 30%, 60%, 100%, 100%).

3. Help. For each time help was requested for this object's component,

update the student modeling variable by —— on (0, 20%, 40%, 60%, 80%).

A subpath object can accumulate the expert and trainee scores over the components of the subpath and perform the same kind of calculations. Variables that refer to such skills as using particular meters to make measurements can be updated by rules that trigger on particular conditions. For example, Table 3.3 shows the triggering conditions for a rule that we use to update the variable that measures ability to use the hand held multimeter. The plus and minus strings refer to upgrades or downgrades of different magnitudes. By initial distribution, we mean the level a trainee is assumed to be at when he starts using Sherlock II.

We are currently conducting a range of simulation exercises to determine differential update rates. The basic approach[9] is first to choose update amounts so that consistently good performance will push the student model entries to the level of expert at about the rate we would expect of a very able trainee. Then the student's "raw" modeling scores can be adjusted by comparing his progress to that of the idealized able learner. We have much to learn yet about how to do this as efficiently as possible, but the approach seems serviceable and promising.

The Condition-to-Variable Mapping

The basic approach we are taking involves substantially redundant measurement. For example, whether or not a trainee places meter probes on the correct test points, and also whether or not the correct probes are used, reflects on several different student model components: knowing how to test the component in question, ability to use schematic diagrams, probe placement skill per se, and understanding how the system and the component being tested work. The approach is redundant partly because we want to use Sherlock as a research vehicle to determine which aspects of student performance are most important in specifying overall competence and in tailoring training. Partly, it reflects the reality that an action can be part of differing plans and/or motivated by different aspects of conceptual understanding.

In practical terms, one could go either of two ways with a scheme in which behaviors map redundantly onto modeling variables. One approach is to base all such relationships in detailed cognitive analyses of the knowledge being traced. Anderson (this volume) has taken this approach strongly, and we have taken it somewhat more weakly. The approach allows a clear specification of trainee capability at any given time, in terms of both underlying cognitive knowledge and predicted specific performances. This cognitive level of specification motivates the tailoring of coaching as well. That is, we can interpret the trainee's actions in terms of knowledge he is missing and can then focus coaching on the

---

[9]Maria Gordin, one of our colleagues, proposed this approach.

missing knowledge. However, real-life task analyses are inherently incomplete, especially when one considers transfer as a critical concern of the analysis. Our approach separates measurements that derive from empirically supported theory from other measurements that, at bottom, are really expert judgments. We prefer this to the millenial assumption that all aspects of performance worth measuring will always be grounded in complete task analyses fully driven by cognitive theories of the domain.

It is also interesting to note, however, that the basic scheme in which the presence or absence of various noted behaviors leads to relatively simple modifications of variables, with the values of those variables then being accumulated into higher-level variables, is remarkably close to being a connectionist network. This leads to the interesting possibility that training systems might have both an "innate" and a "learned" capability to analyze student performance and tailor coaching. The "innate" side would be motivated by the cognitive task analysis underlying the instructional system's design, while the learned side would be driven by back propagation of feedback on the effectiveness of coaching.

The scenario could go something like this. Student modeling would proceed as we have suggested, with student actions triggering rules that update low-level modeling variables and those low-level variables in turn influencing higher-level variables. When advice was requested, the current student model would be the basis for that advice. If the advice were effective, then the modeling scheme would, in essence, be confirmed. If the advice turned out to be insufficient, then rules recently executed that increased coaching-relevant competence estimates might have their incrementing coefficients decreased and rules recently executed that decreased competence estimates might have their coefficients increased. If a trainee did better than expected, carrying out parts of the problem solution without help when the model predicted help would be needed, the reverse adjustments might be made.

Some of this adaptation might be local and some global. On the local side, simply because cognitive models go beyond the degrees of freedom in situations to which they apply, an empirical mechanism is required to weight the importance to an individual case of various cognitive principles and task analysis components. On the global side, it is important to discover situations where cognitive analyses are insufficient and also situations where theory says some additional knowledge is needed but practice says it is not. The latter problem is a common one in the design of training and results in wasted training time as well as unnecessarily limited opportunity when trainees are required to pass tests on knowledge they need in theory but not in practice.

Possibilities for Applying Psychometric and Scaling Methods

Although the connectionist scheme holds promise for the future, there are some more mundane possibilities that can be pursued right now, and that we plan to use as Sherlock II is field tested. Regression analysis techniques are certainly a possibility. We believe that there is some value in using fuzzy variables rather than merely scalar indicators of competence, because problem selection and hinting rules can be grounded in more complex conditions (e.g., "If you are sure the trainee is not an absolute beginner in using the oscilloscope, then include oscilloscope problems"). However, decisions concerning which local variables are related to one another and which are the most sensitive indicators of competence can be made empirically on the basis of initial experience with a tutor like Sherlock, especially if the central tendencies of the fuzzy variables are estimated by scalars. One can then perform regression analyses in which the global variables, as estimated by experts, are predicted by the medians or means of fuzzy local variable distributions that are in turn generated through the updating process described earlier.

It is also possible to search for indicators of competence using scaling techniques. For example, we have looked at a variety of specific indicators of progress and how they change as trainees get more experience using Sherlock. By applying scaling techniques such as factor analyses and cluster analyses to means or medians of local fuzzy variables, we can examine the covariation of these indicators. That in turn suggests possible global student modeling variables, one for each cluster. The indicators that cluster together tend to give clues about which local variables might be aggregated to produce the corresponding global variable. It is important to note, however, that not all local variables need to be fixed by simple empirical observation. Rather, some may have their values inferred from relatively complex qualitative patterns over multiple observable events. For example, some student modeling variables may operate on implications of actions, such as an index of the extent to which measurements made by the trainee rule out possible fault loci or fail to do so.

STUDENT MODELING AND HINTING

We believe that it is possible to use student responses to hints as a further basis for assessment. To illustrate our current thinking, consider the following example of a trainee impasse situation within Sherlock II. Suppose the trainee successfully identifies a subpath that is still suspect, and selects a component to test on that subpath (perhaps even a central component). He might then perform a couple of measurements on the component but not know what else to do. Suppose he then asks for a component-level how-to-test hint. The hint only tells him what measurements he has performed, and the readings he received. This is inadequate because the student's problem is not with history-taking; he has already jotted down his tests and readings. So he asks for help again. The next hint he receives supplies one type of information in addition to that contained in the previous message: an interpretation of each measurement he has already made on the current component. Seeing that the card's outputs are bad and the inputs are good, the student might properly proceed to check the control signals to the card, and carry out each measurement correctly (i.e., set up test equipment correctly for range and type of signal and place probes correctly).

In this example, it would appear that the student's problem was with interpreting the results of his measurements, because once the measurements were interpreted, he proceeded optimally. We believe the system should use this information to downgrade the variable for ability to interpret test results. Furthermore, it should upgrade the measurement-taking variables (probe placement and test equipment usage), because the trainee successfully took measurements without help, and it should upgrade the variable for testing the type of component he is focusing on, because the student did not need to be told to check its data signals. In contrast, had the trainee swapped the component after receiving the second hint, the system might infer that he is weak in testing that type of component and in system understanding (i.e., he doesn't know that the card's control inputs need to be checked in order to conclude that the card is good or bad), and these variables might be downgraded. Sherlock would also downgrade the swapping versus testing variable, because the student swapped a partially tested component; the degree of downgrading should be less than if the student hadn't tested the component at all.

We are just beginning to experiment with this kind of an approach, and we will surely encounter some difficulties along the way. However, it is illustrative of a general difference between human tutors' assessment approaches during training and extant external or even computer-based assessment approaches. Human tutors pay attention to what they are saying and to how students respond to their coaching, whereas other assessment forms attend only to student products (right answers) or, in the best case, to student processing behaviors in solving problems. Extending systems to take account of the coaching context, a Vygotskiian notion in part, seems highly worthwhile.

AN APPRAISAL OF THE SHERLOCK APPROACH

Having introduced the approach being taken in the Sherlock project, we now turn to several specific evaluative questions posed by the editors of this book. In doing this, we note that our ideas about coached practice as a means for training complex skills are reasonably well developed and embodied in two computer systems, one of which has been field tested and the other of which is scheduled for field testing shortly. Our ideas about performance assessment, in contrast, and indeed most of our ideas about student modeling, have not yet been fully worked out nor tested. As a consequence, some of the claims we make are well supported, whereas others are preliminary and speculative. We begin by considering the theoretical basis for the approach.

Theoretical Basis

Like all design activities, the Sherlock effort is somewhat eclectic. Partly, it is grounded in the cognitive modeling tradition. That is, we assume that it is possible to study expertise and to develop computational models that embody much of that expertise. Once a machine can operate expertly, it begins to have some amount of capability, at least in principle and subject to computational complexity limitations, to diagnose others' performances. In the worst case, a machine might combinatorially try to emulate a trainee's performance by trying to function with every possible subset of knowledge components until it finds a combination that matches the trainee's performance. In reality, better modeling tools can likely be developed, though not perhaps with as clear a theoretical justification. That is, a computational system can do better than the combinatorial worst case, but it may not be able to explain as readily what it is doing.

The problem is made more complex when abstraction is considered. For any one action, it is not possible to know how abstract and conceptually understood procedural capability is. Even when a capability is manifest in a number of different circumstances, it is difficult, perhaps impossible, to determine the level of abstraction of the knowledge that has been exercised. We can see this if we look at the object-oriented programs of which Sherlock is an example. When Sherlock does something, we cannot, merely by observing it, know whether it executed a very general routine whose parameters were bound to situational specifics or a very specific routine that cannot generalize to any other circumstance.

In order to make some headway on this issue of level of generality of exhibited knowledge, we must make some assumptions. The simplest assumption we might choose to make is strong cognitive economy, that a given procedure capability is stored in a form generic to the range of circumstances in which we have seen it executed. So, for example, if I have seen a trainee correctly troubleshoot two different relay cards, I will assume that he can troubleshoot any other relay cards that can be handled by the minimal generalization of the specific procedures for the two cards. In reality, one could well learn the two procedures entirely separately and by rote, so there is no reason to be sure that the abstraction has occurred. This leads us to a principle of weak cognitive economy, which is that the more often a capability is manifested and the more efficiently it is carried out, the greater will be our confidence that it has been abstracted over the situations in which it has been exercised. Sherlock implicitly assumes weak cognitive economy, and that is the basis for the aggregation scheme of student modeling variables that we discussed previously.

Another theoretical basis for the Sherlock work is the multilayered theory of curriculum proposed by Lesgold (1988). There, it was suggested that the objects of a curriculum knowledge layer in an intelligent training system were different from, but mapped onto, expert knowledge objects. This very general vision is implemented in the multilevel fuzzy student modeling scheme that is being used for Sherlock II. The point is largely one of the orchestration of knowledge and can perhaps be made more clearly in the context of Newell's SOAR model (Newell, 1990).

Newell has suggested that cognitive activity involves a continuing movement from problem space to problem space, each with its own associated knowledge and representational character. Whenever an impasse is reached in satisfying a currently active goal structure, SOAR initiates a new goal of solving the impasse. This is, in essence, a new problem with a new problem space (i.e., different possible actions and outcomes, and different knowledge about when to take which actions). It is tempting to say that each problem space within Sherlock should be represented by an object that knows how to represent the states of that problem space using its variable slots and also knows how to solve the problem. This would be the equivalent of weak cognitive economy.

However, in order for transfer capability to be acquired, these very specific problem space objects would need to be generalized. Accordingly, we have to assume that there is some mechanism for inducing more abstract objects from specific ones. Further, these more abstract objects, we propose, sit above their specific variations in an inheritance hierarchy. When we look at how induction takes place, we see that it has a strong comparative component. For example, Medin and Ross (1989), in discussing abstraction, make the case that rather than being an automatic byproduct of cognitive activity, abstraction is conservative, with generalizations being made only when they prove useful.

Such a scheme has two possible mechanisms of transfer. The first is that abstractions do occur, because even within the original task they are useful. These abstractions then are available for use in other related tasks. The second possibility is that abstractions inherent in doing the first task are insufficient by themselves to produce the capabilities needed for the second task and that the performer must operate on his first-task knowledge to modify it for use in the second task. There is insufficient data to decide between these alternatives, but they have important implications for assessment. Under the first view, performance must be judged partly by whether it exhibits knowledge at a level of abstraction that can support the transfer task. The second view instead requires assessment of some metacognitive skills of transfer that can search one's knowledge for the closest examples from past experience and can then modify the procedural knowledge attached to those examples to make it usable in transfer tasks.

Supporting Data

The editors specifically asked what data support the approach we have been taking. As we noted earlier, Sherlock has done well in its initial field evaluation, and we expect that Sherlock II will also look good. However, this does not mean that every aspect of the approach is validated. The study of apprenticeship learning is in an early stage, and it will no doubt emerge that some of what is designed into Sherlock is critical to effective training while other details are less critical. Unfortunately, the supply of real trainees and the economics of field evaluations make it difficult to return continually to real job sites for detailed followup studies. Instead, we hope shortly to begin laboratory studies of Sherlock II that focus on very specific questions in the system's design and attempt to evaluate more specifically the various design principles that Sherlock embodies.

One important area we hope to examine is the role of detailed student modeling in conditioning problem selection and the specifics of coaching. Our original view was that we should adjust the specificity of initial coaching to match the student, giving less help when we thought less was needed and more where we thought the student lacked knowledge on which to proceed. However, we ended up giving all trainees the same series of problems to perform.[10] Over time, we have come to wonder whether students might not be a better source of tailoring information than our models of them. That is, would we be better off giving students a chance to influence which problems they get and how specific is the feedback they get, or is it better for us to decide these questions based on the student model? There are a number of other similar questions that demand controlled laboratory study as well.

Range of Applicability

Another question posed by the editors is the range of applicability of the approaches embodied in Sherlock. In general, we feel that the approach we have described is widely applicable, at least to training and assessment of jobs that involve something equivalent to diagnosing and repairing complex systems. The same basic approach can probably also be extended to jobs that involve complex decision making by an individual, based on information available from a relatively fixed set of sources. For example, training for logistic planning tasks should be able to use the same basic approach.

Two additions could make the scheme much more widely usable. The first is to take account of the speed of performances. Nothing in the Sherlock scheme does this, so far, because the sequence of actions sufficiently constrains the overall effectiveness of a solution so that knowing how quickly successive steps were taken would add little. However, some tasks, such as air traffic control, can be successfully completed only if performance is fast enough. Further, when performance is too slow, an assessment should reveal why it was too slow, which requires some type of comparison of each component of overall performance

---

[10]Our motivation was to get trainees discussing problems afterward, which was possible only if they shared problem experiences and realized that they did.

with a speed norm. This certainly can be done, but it involves significant design work that is outside all the Sherlock efforts to date.

A second addition, which could be made more easily, would be to provide some means of assessing the quality of a performance's final outcome. In a sense, Sherlock does not do this; the final outcome is replacing the faulted component and demonstrating that the system now works. It has either been done or not. On the other hand, it would be quite easy to add more elaborated "scoring" of the solution, and we plan to do so shortly. Basically, each action taken while searching for a fault can have a cost index assigned to it. Most measurements are cheap, but it is cheaper, for example, to take at the same time all measurements requiring a particular machine configuration, use of a particular extender board, and so forth. This is an area of minor cost variation. Unnecessary swapping of components is a larger cost because each good component that is swapped represents either a lost resource, if it is discarded, or an additional troubleshooting cost, if it is tested further at a parts depot. We expect to add to Sherlock a scoring scheme that takes account of such costs.

Required Knowledge Engineering Methods

The editors also asked about the knowledge engineering methods that are required for the Sherlock approach. There are three aspects to our task analysis approach, and we think all three are important. The first is the empirical methodology, which was developed by AFHRL with our inputs. This methodology, called PARI (for precursor-action-results-interpretation), is a powerful means of tracing expertise in problem solution. It is a standardized interview scheme for following a person's solution of a problem. The person states each step that he wants to take, and the analyst tells the person the results of that step. Along with this basic interaction, four questions are asked at each step. First, the person is asked to describe the current problem context; what is known and what is the next goal. Then, he is asked to state the action he wants to take. Next, he is asked to predict the results of the action. Finally, after the actual results of the action are given, the person is asked to interpret the new data and its implications for problem solution.

In order to apply the PARI approach successfully, there must be a procedure for developing tasks to be used for this purpose. One approach to task specification is to have experts concoct problems that they think will reveal their abilities and also problems that they think would reveal weaknesses in job novices.[11] Another approach, which we used, is first to examine data about job tasks' criticality and trainability. The Air Force maintains a data base of occupational survey reports that include supervisory ratings of job tasks in terms of difficulty,

---

[11]Allan Collins first proposed this scheme of task analysis by watching experts pose problems to each other.

criticality, and trainability. We intentionally focused on the hardest and most critical tasks for the domain, on the assumption that a relatively expensive approach like Sherlock could only be justified by success in producing real experts who could do parts of the job that many job incumbents find too difficult.

A second aspect of our approach is the search for core mental models for the domain. From the PARI data and other expert interviews, we try to specify the small number of mental models that experts rely on in doing their work. For our domain, two critical mental models are the model of a test and the model of a switching system (such as a phone exchange or a test station). Once one knows that any test has four basic components (stimulus, measurement device, unit being tested, and load) and once one realizes that a test station is a system that configures circuits to carry out tests, then one is ready to constrain and solve test station troubleshooting problems. The knowledge of experts is best captured in terms of these core mental models so that the training system is intelligent enough to be able to explain proposed solutions in terms that an expert would use.

Another concern in task analysis is procedural abstraction. That is, if one hopes to provide training that will transfer to related jobs, then it is important to understand the other jobs well enough to recognize which aspects of expertise will transfer and which components of the second job require separate training. As we have discussed, the specific theory of transfer one holds will influence what work needs to be done in task analyses for transfer, but it will always be necessary to build models of expertise and to identify explicitly the level and nature of knowledge objects that are shared between jobs.

Development of the student model also requires knowledge engineering. In addition to the expert model knowledge that underlies the local variables in our student model, information from our expert trainer about the ways in which he appraises trainee competence also anchors global variables. In addition, the expert is the only source of knowledge about the areas of strength and weakness to be expected in trainees when they first start using Sherlock and the rates of improvement we should anticipate. Like other aspects of expertise generated through knowledge engineering, these inputs are a starting point that must be tuned with experience in using Sherlock.

TRAINEE RESPONSIBILITY

We conclude by commenting on training responsibilities. We think it is important to establish clearly what the trainee's job is and, building on that, to specify clearly what the training system must do successfully to fulfill its responsibilities. With Sherlock, we give the student major responsibilities. He or she must practice the hardest parts of the real job. Further, practice must be followed by review of performance and an effort to reflect on how it could be improved. We provide opportunities for understanding better why certain procedures are optimal, but these help only if they are used. The same fuzzy variable scheme discussed earlier can be used to track students' use of the reflection tools we provide, so that Sherlock could, in future versions, remind a student of his or her responsibilities. Sherlock's responsibilities, of course, are also substantial. The system must be ready to simulate the effects of any relevant action a student wants to take in manipulating or testing the test station. It must be prepared to offer advice on how to proceed and to offer explanations of how the system works, what it is trying to do, and how it can be diagnosed. Thus, although Sherlock is a very supportive learning environment, it is also a very challenging one.

Sometimes, when we reflect on education and training, we may be tempted by the sink or swim approach. Those who learn to swim this way generally are good swimmers and confident. However, many give up or fail to jump in. Sherlock puts the student in the deep water and makes it clear that hard work is required for learning to occur. However, it supports performance so that sinking is impossible. Also, it provides tools for the student that are sufficient so that doing the hard work of learning will pay off in mastery. We believe that there is great power in this type of approach, partly because it reflects current theory of human cognition and learning and current intelligent systems technology but partly also because it establishes clear duties for both the training system and the trainee, and these duties are relevant to the goal of gaining job competence.

REFERENCES

Anderson, J. R. (1983). *The architecture of cognition*. Cambridge, MA: Harvard.

Gott, S. P. (1989). Apprenticeship instruction for real-world tasks: The coordination of procedures, mental models, and strategies. In E. Z. Rothkopf (Ed.), *Review of Research in Education, 15,* 97–169.

Hawkes, L. W., Derry, S. J., & Kandel, A. (1991). Fuzzy expert systems for an intelligent computer-based tutor. In A. Kandel (Ed.), *Fuzzy expert systems*. Boca Raton, FL: CRC Press.

Lajoie, S. P., & Lesgold, A. (1989). Apprenticeship training in the workplace: Computer-coached practice environment as a new form of apprenticeship. *Machine-Mediated Learning, 3,* 7–28.

Lesgold, A. (1988). Toward a theory of curriculum for use in designing intelligent instructional systems. In H. Mandl & A. Lesgold (Eds.), *Learning issues for intelligent tutoring systems* (pp. 114–137). New York: Springer-Verlag.

Medin, D. L., & Ross, B. H. (1989). The specific character of abstract thought: Categorization, problem solving, and induction. In R. Sternberg (Ed.), *Advances in the psychology of human intelligence* (Vol. 5, 189–223). Hillsdale, NJ: Lawrence Erlbaum Associates.

Newell, A. (1990). *Unified theories of cognition* (The 1987 William James Lectures). Cambridge, MA: Harvard University Press.

Nichols, P., Pokorny, R., Jones, G., Gott, S. P., & Alley, W. E. (in press). *Evaluation of an avionics troubleshooting tutoring system*. Special Report. Brooks Air Force Base, TX: Air Force Human Resources Laboratory.

Owen, E., & Sweller, J. (1985). What do students learn while solving mathematics problems? *Journal of Educational Psychology, 77,* 272–284.

Sweller, J. (1988). Cognitive load during problem solving: Effects on learning. *Cognitive Science, 12,* 257–285.

Sweller, J., & Cooper, G. (1985). The use of worked examples as a substitute for problem solving in learning algebra. *Cognition and Instruction, 2*, 59–89.

TRANSCRIPT OF DISCUSSION

John Anderson: I'm interested in more details of methods you've had throughout the updating of local variables. The example you gave, at least, was one in which it seemed like you sort of had a distribution that was shifted upward. Are there more complex rules for changing distributions?

Alan Lesgold: The rules all involve three or four basic distribution patterns: A novice pattern that is heavily biased toward the low end of the distribution, an expert pattern that is heavily biased toward the high end and in which the probability that the person knows nothing is strikingly low, where essentially you are not quite sure whether there is a "complete expert" or an "almost expert." And an intermediate level we call a journeyman level, where you are pretty sure that the person has some knowledge, but you expect that the knowledge may not be fully developed or fully automated. So there are several prototype distributions that everything is anchored to. We specify starting distributions for the variables as we make a guess about whether we know something about the trainee or not at the beginning. Of course, it is nothing, because we know nothing about the person. We specify a starting distribution, and the rules essentially say: "If the person exhibited this behavior then take a step in the direction of this prototype." The question then is, "How big are the steps should we take?" We've been doing all kinds of simulations that tell us things like: Given a certain step size, how many steps would you take to get to the next level? And we tried to anchor that with some of our experts' evaluations with about how much experience it seems to take, for instance with our Sherlock I data. For example, if it turned out that our best belief is after about 12 problems most people had progressed from novice to journeyman in making DC voltage measurements, and it turned out in each problem that there were about 10 opportunities to make such a measurement, then that would say on the average after about 120 opportunities, people tend to make it from novice to journeymen, we then choose a weight and a function for updating that produces journeyman status after 100 to 120 positive updates. That's the place where we need to do more work—we are not entirely happy with that. But we also are not happy with any kind of notion that says that from some behavior you can make a really enduring determination of the person, that the person knows something. We think there's something really fundamentally stochastic about our ability to measure these capabilities, so we're taking our best shot at it.

John Anderson: Your variables are discrete or continuous values? Is there anything critical about that, or do you just have continuous values of expertise and spread the distribution over that?

Alan Lesgold: No. In fact, this is purely a function of trivia variables, like how big a machine you have, how many have floating point processors, and all that kind of stuff. In principle, you can go to a single index and you lose some sense of noise in the variable, which we would like to preserve. But in the end, it may not turn out that the variance estimations are particularly important. You could go in the other direction of having a full distribution, or continuous distribution or something close to it, and again that is computationally more expensive, and we don't know if it would add anything yet.

Walt Schneider: I like the idea of assessing the focuses of knowledge and trying to track those and making new predictions off of it. Do you have in the project an assessment of those to track how well you're doing that job? That is, in essence, you're building an internal representation of the individual and at the moment I see you've got this, "Well, you come in with some ability and then you've got this final performance." And then you've got things along the way where you say, "Well, let's see how they rank on their test on the oscilloscope knowledge . . ." like 20% of the curriculum, 40% of the curriculum, that sort of setup.

Alan Lesgold: You could do it in the middle as well. In fact, the scaling studies (done by one of my co-authors in this chapter—Gary Eggan) we conducted to get us into this scheme had three stages over the course of progressions through Sherlock I. And we essentially looked at some counts of behaviors that we had available from Sherlock I and looked at their intercorrelations and their magnitudes, and how they progressed over the course of experience in Sherlock. And there is no reason why we couldn't do any of this anywhere along the way. We have done some of it. Most of the work has been internal evaluation. You're absolutely right, once you know you've got something that more or less works, the interesting question is not "Did it work at all?" but "Did you really need 20 hours?" "Would you do better if you had 40 hours?" "Would 10 hours be enough?" These are becoming important questions. There is no reason why they can't be addressed in exactly the same way. We have got the measures that have been taken continually, and all that is needed is an external reference, that is, an expert looking at the replay of a person's performance and making a judgment about how good the performance is. Or, the extent that we can look at other things, like the number of steps that they took, it is relatively easy to assign a cost to each action at the time, and essentially say, "What was the course of their getting cheaper?" and try to use that as a sort of superglobal measure.

Dan Fisk: Is this an adaptive type training situation, or do the tasks become progressively harder?

Alan Lesgold: Yes, in two ways. The problem selection issue in its simplest form is an ordering of problems, such that the probability of getting an easy problem at the beginning is very high and the probability of getting a hard problem at the end is very high. You can go one step further and try to tailor that to the individual's needs. The prior view of HRL coming into this work has been that tailoring it to individual students' needs is very important. I think that it is an empirical issue that we will find something more about as we proceed.

John Anderson: How do you know when to promote someone from one problem to another?

Alan Lesgold: Well, an expert, presumably, if he can order people on these global variables, can also order problems on these global variables. Then the question is, "Should we try to select a problem whose profile exactly matches the student or not?" Well, we want to sort of do that. But there are some dangers in that. If you start telling the student, "Your problem is really in the oscilloscope"—then all of a sudden, he starts knowing that from now on he needs to use the oscilloscope every time he has to do something. You might not be teaching quite the right things. There has to remain a certain amount of randomness in problem selection. But you want a bias in the direction of problems that exercise the particular learning possibilities that you know are still needed. We have a scheme for doing that. You can think of it as sort of an "urn model." That is, out of all the problems that are available, we are going to take a subset of those problems and stick them in an urn and we're going to sample one of them. We are going to heavily favor getting into the urn the problems that load on the variables that we think are important. These are not going to be the only problems that get in. Because if only these problems get in, then we are going to be giving away the story. That seems to be a little bit complicated, but there's an extraction of that which turns out to be very simple. And that's how we're doing it. You don't want to be quite that complicated about it. There's a very simple problem-ordering scheme where we can raise and lower the problems in the ordering, according to whether the most recent performances show the need for that kind of problem. And then you can have a biased selection rule for where you selected that order.

Pat Kyllonen: Are you actually going to collect enough data to be able to evaluate this complicated tutoring model?

Alan Lesgold: I think that we can collect enough data to get a sense about it.

Pat Kyllonen: Where each unit of knowledge is independent?

Alan Lesgold: You are raising an important question. That is, there are not enough people out there to tell us everything that we need to know about every variable. But to the extent that we can make some guesses and verify a subset of those guesses, I think we can reasonably follow this strategy. There is another thing that we can do. Because of the design of Sherlock, you can stick any circuit in there. That is more or less like a test station. You can stick a flashlight in there, some simpler resistor network, those kinds of things, and diagnose them. So we think that we can try out a number of ideas about how to deal with those variables without using people in this job. There are probably only a few thousand people on this job worldwide that are in there for at least 4 years. . . . Do you know what the number is? It is not real big. At any given base, there may be only 20 people that are in their first 4 years of that job. So there is no way we are going to be able to have thousands of variables to be verified by getting expert judgments. We can get some of them verified. We can go and try the same scheme on simpler problems and use students in tech school or something like that. I think we've got a lot of potential for tuning the scheme to the point where it is practical. But sure, you are right. In the end analysis, you need to have a scheme that to some extent involves judgments about the domain being made and not universally verified.

Pat Kyllonen: You raised the question to Valerie, which was: "What is the utility of these more global aptitude variables?" I think that is a real interesting question. But one reason why global aptitude variables might be interesting is that it might give you some indication for how quickly a particular person might be moving from the state of "doesn't know" to the state of "knows this particular thing." And there might be a lot of variance in that for a class of variables. And the variables that you are looking at might be correlated across individuals in the sense that people who move quickly with respect to one variable will also move quickly with respect to other variables that you're looking at.

Alan Lesgold: That is a very nice idea in the sense that you can come up with a relatively global aptitude measure and a few relatively global domain-centered rate-of-learning measures, and then just rely on a cognitive analysis to support the rest.

Jim Pellegrino: You know Sherlock I is relatively successful as far as these things go. You made a lot of changes in it that involved a variety of issues. One of the questions raised was, "How are you ever going to know whether those are the right decisions?" I've got another question for you. After all the investment in these decisions, what do you expect as an incremental increase between the utility of using Sherlock II over Sherlock I?

Alan Lesgold: I didn't expect much out of Sherlock I. I don't expect a major increment in the training effectiveness in Sherlock II relative to Sherlock I. I expect at least near transfer performances. I expect that for far transfer, we should be able to demonstrate considerable effectiveness, which is not something we undertook to do systematically before. Because we are now dealing, I think, with more conceptual issues than before, we ought to expect to get some far transfer. Electronics people, more or less as a group, are toward the high end of the aptitude ranges of the Air Force. I would expect that if they get both procedural capability and some understanding of underpinnings of the domain, then they would show more transfer. Our real goals though with Sherlock II have much more to do with "Who is the next witch practicing the witchcraft?" than they do with improving the quality of witchcraft. Our concern has not been, "Can somebody that has been hanging around in the cognitive science world for a while scratch his head and come up with a way to teach something if he has to?" But to what extent can you systematize it and have a prayer of hope that the "Beltway Enterprises" that bid on building the next 40 of them are going to be able to do as well as you did? And that is really the direction we are aiming for in Sherlock II—the systematization, not really improvement, of the effect. I think most people would settle for the effects of Sherlock I.

4 General Principles for an Intelligent Tutoring Architecture

John R. Anderson
Albert T. Corbett
Jon M. Fincham
Donn Hoffman
Ray Pelletier
Carnegie Mellon University

We have developed a number of intelligent computer-based tutors for the domains of LISP programming, geometry theory proving, and algebra. The state of this research as it stood in 1987 is summarized in Anderson, Boyle, Corbett, and Lewis (1990). These tutors had modest success in real classroom situations producing improvements on the order of one standard deviation or one letter grade. More recently, we have been trying to identify the essential features of our tutoring methodology, the theoretical bases for these features, and have been trying to develop a tutoring architecture that facilitates creation of tutors with these features. This report identifies what we feel are the core principles for intelligent tutoring. In particular, we describe (a) a first-pass architecture that partially embodies these principles, (b) our experiences in implementing tutors for LISP, Prolog, and Pascal in this architecture, and (c) the current status of our work on creating a new system that is a development system for tutors of this general type.

We call our approach to tutoring a model-tracing methodology. This involves first developing a cognitive model that is capable of solving problems in the same way we want students to solve the problems. This cognitive model is then used to interpret the student's performance of some task at the computer. Basically, the tutor tries to find some way of solving the problem within the cognitive model that matches the student's problem solving and uses this way as the interpretation of the student's performance. All instructional decisions are based on this interpretation. In our view, the success of our tutoring methodology is basically a result of our use of a cognitive model, which in turn was derived from basic principles of skill acquisition as embodied in theories like the ACT* theory (Anderson, 1983, 1987). In the next section of this chapter, we describe the basic implications of that theory for tutor design. These implications turn out to be surprisingly simple.

KEY ELEMENTS OF THE MODEL-TRACING METHODOLOGY

According to the ACT* theory, a cognitive skill is represented as a set of production rules. There is considerable evidence for this assumption (e.g., Anderson, 1983, 1987; Just & Carpenter, 1987; Kieras, 1982; Kieras & Bovair, 1986; Newell & Simon, 1972; Singley & Anderson, 1989), and the general success of our approach to tutoring can be seen as further evidence. A production rule is a condition-action pair that specifies taking some problem-solving action when a certain condition is met. We have found that the skills being taught in a course can be decomposed into many hundreds of production rules.

Working within a production system architecture like ACT* places a lot of constraints on the representation of a skill. The necessity of representing the skill as productions provides some constraint, but much further constraint comes from style rules (Bovair, Kieras, & Polson, 1990) imposed by the particular theory.[1] However, for complex tasks the skill representation is not unique. For example, in programming, top-down and bottom-up code generation requires different productions. In addition, the grain size of productions may vary. Consider the skill of writing extractor sequences in LISP. A function call of the form (car (cdr (cdr lis))) returns the third element of a list. LISP evaluates such function calls "inside out" and so will apply cdr twice to skip over the first two elements in the list, then apply car to extract the next element. If the list were (a b c d), this function call would return c. One can write productions that successively generate the three functions in top-down order (starting with car) or bottom-up (starting with the innermost cdr). In the first case, the first production to apply would be:

P1   IF   the goal is to get the nth element of the list
      THEN   use car as the first function
                  and set as a subgoal to code an argument to car
                  that will get the $(n - 1)$st tail of the list

In the second case, the first production to apply would be:

P2   IF   the goal is to get the nth element of the list
      THEN   use cdr as the most embedded function
                  and set as a subgoal to get the $(n - 1)$st element
                  of that list

---

[1] For example, in ACT* all production rules require explicit reference to goals. More recent versions of our production systems further require all other parts of the production rule to be explicitly connected to the goal. Another style rule in ACT* and in Bovair and Kieras is that there be no more than one external action connected with a single production rule.

The first production rule would guide coding as in our original LISP tutor, whereas the second production rule would guide bottom-up tutoring more in the style of the GIL tutor of Reiser, Ranney, Lovett, and Kimberg (1989). The theory provides no direct guidance on the issue of which method to teach to students.

However, there can be important consequences of the model taught. Students may find one method more in keeping with their prior methods. Thus, in this case one could argue either that the first method is consistent with left-to-right problem solving or that the latter method is more in keeping with forward causal reasoning. It remains an empirical issue to evaluate the two. Also, one method might just be more powerful than another. For instance, Koedinger and Anderson (1990) present a model of geometry problem solving that is capable of solving more difficult problems than the cognitive model embedded in the original geometry tutor of Anderson, Boyle, and Yost (1985).[2] Another possibility is that one method leads to greater transfer. For instance, Singley, Anderson, and Gevins (1989) describe a model for solving algebra word problems that leads to greater transfer than the method typically taught in algebra textbooks. Perhaps the most important issue about choice of cognitive model is that there can be a clash between the method advocated by the tutor and the methods taught elsewhere to the students. A major source of difficulty in our work with the algebra tutor was that the methods it employed, based on one textbook (Keedy, Bittinger, & Smith, 1978), conflicted with the methods students had learned in the classroom.

In our view, development of the cognitive model is the most important aspect of tutor development and the most time intensive. It is basically the problem of developing an expert system to solve a problem, with the added constraints that the system solve the problem in a cognitively plausible way, that it satisfy some measure of optimality among alternative methods, and that it be consistent with the methods being taught to the student elsewhere. It is not a task that can be done well without intensive study of the domain and the context of its instruction. It is a task that no amount of prior cognitive theory nor development of authoring tools will eliminate.

The work and difficulty involved in developing an adequate cognitive model are the major obstacle in this approach to tutoring (see Bovair, Kieras, & Polson, 1990, for similar comments). Once this is accomplished, the rest of the task is relatively easy and can be supported with various authoring aids, as we describe later in this chapter.

Declarative Instruction

Developing a production-rule model amounts to identifying the instructional objectives. Each production rule is another piece of knowledge that one wants to communicate to the student and have the student master. The ACT* theory

---

[2]This greater power is achieved by planning in an abstract proof space, which is much easier to search by virtue of the fact that it is much smaller.

provides strong guidance on the issue of how these production rules are to be communicated. According to the theory, production rules are acquired by analogy to examples of solutions that were produced by these productions. Thus, if we wanted to teach a student productions P1 or P2, we should center our instruction around an example involving this production. Thus, we might show them the example

$$(car \ (cdr \ '(a \ b \ c)) = b$$

The critical issue is not just presenting the example but attaching to it information to explain how the example relates to problem-solving goals. Essentially we need to attach to the example the production rule it is supposed to illustrate. If we were using the previous example to teach P1, we would need to also present P1 and see if the students understood the application of P1 to the example. We advocate doing this through a series of questions that make sure the subject can map each clause of the production onto the example:

What is the goal of this code?
    Answer: to get the second element of (a b c)
What function do you use?
    Answer: car
What is the function's argument?
    Answer: (cdr '(a b c))
What is the goal of the argument?
    Answer: to get the first tail of (a b c)

In our view, appropriate declarative instruction consists of presenting the production rules in English, providing examples of the application of these rules, and interrogating the student so that the student understands the application of these rules to the example.

Model-Tracing Practice

Once such rules have been explained, the next step is to have the student solve problems that involve the target production rules. There are two goals in such problem solving. One is to determine if the declarative instruction has really been properly encoded. The second is to give the student an opportunity to compile declarative knowledge into production rule format and to practice those rules. Both goals require that we be able to interpret the student's problem-solving behavior and identify what rules he or she is applying, correctly or incorrectly. This is where the model-tracing methodology becomes involved. Simply put, we try to find some sequence of production rules in the underlying student model that will reproduce the behavior. If we can, then we give the student credit for understanding the rules. If not, we try to determine the places where the student's behavior is discrepant from the ideal model. These points of discrepancy will be points where a particular production rule should have fired but did not. That failed production rule becomes a target for further instruction and remediation. Besides needing to deal with errors in problem solution, the tutor needs to be able to help the student when the student is stuck. This again requires interpreting the student's current problem solution and determining what production should apply next. That production becomes a target for advice.

The task of model tracing is difficult because of ambiguity—more than one sequence of production rules could have produced a particular surface behavior. This makes it impossible to proceed with any certainty and creates computational problems as we need to follow a potentially exploding number of alternative interpretations. Our methodology develops its distinct character because of the strong measures we take to tame that ambiguity. One measure is to insist that a student never deviate from a correct solution path, as we do in our immediate feedback tutors such as described in Anderson et al. (1990). Another measure is to present disambiguation menus to students as soon as they produce behavior that can be generated by more than one correct production rule. A third measure is to try to impose strong stylistic constraints on the student to restrict the number of acceptable solutions. These measures simplify the task of model tracing, but the constrains they impose on the student's problem-solving behavior have potentially important side effects on the learning process. Whether these effects are positive or negative on balance is an empirical question. For example, requiring students to remain on a correct solution path decreases problem-solving time dramatically, but may deprive students of the opportunity to learn recovery skills. Presenting disambiguation menus unavoidably provides clues to a correct solution. Style constraints require the students to practice optimal solutions, but the rules can border on the arbitrary in some circumstances,[3] and students who can generate nonoptimal solutions may be confused when they are rejected. Much of our research has examined the consequences of these constraints, and research described here is devoted to finding ways to maintain the interpretability of behavior while avoiding these constraints.

The system needs to be able to respond to holes in the problem solution, whether these holes reflect overt errors or points where the student simply cannot progress. Our method is to essentially reinstruct the needed production rule.

---

[3]For instance, rules about style of solution, although generally well motivated, can be pretty arbitrary in particular applications. An example concerns when to introduce temporary variables in a computer program. One rule we have used is that temporary variables should be used to store the results of repeated computations. Although generally a good idea, sometimes the savings is not worth the cost of creating the variable. It is a subtle problem just when it is worthwhile and when not. This is not something we want to burden the beginning student with so we use the blanket rule—create a temporary variable every time it can prevent you from recomputing a quantity. This means the student is forced to create a temporary variable when it is perhaps not the best thing to do.

There is a danger in simply representing the rule, as that may provide students with more information than they really need. There is ample evidence that people remember better what they can generate for themselves than what they are told (see Anderson, 1990, for a review of research on the generation effect). It is also possible that processing elaborate feedback will interfere with problem solving. A final danger is that subjects will process the feedback we present just to extract the answer and not really understand why it is the answer. Thus, we have adopted a successive hinting strategy in which we provide students with minimal information and then only more as needed.

One could imagine a scheme in which there were many layers of progressive hints, but our students find such a scheme frustrating. Rather, we tend to use a two-hint scheme in which the first level basically frames the task and leaves it to the student to solve it while the second level explains the correct solution. Thus, for P1 we would present at the first level: "You need to come up with some sequence of extractors that will produce the third element of a list. Remember that LISP evaluates its functions inside out."

The second level would present: "To get the third element of a list you need to get the second tail of the list and then apply car to get the first element of that list. Since LISP evaluates its functions inside out, the first thing you will code is car and then you will code its argument that gets the second tail."

An interesting aspect of this approach to tutoring is that it places no value on providing bug diagnoses to students, which has been the traditional heartland of intelligent tutoring research (e.g., Sleeman & Brown, 1982). The students' problem is that they do not know the correct rule, and this is what needs to be repaired. They generally do not need an elaborate explanation about what mental state led to error but instead need an explanation about what needs to be done. There is now research finding that reinstruction helps, whereas bug reports do not (Sleeman, Kelly, Marlinak, Ward, & Moore, 1989).

There needs to be one strong qualification placed on this rejection of bug reports. A student needs to be told what is wrong about his or her thinking if the bug belief actively interferes with student's incorporating the correct instruction. There are two ways this can happen. First, the student can have some misconception that causes the student to systematically misinterpret the instruction. This appears not to be a great difficulty in the domains of programming and mathematics where students do not harbor elaborate and strongly held misconceptions about the subject matter. It may be a serious issue in other domains like physics, where strong misconceptions have been shown to interfere with learning the target domain (McCloskey, 1983). The second way misconceptions can interfere is that the student simply refuses to process the instruction, convinced that he or she is right. In contrast to the first category of distorting misconception, this category of obstinate misconception is quite prevalent in the domains of programming and mathematics. Here the students really need not have their misconceptions explained, they only need be convinced that their belief is incorrect.

Sometimes, a simple "error diagnostic" rather than a bug message is sufficient. Thus, if the student enters "write" rather than "writeln" for Pascal, we will deliver the message "You need to issue a line feed and write does not do this." On other occasions, a certain exploratory component to the tutor is useful. Students can try out the code they believe in and see that it does not produce what they believe it will.

Knowledge Tracing and Mastery Learning

The outcome of the model tracing process is a scoring of the production rules in a problem-solving episode as to whether they were performed correctly or not. We can use this scoring to estimate the probability that the student has mastered the target production rule. Over problems, we can keep updating our estimates of what the student knows. We call this knowledge tracing, in contrast to model tracing. We have developed an algorithm for performing such knowledge tracing based on work by Atkinson (1972). Our application of their technique is described in Corbett, Anderson, and Patterson (1990).

There are a number of things one can do with this model of the student's knowledge state. One is to simply communicate this model to the student or teacher, which we believe can be very useful. The more elaborate use we make of it within our tutors is to implement a remediation algorithm in which we select problems designed to provide practice on productions designated as weak. We divide the material up into a large number of curriculum units where each unit involves introducing the student to a small number (less than 10) of production rules. As in standard mastery-based methodology (Block, 1971), we try to assure the students have mastery of the elements in the current curriculum unit before promoting them to the next unit. We continue to present remedial problems to the students until all the target production rules exceed a certain threshold defined as a probability of mastery. In our applications, we have had pretty good success (Anderson, Conrad, & Corbett, 1990) in using a mastery level defined by a 95% confidence on our part that the student has mastered the target production rule.[4] Given the way we typically parameterize the knowledge tracer, this means that the students typically practice a rule between two and four times. That is to say, a couple of successful uses or an error and three successful uses is enough to raise the production rule above threshold.

Summary: The Critical Intervening Learning Variable

We have now reviewed the essential ideas involved in creating a model-tracing tutor. They are clearly centered on the production rules and providing students

---

[4]The underlying logic is a Bayesian inference scheme by which we estimate the probability that they have transitioned to a learned state in a two-state Markov learning model.

with example problems that illustrate their use. To a first approximation, the intervening variable that determines learning rate is the number of problems solved and understood. Each problem solved and understood gives the student another opportunity to compile and strengthen production rules. Ultimately, the critical variable is the number of productions involved and the number of opportunities to fire productions in obtaining these solutions. Note that it does not matter how students actually achieve the problem solution, only that a solution is understood. We have found, in fact, that students following very different trajectories to final solution and understanding are nonetheless equivalent in their resulting problem solving skills (Anderson et al., 1990; Corbett & Anderson, 1990). This argues that within the constraint of achieving understanding, one wants to do everything possible to maximize the rate of progress through relevant examples. There are really three critical criteria by which one wants to judge instruction. First, one wants the student to achieve understanding. Thus, it would not do to simply tell the student what to do in problem solving and have the student blindly follow the instruction. Second, the problems have to be relevant to the instructional goals. Thus, for instance, it does no good to give students massive practice on components that reflect only a fraction of the target skill. The third constraint is speed through the material. A pure discovery environment (assuming understanding can be achieved) is a poor idea because some things are very hard to discover without guidance. There is a growing body of data that is consistent with the benefit on instruction that emphasizes these three conditions (Anderson et al., 1989; Black, Bechtold, Mitrani, & Carroll, 1989; Carroll, in press; Carroll & Mack, 1985).

We feel that knowledge tracing achieves the relevancy criterion and that our example-based instruction and incremental feedback achieve the understanding criterion. The criterion that is actually the most challenging is that of maximizing rate of progress through the problems. The challenge is to create an interface that minimizes irrelevant time and maximizes profitable learning. We believe that most paper-and-pencil or standard computer-editing environments leave too much unnecessary detail for the student to manage, and that optimal skill acquisition rates can be obtained with a "structured interface." A prototypical example of a structured interface is the structured editor in programming, which is a system that can take care of all the low-level details of syntax in programming without really understanding the goals of the student. More generally, a structured interface provides as much support as the technology allows without knowledge of the students problem-solving goals. In our word problem tutor (Singley et al., 1990) we provide students with automatic symbol manipulation facilities. In the context of geometry theorem proving, we provide students with a proof-checking facility among other on-line tools.

Structured interfaces do for the student some of what is the target of traditional instruction. For example, structured editors in programming eliminate the need for students to learn syntax. This often provokes the criticism that tutors that use them do not teach certain skills such as syntax of the programming language, algebraic symbol manipulation, or proof checking. We have two responses to such criticisms. The first is to note that these are typically not the skills students have difficulty mastering. The second is that there is no reason for students to master these skills since they can be automatically provided. Thus, we feel that we are justified in providing these computer-automated components if they can accelerate the acquisition of those problem-solving components that cannot be automated.

THE MULTIPLE PROGRAMMING
LANGUAGES PROJECT

The initial product of our multiple languages project was a tutor that embodies the philosophy just discussed. This tutor and philosophy in turn serve as the basis for our research into an authoring system that can make the technology more accessible to experts who are not cognitive scientists. This system used a common production system, interface, and tutoring architecture to teach LISP, Prolog, and Pascal. We illustrate the tutor with a Pascal exercise.

Figure 4.1 shows the system as it appears when a Pascal problem is initiated. There are four windows on screen. At the top is a scrollable window that contains the problem statement. Below the problem statement window is another scrollable window that contains a code template. Students can enter code into this window by means of a menu of coding actions or by typing. The tutor provides help messages to the student in the third window down, and the bottom window serves as a type-in buffer. To the right of the screen is the menu of coding actions. Note that one node in the code template is highlighted. This is the node that will be expanded by the student's next action, unless the student shifts the focus to another node (by means of a mouse).

Figure 4.2 shows the code window at a later point during the learning process. The student has chosen to expand the highlighted node as an arithmetic expression; a submenu of arithmetic expansions has been brought up, and the student has chosen to expand this as "multiplication." Most of the code entry takes place by means of menu selection. The student is required to type in names of identifiers and other such terms. Students have the option of typing larger chunks of code, however. These chunks are analyzed into a set of new actions by a parser. Then these new actions are implemented in sequence. Our model for this interface was taken from the system used at Carnegie Mellon University (CMU) (Goldenson, 1989; Miller & Chandok, 1989) for the instruction of introductory programming to the bulk of CMU undergraduates. This course uses a structure editor but not a tutor. Considerable success has been reported for it (Goldenson, 1989).

The error feedback in the tutor is quite primitive. We recognize a few common

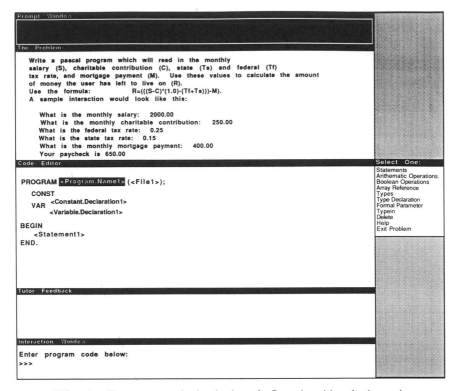

FIG. 4.1.   The screen at the beginning of a Pascal problem in the multiple-programming languages tutor.

bugs, such as when students confuse write and writeln in Pascal, and provide explanatory feedback, but most of the time when the student makes an error we simply respond by stating that it is an error. Most of our effort at instruction takes place upon requests for help from the student, in which case we present a series of successively stronger hints culminating in telling the student what to do. However, the design of the hints was purely a matter of intuition. In redoing the effort, we intend to use the two-step hinting procedure illustrated earlier.

The current tutor is an immediate-feedback tutor that insists that the student stay on the correct path. However, we would also like to implement something closer to the version of the LISP tutor, which we call the flag tutor (Corbett & Anderson, 1990). In the flag tutor system when a student makes an error, the tutor places the erroneous code in bold face to indicate that it is an error, but the student is allowed to continue coding. This is something that is easy to do in a syntax-based editor. We have observed that 80% of the time when the student's error is flagged the student will spontaneously correct it; 10% of the time students ask for help; and 10% of the time they continue coding despite the warning

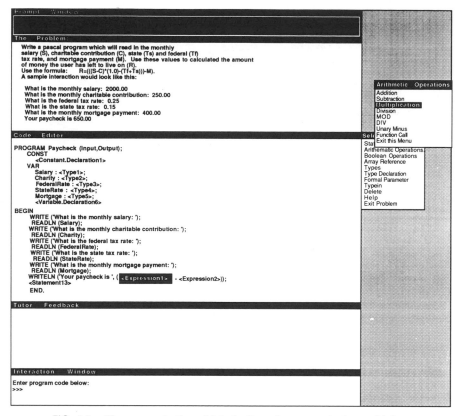

FIG. 4.2. The screen in the midst of a Pascal program in the multiple-
programming languages tutor.

that they are in error. Occasionally, students are actually on a correct path of solution and the tutor will accept this if it works. More often, students will become convinced they are in error and go back and seek help from the tutor at the point of error.

This flag tutor has the advantage of the immediate-feedback tutor in allowing students to quickly correct mistakes. It minimizes time spent processing feedback and allows students to self-correct without any feedback. It also allows students, when they are set on their erroneous solution, to become convinced that they have a problem before processing the tutor's feedback. It also allows the student to express innovative solutions. We like this system because we perceive that it allows the student greater freedom without any substantial cost. We also perceive that most colleagues and potential users like this system upon hearing it described. However, our evaluations of it have not produced any significant positive results on measures like final achievement tests or student evaluations after using it. Further, students generally take longer to get through the material using the flag tutor than the immediate feedback tutor. This raises interesting questions about what one does if one has an instructional system that is philosophically superior but does not perform as well. Our attitude on this score is to leave the choice with the student or teacher and have the tutor setable for immediate feedback mode or flag mode.

One of the major technical achievements of the tutor was the use of a new production system—Tertl. This system was designed to take advantage of the constraints of tutoring in a model-tracing paradigm. In such a paradigm, as long as the student stays on the course of an interpretable solution, only one production will fire at each point, and that production will apply to a part of the solution the student designates. In this case, a production system can be written that identifies the correct production in the time proportional to the logarithm of the number of productions and independent of the size of problem representation. This means that we are relieved of the complexity barrier and have been able to tutor many-hundred-line programs. Problem complexity had always been a major limitation in our previous efforts at tutoring.

Another efficiency we have added to the tutor is the ability to enter tutoring exercises in the form of code solutions. A parser has been implemented that, in effect, reversed production rules and produces a general working memory representation of an exercise from a canonical solution. This parser is a revision of the parser required to translate code chunks into menu actions. The canonical solutions have to be augmented with English phrases for tutoring and with information on ordering constraints, but they are far less elaborate than the working-memory representations that were previously entered by hand.

Another interesting feature of this multiple programming languages tutor is that it served as the basis for transfer to another application. Researchers at NYNEX (Gray & Atwood, in press) were able to take this system and adapt it to provide a tutor for COBOL, which is taught internally within NYNEX. Their tutor is also used at Metropolitan Life, and they are exploring the options of using it at other locations.

Classroom Experience

In the fall of 1989, we completed a classroom test of the tutor in which it taught a semester course to undergraduates in the School of Humanities and Social Sciences at Carnegie Mellon University. These students were selected on the basis of never having had a programming course before. In that semester course, students mastered LISP, Prolog, and Pascal to the point where they could write in each language a program that would solve an arbitrary eight-puzzle problem (Nilsson, 1971). Although there is no comparable nontutor course, we view this as a dramatic level of achievement for beginning students. We believe that one basis for the success was the transfer of skills across programming languages. However, the order of learning the programming languages was not systemat-

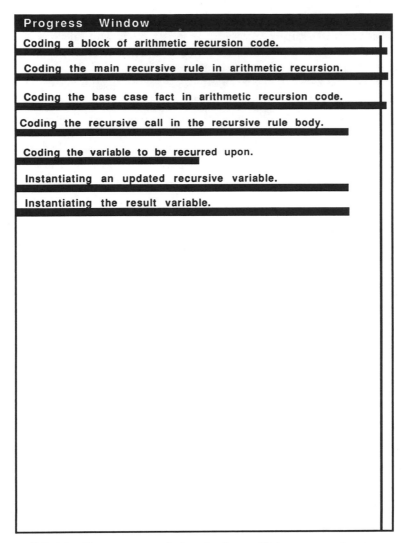

FIG. 4.3. The progress window in the multiple-programming languages tutor show level of mastery of the individual productions being monitored in the LISP lesson on recursion.

ically manipulated. (It was always Pascal, then LISP, then Prolog.) It remains a goal to manipulate language order and see the effects on learning.

In the class we experimented with a feedback facility that proved to be popular with students and that illustrates a general direction we need to go in developing a general tutoring system. We graphed for students how well they were doing on the various production rules that we were monitoring. Figure 4.3 shows an illustration for a lesson on recursion. The length of each bar represents our estimate of the probability that the student has mastered each of the rules. Upon each action that the student takes an appropriate production rule will grow or shrink. The line to the right represents the 95% confidence threshold that we use for assuming the student has mastered the production rule. Students appreciate this access to the system's internal model of them. In the future, we intend to attach declarative, example-based text to each of these bars so that students can bring up instruction relevant to a rule they are having difficulty on. This effort reflects the direction of making the inner workings of the tutor available to student and teacher. We feel that it is important that the tutor's behavior be as transparent as possible so that it does not appear as a mysterious burden being forced on everyone. Another step in this direction might be to let students choose which rules they wanted remediation on, rather than leaving this step in the hands of the tutor.

The system was not without its difficulties. Besides the problems associated with new software, students found the option of typing in code and having it parsed tempting but frustrating.[5] It often seemed attractive but they were constantly making errors in their syntax and so would go back to menu-based entry.

Students also complained about getting lost in the large programs. The tutor would be providing feedback about the next line of code in some submodule while students had lost track of what the submodule was supposed to do. This suggests the need to provide appropriate explanation to students of what various submodules were supposed to achieve.

An interesting outcome concerned the use of recognition-based code entry through the menu system. We did a comparison of this with recall-based entry as in the LISP tutor where subjects are required to recall and then type the code in. Students trained on a recognition-based system did not do as well as recall subjects when they were asked to do paper-and-pencil tests. We have subsequently obtained evidence that this reflects at least in part a mismatch between the mode of training (recognition) and the mode of the paper-and-pencil test (recall). If tested in a recognition mode they are equivalent to recall subjects. This raises serious questions about the criterion for which one is training. As we stated earlier, we have adopted the view that we are training students to do well in a recognition-based structured editor and so are not necessarily bothered by these results. However, others might take the view that paper-and-pencil recall-based performance should serve as the criterion and would want a recall-based tutor.

The tutor provoked a lot of complaints from those who had to develop software on it. Developing a tutor for a language required the mastery of a lot of obscure details, and there were relatively few facilities for debugging the software. As long as such development is done in-laboratory these were tolerable inconveniences. However, it is clear that the development environment will have to be substantially cleaned up if we are to see it used outside the lab.

---

[5]Actually, we created this system in response to student requests for such a facility. This is one example (among many) of a feature that students demanded only to complain when it was provided.

AN AUTHORING SYSTEM FOR MODEL-TRACING TUTORS

We think we now sufficiently understand the model-tracing methodology that we can create an authoring system for this style of tutor. There are two related motivations for going in this direction. One is that we would like to extend the range of people who can create such tutors and extend their use beyond laboratory classrooms. The second is that we want to formalize our theory of tutoring and lay the groundwork for extensive empirical testing of this theory. Our claims of success will always be received with a certain justified skepticism as long as it is we who are testing our own handcrafted tutors. We see this as a necessary step for the field of intelligent tutoring in general. The time has passed when one's ideas should be given the protection of one's own laboratory and the only basis for deciding among alternative proposals is rhetoric. It is time these ideas get out into the world in a form that can be explored and tested. It is also critical when this happens that they be subject to rigorous experimental test and not more rhetoric.

In keeping with this goal, we are trying to create an appropriately portable system, implemented in CommonLISP and able to run on commonly available systems like the MAC II. We need to eliminate the difficulties currently associated with the system, and we also need to release the tight connection between our systems and a prescribed curriculum and instructional mode. Clearly, educators want the freedom to choose what will be taught and how it will be taught. Similarly, researchers want a tool that will allow flexible implementation of these variables.

When we talk about an authoring system for intelligent tutors, it is important to appreciate that there are levels of authoring and different users would like to have differential access to these levels. Our discussion with teachers suggest they most would like control over the problems that are used and the sequence of the curriculum. For them a system that allowed them to enter problems to be tutored and specify the sequence of problems would be adequate. Many teachers are also very concerned that the language the tutor uses be congruent with the language they use in the classroom. As teachers do not agree as to what language is appropriate, it is important they can also have access to this option without having to master the more technical aspects of the tutor.

As we discussed earlier, if someone is actually going to construct new educational software in the tutor, there is no way to avoid the task of developing production system student models. We think this can be facilitated in various ways, and one of our research goals is to study the acquisition of production system modeling skills and perhaps tutor them as we have other skills.

A person doing production system modeling is still removed from the internals of the system. We suspect that the task that will take the software developer closest to the internals of the system involves developing the structured interface. In certain applications, it may be possible to borrow a structured interface. For example, NYNEX was able to borrow our structured editor interface for programming. However, to develop a completely new domain one will have to go down to the level of code that will require mastery of Commonlisp and its relationship to the tutor.

The steps involved in creating a tutor for a new domain are outlined here. They are listed roughly in the order that they will have to be addressed in development. One might imagine software developers doing the early steps and end users, such as teachers, doing the later steps. With each step we discuss some of the issues involved and some of the special considerations that arise in these steps with respect to our programming applications. For contrastive purposes, we also discuss the application of these steps in the anticipated conversion of the word problem tutor from its old implementation (Singley, Anderson, & Gevins, 1990) to one in the current architecture.

Step 1: Develop a Structured Interface

In our view, the first step in developing an interface has to be specifying the structured interface for problem solving. This is a system that can be used without the tutor. One needs to construct and test out such a problem-solving environment before actually developing the tutor. We see problem solving as not independent of the interface in which it takes place, and so one cannot develop a cognitive model until one has settled on the interface. Then one can observe problem solvers with that interface and try to develop a cognitive model. This observation process may also lead to suggestions for improvements in the interface. The goal in developing the interface should be to design the best problem-solving environment that nonintelligent technology will permit.

In the case of our programming application, this structured interface becomes the structured editor. We have developed a set of facilities for taking a BNF specification of the grammar of the language plus some pretty-printing information and automatically compiling the structured editor for that language. Thus, in the programming languages domain it is relatively painless to get a tutor for a new programming language provided one accepts this sort of interface.

In the case of the word problem tutor, we want to create an interface that replicates the existing interface illustrated in Fig. 4.4. This system consists of a set of facilities for bringing up diagrams, labeling them, writing equations, and solving them. In particular, we provide the student with the power of a symbolic calculator and relieve the student of the need to actually compute expressions. Given that the interface already exists, one might question the need to recreate it. There are two reasons for reimplementing this interface: (a) It only resides on an outdated AI machine (the Xerox 1100 series), and (b) it is necessary that the interface have hooks into the production system.

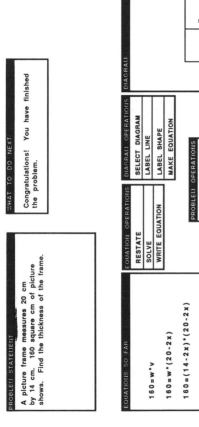
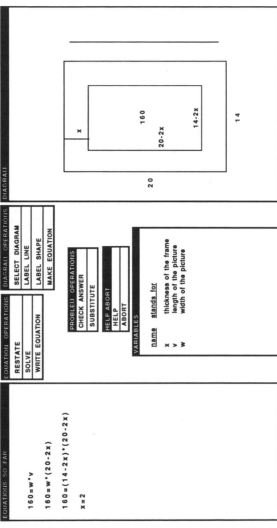

PROBLEM STATEMENT

A picture frame measures 20 cm by 14 cm. 160 square cm of picture shows. Find the thickness of the frame.

WHAT TO DO NEXT

Congratulations! You have finished the problem.

EQUATION OPERATIONS

RESTATE
SOLVE
WRITE EQUATION

DIAGRAM OPERATIONS

SELECT DIAGRAM
LABEL LINE
LABEL SHAPE
MAKE EQUATION

PROBLEM OPERATIONS

CHECK ANSWER
SUBSTITUTE

HELP ABORT

HELP
ABORT

VARIABLES

name	stands for
x	thickness of the frame
v	length of the picture
w	width of the picture

EQUATIONS SO FAR

$160=w*v$

$160=w*(20-2x)$

$160=(14-2x)*(20-2x)$

$x=2$

DIAGRAM

x
160
20-2x
14-2x
20
14

FIG. 4.4. The screen image for the word-problem tutor showing problem statement (top), equations window (left), operations and variable window (middle), and diagram (right).

Step 2: Specify Solution Syntax

It is necessary that the production system model be able to read the existing state of the solution and modify that solution state just as a student can. In a production system, access to all knowledge is through a working memory. This requires that we specify a syntax for representing the current screen structure in working memory. Each time a change takes place to the screen it is necessary to update the working memory's representation. In the case of programming, this is a hierarchical representation of the code structure. In the case of the word problem tutor, it is a representation of the state of the diagram and of the equations with variables providing cross-references between corresponding quantities.

Step 3: Specify Syntax of Problem Representation

One must also keep a representation of the problem. In the case of certain formal domains like geometry or algebra symbol manipulation, the domain already has a set of formal conventions and notations for encoding problem states and one can represent the problem in those terms. Domains like programming or algebra word problems are much more difficult because they traditionally use informal English specification of the problem. An entirely "honest" problem representation would include a string of words, but this would require the very difficult process of natural language understanding. It is also the case that the students really do not have difficulty in the language-understanding components. It is thus somewhat irrelevant to try to model the natural language processing. This motivates one to search for some internal representation that represents the immediate product of the natural language understanding process. In the case of word problems, we hope to use something like the propositional representation that Kintsch and colleagues (Kintsch & Greeno, 1985) have used with some success to model word problem solution.

We have problems with such a propositional representation in the case of programming because there is the rather unbounded process of design in going from this to an algorithmic representation. Thus, we would like to have a representation that encodes the algorithm in some code-free way and then focuses on tutoring the realization of that algorithm in some target programming language. This leaves open the option of also teaching algorithm design in certain restricted applications such as sorting algorithms.

We have chosen to represent the programming algorithms in an internal representation that is rather closely tied to Prolog. There are a number of motivations for this choice. First, we have found, as have others (Taylor, 1987), that as long as students' Prolog programming involves treating the language declaratively and avoids dealing with procedural details (like the cut) it is a relatively easy language to use. Thus, it provides a somewhat natural algorithmic representation. It is also relatively easy to generate English descriptions again if we ignore procedural issues. However, this being said, the Prolog choice is somewhat arbitrary but does provide us with a algorithmic representation. It does allow us the interesting potential of presenting the system with a problem in any language, have that problem compiled down to the internal representation, and then being able to tutor that problem in any target language.

Step 4: Production Rule Writing

The heart of the task is the production rule writing. With the interface specified and internally modeled and with the problem syntax specified, this becomes a relatively constrained task. The goal of this step is to write production rules that map the current state of the problem solution and the problem representation onto interface actions that the ideal student should take. Having the production system perform actions in the real interface is helpful because it makes the production rules fairly faithful to the task before the student. The idea that the production rules should produce interface actions is a deviation from many of the production system models that we have worked on in the past where the production rules actually specified changes to some internal representation of the solution. Now one can simply specify an interface action and have the consequence of that action be automatically represented in the working memory encoding of the current state of the problem solution.

One of the other features of our production system is that we are going to allow for unlimited number of productions to fire before an interface action is taken. This means that many productions will be invisible in the sense that they produce no external behavior as a sign of their firing. This allows in many cases easier modeling but produces the prospect for serious temporary nondeterminism as there may be many paths of these invisible productions taking place before a production fires that produces a disambiguating external action. The current production system is sufficiently efficient that we can deal with the bounded cases of such nondeterminism that we anticipate in the programming and word problem applications. Of course, people could create systems in which there was an exponential explosion of nondeterminism. However, our attitude is to leave this to developer's good sense, rather than legislating the restrictions on invisible productions and resulting nondeterminism.

Step 5: Attaching Declarative Information to Productions

Once the production rules have been written, one then needs to attach to these production rules examples for instruction and a set of questions that go with these examples. To date, all of the instruction that we have associated with productions has been hand generated. We intend to explore an option of automatic generation of questions from the production form. However, we doubt that we will ever want to eliminate the option of handcrafting instruction. This is one of the points of contact teachers like with the system—to have the ability to determine what is said.

Step 6: Entering and Annotating Problems

Another thing that teachers like is the facility to determine the problems that students see. The ideal mode for entry of such problems varies from domain to domain. In the programming domain, what is ideal is to be able to type in programs and have the tutor be able to tutor that program and equivalent solutions. As we said earlier, this is something we have already developed. In addition to the program, the teacher must enter an English problem statement plus attach English to various components of the code such as stating that a particular variable represents federal income tax.

In a domain like geometry, it is easier to enter the formal problem statement and have the tutor solve it. The difference is that in programming it is the solution that is entered and in geometry it is the problem. The reason for this is that in programming it is easy to formalize solutions and for geometry it is easier to formalize the problem statement.

The word problem situation is similar to the geometry case. The teacher needs to enter a specification of the key mathematical relationships in the problem. However, in addition to this formal specification the teacher needs to be able to enter a natural language problem statement.

Step 7: Specifying the Curriculum

There are two ways in which the curriculum can be specified. One is just to identify the sequence of production rules to be taught. They need to be aggregated into small units that correspond basically to sections in typical textbooks. In principle, this is all the tutor needs to compose a curriculum. It can choose from its stock of problems those that exercise the needed productions. However, teachers often have a desire to control the actual problems. Also, one might want to insist that certain prototypical problems be presented and specify the sequence in which these problems are presented. The tutor can then recruit additional remedial problems as needed. It may also be desired to enable the student to go on after a fixed set of problems even if they have not achieved mastery. This does not strike us as a wise educational policy, but we even more firmly believe in the need to have the end user determine the shape of the system.

If there is going to be remediation and mastery-based learning, it is necessary to parameterize the system with quantities that reflect the ability level of the student and the difficulty of individual productions. These can be set at default levels to be adjusted automatically with experience with the student (see Lesgold's chapter, this volume, for examples of parameterizing such quantities). Alternatively, the teacher may want to actively adjust the parameters that determine the remediation policy and when the student is judged to have mastered the material.

Coerciveness of instruction is another dimension that needs to be adjustable. As mentioned earlier, our tutors are designed to move seamlessly from a tutor to a structured interface for problem solution and back to tutor. This allows one to choose systems. Systems can be created that force the student to stay on a solution path, that allow the student to do anything, or that provides the guidance as in the flag tutor. We intend to do further research on various possible configurations of coercion and freedom to provide an array of options for student and teacher.

What One Gets for Free

We have described all the things that are necessary to create a tutor from scratch. Therefore, it is important to note what comes with the system. One gets the production rule interpreter and facilities for production rule development. One gets the model tracer and with it facilities for presenting production-based instruction. One gets the mechanisms for knowledge tracing and curriculum sequencing. Finally, there are the facilities to fashion one's feedback mode and level of instructional coercion. This represents easily half the work in developing a tutor. In addition, if one is not starting from scratch, one can use existing work on the earlier steps in this sequence.

SUMMARY

As mentioned in the beginning, this chapter has provided a mixture of past, present, and future. We have reviewed our past research that has led us to a particular view of how learning takes place and how tutoring can facilitate it. The key conclusions are that the productions define the critical units of learning and that the critical learning variable is to be number of problems solved and understood. A tutor should strive to maximize rate of problem solution and degree of understanding.

We are currently doing explorations on generalizing the tutoring architecture in a way that reflects the outcome of our research experience. We described the multiple-languages tutor, which is an approximation to the style of tutoring we would like to achieve. Although it would be a gross exaggeration to say that our experiences with this tutor have been uniformly positive, it presents us with a number of achievements that make us confident about the future developments.

Our future plans for an authoring system reflect our desire to get the methodology into the hands of teachers and researchers. The major motivation for the emphasis on flexibility is to facilitate experimentation with the methodology. Enough pieces of the proposed authoring system are in place that we have begun reimplementing the multiple languages tutor. We hope to see the word problem tutor reimplemented within a year and in that time have a fairly general authoring system that can be distributed. It is our intention that the only limitations on what can be tutored on this system will be writing production system models for the skills and creating appropriate interfaces. Of course, we recognize these are no small limitations. However, perhaps the existence of such an authoring system will encourage others to help push back these barriers.

REFERENCES

Anderson, J. R. (1983). *The architecture of cognition.* Cambridge, MA: Harvard University Press.

Anderson, J. R. (1987). Production systems, learning, and tutoring. In D. Klahr, P. Langley, & R. Neches (Eds.), *Production system models of learning and development* (pp. 437–458). Cambridge, MA: MIT Press.

Anderson, J. R. (1990). *Cognitive psychology and its implications* (3rd ed.). New York: W. H. Freeman.

Anderson, J. R., Boyle, C. F., Corbett, A. T., & Lewis, M. W. (1990). Cognitive modelling and intelligent tutoring. *Artificial Intelligence, 42,* 7–49.

Anderson, J. R., Boyle, C. F., & Yost, G. (1985). The geometry tutor. In *Proceedings of IJCAI-85* (pp. 1–7). Los Angeles, CA: IJCAI.

Anderson, J. R., Conrad, F. G., & Corbett, A. T. (1989). Skill acquisition and the LISP Tutor. *Cognitive Science, 13,* 467–506.

Atkinson, R. C. (1972). Optimizing the learning of second-language vocabulary. *Journal of Experimental Psychology, 96,* 124–129.

Black, J. B., Bechtold, S., Mitrani, M., & Carroll, J. M. (1989). On line tutorials: What kind of inference leads to the most effective learning. In *Proceedings of the CHI '89 Conference on Human Factors in Computing Systems.* Boston, MA: Association for Computing Machinery.

Block, J. H. (1971). *Mastery learning.* New York: Holt, Rinehart & Winston.

Bovair, S., Kieras, D. E., & Polson, P. G. (1990). The acquisition and performance of text-editing skill: A cognitive complexity analysis. *Human Computer Interaction, 5,* 1–48.

Carroll, J. M. (in press). *The Numberg funnel: Designing minimalist instruction for practical computer skill.* Cambridge, MA: MIT Press.

Carroll, J. M., & Mack, R. L. (1985). Metaphor, computing systems, and active learning. *International Journal of Man-Machine Studies, 22,* 39–57.

Corbett, A. T., & Anderson, J. R. (1990). The effect of feedback control on learning to program with the Lisp tutor. In *Proceedings of the Twelfth Annual Conference of the Cognitive Science Society* (pp. 796–806). Hillsdale, NJ: Lawrence Erlbaum Associates.

Corbett, A. T., Anderson, J. R., & Patterson, E. G. (1990). Student modelling and tutoring flexibility in the LISP intelligent tutoring system. In C. Frasson & G. Gauthier (Eds.), *Intelligent tutoring systems: At the crossroads of artificial intelligence and education* (pp. 83–106). Norwood, NJ: Ablex.

Goldenson, D. R. (1989a) Teaching introductory programming methods using structure editing: Some empirical results. In W. C. Ryan (Ed.), *Proceedings of the National Educational Computing Conference 1989* (pp. 194–203). Eugene, OR: University of Oregon, International Council on Computers in Education.

Goldenson, D. R. (1989b). The impact of structure editing on introductory computer science education: The results so far. *SIGCSE Bulletin, 21,* 26–29.

Gray, W. D., & Atwood, M. E. (in press). Transfer, adaptation, and use of intelligent tutoring technology: The case of Grace. In M. Farr & J. Psotka (Eds.), *Intelligent computer tutors: Real world applications.* New York: Taylor & Francis.

Just, M. A., & Carpenter, P. A. (1987). *The psychology of reading and language comprehension.* Boston, MA: Allyn & Bacon.

Keedy, M. L., Bittinger, M. L., & Smith, S. A. (1978). *Algebra one.* Menlo Park, CA: Addison-Wesley.

Kieras, D. E. (1982). A model of reader strategy for abstracting main ideas from simple technical prose. *Text, 2,* 47–82.

Kieras, D. E., & Bovair, S. (1986). The acquisition of procedures from text: A production system analysis of transfer of training. *Journal of Memory and Language, 25,* 507–524.

Kintsch, W., & Greeno, J. G. (1985). Understanding and solving word arithmetic problems. *Psychological Review, 92,* 109–129.

Koedinger, K. R., & Anderson, J. R. (1990). The role of abstract planning in geometry expertise. *Cognitive Science, 14,* 511–550.

McCloskey, M. (1983). Intuitive physics. *Scientific American, 248,* 122–130.

Miller, P. L., & Chandok, R. P. (1989). The design and implementation of the Pascal GENIE. In *Proceedings of the 1989 ACM Seventeenth Annual Computer Science Conference on Computing Trends in the 1990's* (pp. 374–379). New York: The Association for Computing Machinery, Inc.

Newell, A., & Simon, H. A. (1972). *Human problem solving.* Englewood Cliffs, NJ: Prentice-Hall.

Nilsson, N. J. (1971). *Problem-solving methods in artificial intelligence.* New York: McGraw-Hill.

Reiser, B. J., Ranney, M., Lovett, M. C., & Kimberg, D. Y. (1989). Facilitating students reasoning with causal explanations and visual representations. In *Proceedings of the Fourth International Conference on Artificial Intelligence and Education.* Amsterdam.

Singley, M. K., & Anderson, J. R. (1989). *The transfer of cognitive skill.* Cambridge, MA: Harvard Press.

Singley, M. K., Anderson, J. R., & Gevins, J. S. (1990). *Promoting abstract strategies in algebra word problem solving* (RC15861 [#69354]).

Singley, M. K., Anderson, J. R., & Gevins, J. S. (1991). Promoting abstract strategies in algebra word problem solving. In L. Birnbaum (Ed.) *Proceedings of the 1991 International Conference on the Learning Sciences.* Charlottesville, VA: AACE.

Sleeman, D., & Brown, J. S. (Eds.). (1982). *Intelligent tutoring systems.* New York: Academic Press.

Sleeman, D., Kelly, A. E., Marlinak, R., Ward, R. D., & Moore, J. L. (1989). Studies of diagnosis and remediation with high-school algebra students. *Cognitive Science, 13,* 551–568.

Taylor, J. (1987). *Programming in Prolog: An in-depth study of problems for beginners learning to program in prolog.* (unpublished doctoral dissertation, University of Sussex Cognitive Studies Programme.

TRANSCRIPT OF DISCUSSION

Doug Towne: I didn't quite follow what you were saying about teaching the three different programming languages in the same environment. Did you say that you were not able to use the same structure?

John Anderson: It turned out that the three developers modified the original tutoring system to fit their tasks. However, there was no real reason to have modified the system. Evidence for this is our new tutor, the Mac II based tutor, where only one person has access to the code. We denied other developers access to the code. It turns out to be quite easy to develop three tutors in the same system. But it is just the fact that we made the code available to everybody, that they wound up essentially going and changing the system given their particular beliefs of how a system should be designed.

Doug Towne: There really was nothing in the languages that caused you to think different about instructing them?

John Anderson: No.

Alan Lesgold: I'm impressed by the overall scheme and I find it very congenial. I have a problem and I think the same problem exists here. It really has to do with the logic of what you're teaching. In the brave new world, if you can write the production rules to do something you can just make the machine do it. But then the question "Why do you want to teach the person?" suddenly arises. I guess that I'm trying to sort out in my own mind what the logic is for deciding on the set of productions to teach. Is it that somehow some experts out there happen to think that those are important productions to learn in order to afford some transfer opportunities, or some generalization opportunities? Or is there some relatively better-rationalized scheme for deciding on what gets taught in the way of introductory or basic skills kind of instruction? The assumption would be that the real goal is to get people able to do some things for which we're not able, in brief design sessions, to write the production rules.

John Anderson: There is one question that's been long asked about this whole approach: If the tutor must be built around an expert system to do the task, then why teach people to do the tasks (because you already have the expert system)? The answer to that presumably is that you can only teach part of the task, such as writing code. We don't have a full expert system to program in LISP, as witnessed by the kind of salaries I pay. So what we have is a complex critical skill for which you can actually develop an expert system for only the beginning parts. The theory is that the tutor can get people going along the right route, and at some point in time, the system has to pull away. What you want to do is be able to launch them on the path toward expertise.

Alan Lesgold: Can you give some guidance? When an instructor comes from using an authoring environment like this, what do we know about what to tell them where to focus their attention to find the appropriate launch pads, if you will?

John Anderson: Well, we essentially just take the beginning parts of the curriculum and try to model what is going on. I don't actually think that there is (in principle) any difficulty with teaching any aspect of these skills. But it takes a long time to codify that knowledge. Probably, there are at least thousands, maybe tens of thousands of rules that define an expert in one of these particular domains. It is just not possible to codify all this. So what you do is you look at what tends to be the early curriculum and try to codify the expertise that underlies that.

Alan Lesgold: I guess my concern is that in the brave new world there are a lot of new kinds of skills being called for which there are no real experts. The traditional approach is relying on a social process to accumulate some sense of what the launching knowledge ought to be. It might break down. One of the hardest puzzles that I see when I look in this area is can we begin to accumulate some wisdom from looking at what kinds of things turn up in the beginning curriculum of courses that would help guide the writing of courses of the . . . for, say, fixing a device that never existed before and operating a device that never existed before.

John Anderson: That's a good problem. I don't know the answer to that.

Geraldine Myers: In teaching this multilanguage syntax, are they taught as individual entities or are do you try to capitalize on the knowledge that you have developed in teaching the first language? In other words, is there any attempt to transfer the knowledge, the understanding of, say, the algorithmic process?

John Anderson: That is probably the main reason why we are able to teach three languages in one semester. We followed that class up with a number of more careful experimental investigations where we looked at learning Language 1 and then Language 2, or vice versa. There was a lot of transfer of the first to the second language. The transfer does seem to be substantially involved with algorithm design, which is common to all languages.

Geraldine Myers: Does the tutor itself capitalize on that, or is that just what the students bring in?

John Anderson: It does in the sense that the production rules are cut out of the same mold. But there really isn't any attempt in the tutor to explicitly draw out links among the languages. We don't say things like, "As you did in one language, you do on another language." Somehow the potential for transfer is kind of self-evident. For instance, students essentially see that there is a lot of commonality in how conditionals are done in LISP and how they are done in Pascal. The transfer is taking place spontaneously without a lot of pushing on the tutor's part.

Pat Kyllonen: How important is knowledge tracing and the sequencing of problems? It sounds like knowledge tracing is giving you the ability to select the problem that's going to optimize learning for a particular student. But how much of a difference does it really make?

John Anderson: We don't have in our own research any careful comparisons of the sequencing produced by our algorithm versus other algorithms. Some other people have used similar knowledge tracing algorithms back 15 or 20 years ago and produced some demonstrations that the kind of algorithm we're using is optimal. We do know that just requiring students to go through a fixed set of problems without knowledge tracing means many will fail to achieve mastery level in final achievement tests. Knowledge tracing appears to guarantee mastery for everyone.

Pat Kyllonen: But are those data clear and convincing?

John Anderson: They are convincing to me. It turns out that on mastery tests students are getting close to perfect scores with the adaptive sequence produced by knowledge tracing. They are not doing badly but definitely worse on the fixed sequence. But there are lots of potential adaptive sequences, so I cannot claim ours is optimal.

Walt Schneider: Let's talk about creating production rules. It's hard for me to think of what one has done in a two-page description of a production, and two pages of lists to describe that production rule. When you go to a new domain, can you make it so that somebody not as familiar with that domain can do what you do? So far, everybody who has ever done that is at CMU or was explicitly trained there.

John Anderson: Two comments. First of all, production rules in the new system are no longer two pages. They are down to half of a page. Development time has been decreased by a factor of 2 to 10. Second, one of the new things we've wanted to do is to build a tutor to teach students how to write production rules. We think we actually have a cognitive model of what is involved in writing production rules. So our image of how the system will eventually be given to the world is that your first interaction with it will be to spend 30 hours being tutored on production rules programming. That's how we are going to try to give that particular skill to the student.

Bill Johnson: Last night, when we were trying to define an authoring system we said something along the lines that it would allow a subject-matter expert, or teacher, or first-time builder on the tutoring system to build such a system. On the last slide that you had out, "What you get for free," what do you have to do? My experience is that putting together a reasonable interface is a really tough part of the job, and it seems like building an authoring system, you would want to have the design and building of the interface on one of the important things that you would get for free.

John Anderson: You can't really get an interface for free, but building an interface certainly could be a lot easier than it currently is. One of the issues that they are doing some research on at NYNEX is how you might aid the actual definition of the interface. Right now, that is something that we haven't made any real progress on. Not that there isn't any progress being made around the table here, it's just something we haven't done.

Bill Johnson: It seems that once you have that interface somewhat defined, it creates the whole structure for the remainder of the tutor.

John Anderson: I think that's right. It is not a trivial task to create a structured interface. For instance, consider the symbolic manipulations that will be part of the structured interface for a word problem tutor. It is hard to imagine that, if you had not anticipated the need for a calculator in your tools for authoring interfaces, you would create tools that would make it easy for the first-time user to create a symbolic manipulator. That's just a major subgoal if you don't already have it available. This gets to the issue of how you anticipate the kind of power you actually want to put into your interface.

Kevin Bennett: I have a question about the model tracing approach. Do you think that it could be extended to deal with either more complex or less well-structured domains?

John Anderson: There are probably limitations somewhere along those combined dimensions of complexity and ill-structuredness on the applicability of this approach. It is really hard to say where those limitations lie. That's one of the reasons why we want to make it available. The key notion is you really have to build an expert model of what is going on. And can you always build expert models to do problem solving in relatively complex and ill-structured domains? Clearly, as you move in that direction, the whole issue of specifying expertise becomes more and more problematical.

5 Supporting Diverse Instructional Strategies in a Simulation-Oriented Training Environment

Douglas M. Towne
Allen Munro
University of Southern California

An intelligent tutoring system (ITS) should have the capacity to deliver instruction according to whatever approach is deemed most effective under the prevailing conditions. Whether the instructional planner making that decision is human or automated, the ITS should place virtually no constraints on the instructional strategy or the technical content to be addressed in the diverse and dynamic environment of technical training.

RAPIDS II, a training system that provides the tools for authoring interactive simulations of complex devices, has been developed with the goal of offering a very wide range of fundamental instructional approaches. Using RAPIDS II, subject matter experts can convey their domain-specific skill and knowledge to others via such approaches as *coaching,* which emphasizes demonstrations and explanations of tasks; *tutoring,* which emphasizes situationally based and opportunistic interventions; *free exploration,* which affords to the learner the opportunity and responsibility to conduct the learning process; and various types of *drills* and *exercises* that attempt to increase speed and accuracy by prompting the learner to make specific responses.

The subject matter that can be trained includes declarative knowledge, such as theory of operation and front panel orientation; procedural knowledge, including the performance of time critical tasks; and problem-solving skills such as diagnostics.

INTRODUCTION

The acquisition of cognitive skills is rarely a smooth and consistent progression from total ignorance to total knowledge. Learners necessarily start a learning unit with some prior knowledge relative to the subject matter, they often emerge with less than total mastery, and throughout the learning process they may progress in a noncontinuous fashion. Sometimes increases in knowledge and ability are gradual and predictable. At other times there are sudden breakthroughs in understanding and performance.

The changes in knowledge during learning also include losses of understanding. It may be that a seemingly learned skill was never really mastered, that the learner simply remembered the directions for performing it long enough to repeat it. Alternatively, a learned skill can deteriorate either with the passage of time without an opportunity for further practice, or with exposure to new information that somehow creates confusion about the old. Whatever the precise mechanisms that enable learning, a single correct performance of a skill may be insufficient evidence that it has been learned for all time. Similarly, deficient performance of a task does not necessarily mean that the entire task must be remediated. In many cases, resolving a small knowledge deficit can produce significant improvements in understanding and performance.

In a sense, human tutors are constantly diagnosing their students' abilities, as are the students themselves. Many knowledge deficiencies appear during instruction of closely related skills, indicating the need for additional instruction of the topic. Other problems are manifested during instruction of relatively unrelated topics, yet the author can recognize that remediation is required. Finally, many knowledge deficiencies are brought to the attention of the tutor explicitly by the learner, who may indicate that he or she has forgotten some point, has become confused, or has failed to grasp a concept.

Few human tutors would claim that their ongoing assessments of their students are absolutely accurate and complete. Thus, even in the very best of conditions, involving a highly skilled instructor and a bright, motivated, and articulate student, there is some level of shared uncertainty about the learning state of the student. Yet the parties to the instructional process seem able to tolerate the possibility of uncertainty and error, knowing either that the unknown deficiencies will be manifested sooner or later, or that those deficiencies will be resolved in the course of the ongoing instruction.

Such opportunistic and error-tolerant instructional intelligence is not easily achieved in automated instructional systems. To avoid serious consequences of error, automated instructional systems must be designed to facilitate recognition of the learner's status, even at unexpected times; they must allow the learner to exert some influence on the instruction according to his or her perceptions of understanding and proficiency; and they must function in a flexible manner, recognizing the unavoidable error that surrounds assessments of individual knowledge. At the same time, the goal of precise cognitive diagnosis cannot be so overriding that the instructional process is riddled with artificial intrusions designed to find out what the students knows. Such intrusions, possibly tolerable during instruction of declarative knowledge, can become extremely counter-productive during instruction of procedural and problem-solving skills.

A model-based instructional system can provide an environment that supports cognitive diagnosis of most types of student performance in learning to operate and maintain complex systems. In such a setting experts can demonstrate and explain complex procedures, and learners can practice performing them, often observing the consequences of their errors. Most performance errors can be evaluated directly, by automated processes that can discriminate critical performance errors from trivial ones. When variation is allowed in the performance of a task, a model-based simulation environment can discriminate between successful and unsuccessful performances.

RAPIDS OVERVIEW

RAPid ITS Development System (RAPIDS)[1] is an automated instructional system that attempts to provide high cognitive fidelity of simulation (Towne & Munro, 1989). RAPIDS was developed to meet two basic objectives: (a) to provide effective instruction over a wide range of devices and task types, and (b) to provide the tools for developing new applications in a cost-effective manner.

RAPIDS automatically guides and exercises learners in performing tasks previously performed on the simulation by a subject matter expert. Those tasks may be ones actually performed on the real device, such as calibration, fault diagnosis, or real-time tracking operations. Alternatively, the tasks may be part-task exercises related to underlying declarative knowledge, such as front-panel drills, fault-effect drills, and functional flow exercises.

The core of the instructional system (Fig. 5.1) is configured of four independent components: (a) an active model of the system being instructed, (b) saved instances of expert performance of tasks on the system model, accompanied by supporting knowledge, (c) the instructional delivery routines that convey the previously captured expertise to the learner, and (d) a high-level instructional plan that specifies the manner in which instruction will be conducted. A fifth major element in the system, the simulation processor, works behind the scenes to maintain the graphical views of the device model as the expert or the learner operate upon it.

RAPIDS also provides the tools with which a domain expert creates the device model and demonstrates procedures upon it, and the tools for producing the instructional plan. The instructional delivery routines then interact with the learner to convey this expertise according to the high-level specifications of the instructional plan.

---

[1]The instructional features and real-time simulation capabilities of RAPIDS were developed under sponsorship of the Air Force Human Resources Laboratory. Prior research in object-oriented device simulation and instruction of diagnostic tasks resulted in IMTS (Intelligent Maintenance Training System), sponsored by the Office of Naval Research and the Navy Personnel Research and Development Laboratory.

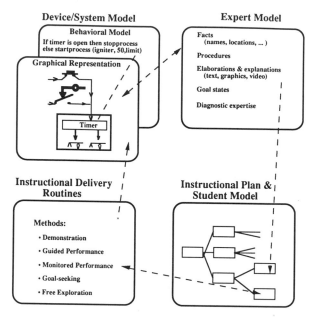

FIG. 5.1.   RAPIDS system architecture.

The Device Model

The interactive device model is the primary vehicle with which expertise is captured and conveyed to the learner. The simulation construction and execution scheme of RAPIDS is partially based on, the significantly extends, object-oriented concepts demonstrated in the STEAMER project (Hollan, Hutchins, & Weitzman, 1984). This approach allows complex systems to be built up from relatively simple objects that follow locally defined rules of operation—that is, an object's operation is specified entirely in terms of values of its inputs, rather than equipment-specific conditions. In this manner, complex devices can be specified and simulated without explicitly enumerating the numerous combinations of conditions that could exist in the device.

Examples

One example of a RAPIDS device model is the leading edge flap control system on a jet aircraft (Fig. 5.2).[2] This model mixes physical representations, such as the flat panel display, with schematic ones such as the auxiliary power unit (APU), shown only as a block. It also includes an abstract object, the graph

---

[2]This simulation model was developed by David Branks and Bettina Babbitt of Northrop Corporation.

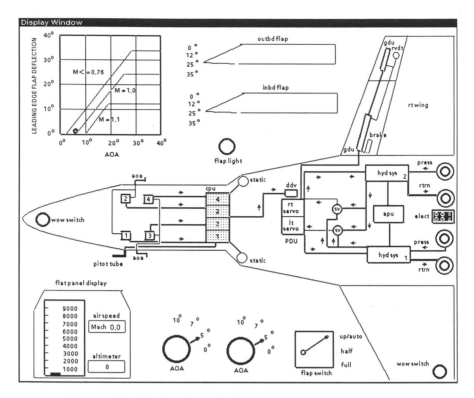

FIG. 5.2.   Model of leading edge flap control system. This simulation model was developed by David Branks and Bettina Babbitt of Northrup Corporation. Reproduced by permission.

showing flap deflection as a function of angle of attack, as an aid to learning. This graph, like many other of the objects, changes appearance as the user operates upon the model, using a mouse.

Figure 5.3 presents the top view of a hierarchically organized course on digital circuitry, including a fully operational four-bit adder. When the learner selects any individual block in the system, RAPIDS displays a more detailed view of that element. This extensive model contains 22 screens of operational digital logic circuitry, organized in a six-level hierarchy. At the bottom level are basic digital circuits involving such primitive functions as OR, NOR, and NOT. The instructional sequences explain digital functions in general, and they demonstrate the internal behaviors of various digital systems, allowing the learner to manipulate inputs and to predict results.

Figure 5.4 depicts an equipment front panel in a large shipboard satellite communications system. The model, developed to train fault diagnosis, is comprised of 25 screens of operational front panels and test point panels, involving

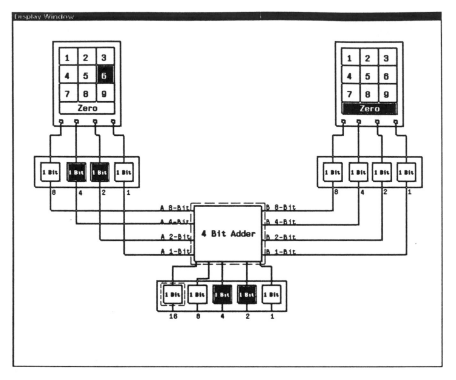

FIG. 5.3.   Section of a digital logic model (1 of 22 screens).

all the equipment in the real system. While the behaviors of the device model are complex, the underlying rule base is a relatively superficial listing of the interactions among individual front panel controls, front panel indicators, test points, and malfunctions.

Model Construction

To produce a device model, the domain expert selects objects from a library of previously defined parts and positions them on the screen to form a graphical figure. Then, as required, rules are entered that specify what values are passed between the objects in the model.[3] As objects are brought into the emerging representation, their underlying rules are automatically added to the rule base for the system. Large system models may be organized into many screen-sized views. Any combination of front-panel views or internal views may be produced in physical, functional, or schematic form.

---

[3]In a previous version, objects were connected automatically, based only on their physical proximity in the graphical representation. This approach was found to be overtly constraining. Simulation authors can now connect objects either automatically or manually to suit their needs.

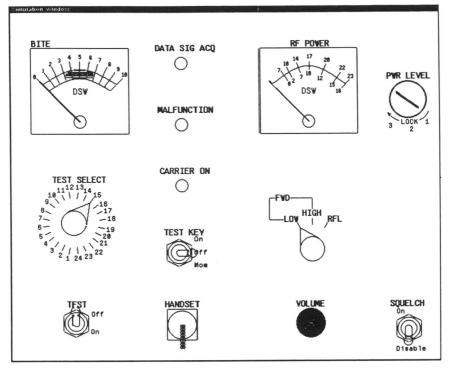

FIG. 5.4.   Model of an equipment front panel.

Following the development of the detailed device model, the author may choose to produce a set of simplified models. The training effectiveness of simplified representations has been explored and demonstrated extensively (White & Frederikson, 1987). Each such representation is produced quickly by removing objects from a copy of the complete model. Because the rules of the complete model are always executed, regardless of the version manipulated by the student, the simplified representations reflect correct behaviors even though some parts are not shown.

New objects may be produced and saved using the authoring tools provided. An object may be any entity, including a front-panel element such as a switch or indicator, or an internal element, such as a relay or servo (internal components are usually represented schematically). If desired, large units of hardware can be represented as single objects in models not requiring detailed understanding of those particular elements. Thus power supplies, amplifiers, or even entire aircraft can be represented as simple objects in models requiring these elements for proper function, but not requiring detailed views. A typical representation of a system includes highly detailed models of the parts being learned, in a context of less-detailed representations of peripheral units.

Objects may also be abstract entities included for instructional value. Examples include graphs reflecting important characteristics, and artificial switches that allow the student or the courseware to alter conditions of the simulation (such as flight condition vs. on-ground operation).

Defining a new object involves describing its behaviors using a small number of rule types and specifying how the object will appear under various conditions. The rules may be quantitative or qualitative, depending on the nature of the application. At the option of the user rules may be entered entirely via response to menus, thereby guaranteeing syntactic correctness (Munro, 1990). The graphical appearances of the object may correspond to multiple discrete states, or they may be defined to change continuously according to values of their inputs.

Expert Models of Knowledge and Performance

When the device model has been completed, the expert manipulates it to demonstrate and explain such topics as device configuration, operational or maintenance procedures, and internal device functions and causations. As procedures are performed on the device model, RAPIDS executes the underlying behavior rules to update the graphical image of the system. Because the simulation process executes continuously, the expert can perform and explain such tasks as adjusting a control according to some secondary indication or tracking a simulated radar blip with a cursor.

As the domain expert manipulates the device model, he or she may provide supporting knowledge to explain the reasons for performing various actions, and the underlying device functionality that produced the observed effects. These instructional elaborations may be in the form of written text, video, and graphics that overlay and highlight pertinent sections of the device model. The expert can also intersperse questions that require learner response in the appropriate instructional modes.

When the domain expert completes a body of instruction, he or she assigns it a name under which it is saved. Instructional *plans* (see later), refer to these specific blocks of expert knowledge and performance via these names, in order to invoke particular units of instruction.

Predefined Exercise Types

For maximum efficiency in producing instruction, a number of drill types have been predefined within RAPIDS. To produce instruction of a predefined type, the domain expert selects its name from a menu and then makes the correct student responses for that type of exercise. To produce a front panel identification drill, for example, the author selects that drill type, then selects the elements to be included in the exercise.[4] To produce a classification drill, the author enters a

---

[4]Usually some objects in a model are provided for cosmetic purposes and would not be included in an equipment orientation drill. Other objects, such as wires, are necessary for the device model to function, but may not be considered worthy of inclusion in drills.

statement identifying the class, such as "All the components that process the CGY signal," then selects the corresponding elements from the device model. Likewise, drills can be produced that each what switches are involved in different operating modes, or what components could produce a particular abnormal symptom.

Instructional Delivery Routines

The instructional delivery routines in RAPIDS convey the expert knowledge to the learner while automatically recording measures of the learner's ability and handling low-level learner errors. Instruction is delivered under any of five predefined methods, defined as follows:

1. Demonstration/instruction
2. Directed performance
3. Monitored performance
4. Goal seeking
5. Free exploration

Demonstration/Instruction Method.   Typically, instruction of declarative and procedural knowledge is presented initially with the demonstration/instruction method, which allows the learner to observe the expert's performance and explanations as they are presented on the device model. The actions presented may identify various parts of a device model, they may cause the device model to operate in an instructive manner, or they may be components of operational or diagnostic procedures. The learner's only overt responsibility in this method is to pace the rate of the presentation by clicking the mouse following each step. As time allows, the learner may repeat the presentation to study difficult parts more thoroughly.

Directed Performance Method.   Most instructional plans will follow up demonstrations of declarative and procedural knowledge with the directed performance method, which has the learner perform the actions in response to step-by-step prompts such as "Now find the rear flow-deflector control" or "Set the mode switch to STANDBY" (such prompts being generated automatically by RAPIDS). Typically this method of instruction is employed until the learner can perform correctly and within a specified time. After instruction under this method, a learner can perform the prompted actions and has begun to learn the order or conditions in which those actions are performed.

Monitored Performance.   The monitored performance method of instruction assists the learner in performing a complete task independently. Thus the learner must know what actions to perform as well as how to perform them. If the leaner makes mistakes or cannot proceed, RAPIDS automatically provides assistance. Because this method provides assistance only when necessary, the student can progress from fully guided to fully independent performance in a manner that suits his or her own particular demonstrated abilities. At the conclusion of instruction in this method, a learner can perform a complete and well-defined task correctly. As mentioned at the outset, there is no guarantee that the learner will retain this ability for all time, in the face of new, and possibly confusing, information. Further, there is no guarantee that the learner can generalize the learned task in a manner that allows tailoring it to meet slightly differing conditions. Practice in this latter skill is provided in the goal-seeking method.

Goal-Seeking. Instruction in the goal-seeking method allows the learner to practice operations for which there are many acceptable approaches. Under this method, the device status produced by the expert is used as the measure of student proficiency, rather than the individual actions the expert happened to perform to demonstrate his or her approach to the problem. Example operations include putting the simulated device into a particular operational status (not necessarily a fixed combination of switch settings) or carrying out a tactical operation. Typically, this instructional method is used following instruction of a number of example cases in the monitored performance method.

Guided practice in isolating simulated malfunctions is also provided under this method. A generic diagnostic expert built in to RAPIDS evaluates the learner's diagnostic strategy, and it supplies assistance in choosing tests, assessing the normality of test results, and drawing inferences from the symptom information evident in the device model.

Free-Exploration. In the free exploration mode, the learner is allowed to manipulate the device model as he or she wishes, for the time allowed. The learner may repeat procedures practiced previously or try new ones. Additionally, in this mode, the learner may wish to introduce various malfunctions (single or multiple) into the simulation, to explore the symptoms that result. Thus, under this instructional method, the learner has control of the learning objectives as well as performance of tasks.

Figure 5.5 summarizes the functions of the learner under each of the five instructional methods.

The Instructional Plan and Student Model

The instructional specialist produces a course plan that specifies the order in which topics will be presented and the manner in which they will be instructed. The plan is produced using an interactive graphical editor. Figure 5.6 illustrates the structure of a course plan, decomposed into topics, subtopics, and ultimately units of domain-specific expertise called content units.

Instructional Method	Learner Functions				
	pacing	performing	action decisions	task decisions	learning decisions
demonstration/inst'n	√				
directed performance	√	√			
monitored performance	√	√	√		
goal seeking	√	√	√	√	
free exploration	√	√	√	√	√

FIG. 5.5.   Learner involvement under five instructional methods.

Here, the two content units at the far right might be Front Panel Drill and Mode Drill, respectively, grouped under the topic Basic Equipment Orientation. Each of the two content unit names corresponds to the name of a drill or instructional sequence produced by the domain expert.

For every block in the course structure (every content unit and topic) the instructional planner may specify:

1. The maximum time to allocate to the unit or topic.
2. The minimum and maximum number of presentations made.
3. The speed and accuracy criteria for successful completion.
4. Conditions for presenting or skipping the unit or topic.

By setting the time allocations and proficiency criteria in various ways, the instructional planner can produce widely differing instructional strategies. One strategy might allocate a fixed time to a topic, for all students, and another could allow highly individualized pacing. One strategy might ensure that all learners progress through the same material, whereas another might define conditions, in terms of individual proficiency measures, that schedule instruction in an individualized basis. Or, one instructional approach might ensure that the learner

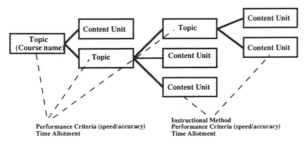

FIG. 5.6.   A RAPIDS course structure.

masters a topic before proceeding, regardless of the time required, and another might ensure that every learner receives instruction on all topics.

Data expressing each student's proficiency on each course topic are automatically recorded in a copy of the course structure. Thus the course organization, with individual performance measures, provides a high-level model of student progress and ability. The measures recorded for each student include accuracy, speed, number of attempts to successfully complete a topic, and time spent on the topic. These measures reflect the student's terminal proficiency upon completing a topic as well as the time required to attain that level.

If the instructional plan is produced prior to creating the instructional content, a subject matter expert can use the plan as the specification for creating the required demonstrations and explanations. Alternatively, the plan may call for domain expertise units that already exist, possibly having been developed for other courses. Thus, adding a significant remedial phase to a course could be as easy as referencing an existing instructional unit for that topic.

ISSUES IN COGNITIVE DIAGNOSIS

The preceding section describes the main components in our approach to automated instruction. This section offers some observations on the concepts and issues that underlie its design, what we have learned about its effectiveness and range of application, and some specific elaboration upon the manner employed by RAPIDS in diagnosing individuals' cognitive skills.

Approach to Cognitive Diagnosis

Cognitive diagnosis usually means, at the least, determining what the learner knows and how well he or she knows it. To the truly ambitious and optimistic, cognitive diagnosis also means determining what the learner incorrectly believes, how strongly he or she believes that, and how one could lead the individual from that person's current flawed knowledge state to a desired knowledge state.

High-Level Cognitive Diagnosis

In RAPIDS, information about what the individual learner knows, and how well he or she knows it, is stored in the form of the individual proficiency measures (speed and accuracy) associated with each unit of instruction in the instructional plan. RAPIDS compares these proficiency measures to criteria provided by the instructional specialist. If the learner has not attained the performance criteria, the instruction is repeated if there is time available. Implicit in the performance criteria are the specialist's conceptions of what levels of performance constitute proof of mastery, what levels of mastery are required for the intended application, and what the costs are of increasing mastery beyond given levels. These crucial considerations affect RAPIDS instruction via the proficiency criteria.

Low-Level Cognitive Diagnosis

The five instructional methods provided in RAPIDS play a major role in supporting cognitive diagnosis of detailed student performance (as well as in reducing the cognitive load in acquiring new information). When a complex subject is instructed via a progression through the instructional methods, the possible causes of student errors at any stage can be isolated to the new cognitive requirements imposed by the current instructional method. The particular manner of instructing and dealing with student errors depends upon the type of knowledge involved.

Part-Task Drills. For part-task drills the student is usually asked to make single responses to well-defined questions or prompts. An incorrect response could be a "slip" (Norman, 1980), caused by inattention for some reason. Alternatively, the error could be evidence of a true confusion among two or more elements. Upon encountering this type of learner error, RAPIDS first explains the nature of the error, then offers the learner a second chance to respond.

If the learner's second response is correct, there is no automatic attempt to determine whether the original error was caused by a slip or a true confusion (RAPIDS allows half-credit in scoring the item). If the second response is incorrect, RAPIDS shows the learner the correct response, and scores the item as being missed. In either case, the item is automatically retained in the list of elements to be presented in the next round, for even if the second attempt was correct it does not represent proof that the item has been learned. In fact, correct responses on a first attempt may not represent sufficient proof of long-term learning. For this reason the instructional plan may require higher performance objectives, such as three correct responses without an error, to consider an element learned.

Figure 5.7 shows the RAPIDS screen at one point in an identification drill, during instruction via the directed performance method (the device model is adapted from Kieras, 1988). Prior to this stage, the learner would have been led through the device model with the demonstration/instruction method. The text shown was incrementally displayed (over time) in response to the learner's actions.

The capability to diagnose learner errors in this instructional condition stems from the limited and highly defined knowledge that is required for correct performance. If a learner is asked to read a particular indicator or set a particular switch, then an error can be addressed automatically with high likelihood of being appropriate. On the other hand, if a learner makes errors in these actions

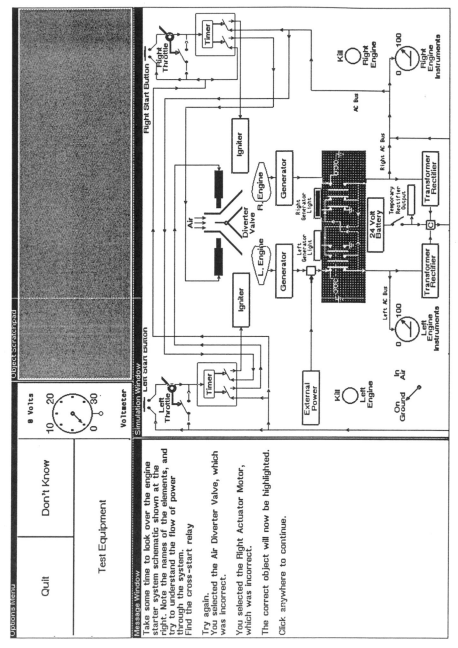

FIG. 5.7.   Sample RAPIDS instruction during front-panel drill.

120

during performance of a complete task, cognitive diagnosis becomes more difficult, especially if the learner has not already demonstrated proficiency in performing the constituent actions of the procedure.

Fixed Procedures.   One common form of procedural skill involves the transformation of a system from an initial state to some desired end state, via the performance of a fixed procedure. If a few particular initial and final states occur frequently in operational settings, then there is good reason to instruct the precise action sequences that will be required for each case. There may also be good reason to explain the underlying device functions that come into play during these operations, so the learner will have a stronger foundation for learning that sequence, and for extending that knowledge to new procedures.

The expert conveys his or her procedural knowledge for a task by setting up the simulated device in a desires initial configuration, then performing the procedure on the device model and producing instructional elaborations to accompany the sequence. The instruction may explain why certain actions were performed, what responses of the device should be noticed, and why those responses occurred. The expert may also demonstrate the implications of common or critical errors.

As with instruction of declarative knowledge, instruction of procedures would typically be presented initially with the demonstration/instruction method, which shows the system responding as the task is done, and the associated instructional elaborations. In the directed performance method, the learner performs the task in response to step-by-step instructions automatically generated by RAPIDS. Finally, in monitored performance instruction, the learner works to perform the task without prompting. Errors are detected by RAPIDS, and the learner is assisted in performing the correct action.

Theory of Operation.   A second type of declarative knowledge that supports performance of device operation and maintenance concerns theory of operation. As with system topology and nomenclature, we would not normally wish to teach aspects of theory that are not required to recall, generate, or perform the skills being taught. Thus it seems that there could be natural ways to embed virtually any theory instruction into the instruction of the procedures that involves it. One useful option for doing this allows the technical expert to tack explanations onto the basic device model, as shown in Fig. 5.8.

Determining the learner's understanding of device operation can be done in a number of ways, including the following:

1. Asking the student to identify system objects related to particular functions, for example, "Find the object through which all electrical power is routed."
2. Asking the student to make explicit predictions about the system's behav-

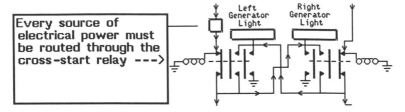

FIG. 5.8.   Overlaid text in instructing theory of operation.

iors under various conditions, for example, "If the cross-start relay fails, can the engines be started using battery start procedures?" (in this case the author would also provide a Yes/No menu for the response).

3. Asking the student to manipulate the device model to achieve various results, for example, "Make the settings required to route external power to the ignition system."

Operational Problem Solving.   It often happens that some families of operations involve a very large number of initial and final configurations of a system, and that no student could be expected to memorize all possible procedural responses to those conditions. Instead, the student must learn to produce or invent procedures that satisfy each unique requirement, based on a deep understanding of the device. We call such performance operational problem solving, in distinction from fixed-sequence procedures.

It is also common in such situations that more than one action sequence can be regarded as correct for a particular situation. In fact, there is typically a very large number of unique and acceptable action sequences that will satisfy the requirement (while there will exist at least one optimal sequence, it is not reasonable to expect even an expert to perform that sequence). Sometimes the differences among alternatives are only the sequence in which the actions are performed. In many cases there are alternative approaches that involve different actions.

To an outside observer, a skilled operator performing a variable task might appear to be performing a previously learned procedure. However, the cognitive skills involved, and hence the instructional techniques required, are quite different when the operator must create the procedures. In the extreme, the operator must invent a procedure to address a condition that he or she has never before seen or considered. More likely, one instance is closely related to previously experienced conditions, requiring a procedure very much like ones performed before. Although we would suspect that recollections of similar procedures are tailored to meet present conditions, using knowledge of the device functionality, the crucial point is that the approach for instructing the production of variable tasks is quite different than that for fixed procedures, even though their performance may appear identical.

One reasonable manner of initiating such instruction in RAPIDS is to demonstrate a number of typical situations, showing good procedures for each, and elaborating the underlying reasoning that motivated each performance sequence. Such instruction would be provided under the demonstration/explanation method, and might not appear much different from initial instruction of fixed procedures, although the expert's elaborations might well describe alternative options at various stages.

To then provide practice in producing procedures, the instruction can present problems in the goal-seeking method. For each problem the learner sees an initial device configuration and attempts to achieve a specified end state.

The expert creates such problems by:

1. Establishing the initial configuration of the model.
2. Manipulating the device model to achieve the ending state.
3. Identifying those objects whose states are critical in duplicating the objective, thereby allowing RAPIDS to dismiss inconsequential differences between the expert's final state and that of the student.

As with declarative knowledge drills, the ratio of student practice time to authoring time can be extremely high for this type of instruction.

RAPIDS diagnoses the learner's performance automatically by comparing the significant final conditions produced by the learner with those produced by the expert. If the learner achieves the objective status, within the time specified in the instructional plan, the performance is successful. In essence the device model, as updated by the simulation processor in RAPIDS, reflects whether the student performed acceptable actions, in an acceptable sequence, and did not perform any prohibited actions. Furthermore, the time taken by the student to achieve the final device configuration reflects the student's skill.

In addition, the device model is tolerant of minor errors, subsequently corrected, if the real device is correspondingly forgiving. On the other hand, if the learner commits a critical error that would damage the real device, the RAPIDS device model will similarly fail, by changing the state of the affected parts to failed conditions. To achieve this level of behavioral fidelity requires that the domain expert add rules about how and why objects fail, if the involved objects do not already possess such specifications.

While the device model is an extremely robust vehicle for evaluating the success of a particular performance, it cannot support the identification of particular performance errors for this variable type of procedure. Thus, if the student does not achieve the objective in the allotted time, there are no automatic processes[5] in RAPIDS that can (a) diagnose the particular procedure performed so

---

[5]One approach for diagnosing specific errors of omission, commission, and sequence was developed by Towne (1969), but it involves specifying the complete structure of a task as a separate specification, an often difficult task.

far and (b) direct the learner in completing the task. Some reasonable instructional alternatives are available, however, including (a) repeating the demonstration/explanation of the problem, and giving the learner a second chance, or (b) initiating the instruction of simpler problems.

Fault Diagnosis.   Fault diagnosis is a type of operational problem solving that involves a physical change to the device itself. Part-task exercises to provide the underlying declarative and procedural knowledge required to support troubleshooting can be produced using the instructional methods described above. Possible topics include use of test equipment, assessments of indicator normality, possible causes of abnormal symptoms, effects of various failures, and implications of normal readings.

Whole-task instruction in fault diagnosis can be provided in the goal-seeking method of instruction. In this case, the expert establishes the initial configuration by selecting a particular failure and entering a statement that describes the general nature of the problem, the specificity of which has great impact upon the difficulty of the problem.

RAPIDS simulates a malfunction by replacing an object's normal behavioral rules with rules describing a particular mode of failure. Depending on the particular behaviors described, a failed part can exhibit catastrophic cessation of operation, partial loss of some functionality, or low-level degradation in performance that results in outputs that are out of tolerance. In extreme cases a malfunction will only be exhibited in very special device conditions, and thus the maintainer may spend considerable time just finding some evidence of the abnormality. Whatever the abnormalities simulated, the standard RAPIDS simulation processor maintains the simulation of the device as the student operates and tests it.

The student's task is to perform testing operations to identify the source of the simulated problem to the level of a replaceable part, then perform a simulated replacement, using a menu command, and verify that the replacement restored the device. When the student declares the problem over, or time expires, RAPIDS records whether or not the failure was resolved, the time take to complete the problem, and the number of replacements made.

Throughout the problem, RAPIDS automatically measures the effectiveness of the student's testing process, and it maintains an internal trace of the test results obtained by the student and the inferences that he or she could draw from those results. If the student seeks assistance in selecting a test, RAPIDS suggests the tests that would be most effective, considering the work that the student has already performed. Additionally, the reasoning supporting the selection of the recommended test is presented, in terms of the inferences that could be drawn from possible outcomes. After a problem has been completed, the student may ask to see a complete expert approach to the problem or may ask for a complete critique of his or her performance on the problem.

All of these supporting functions are produced automatically via a model of expert diagnostic reasoning termed Profile (Towne, Johnson, & Corwin, 1982, 1983). This generic model operates on fault effect information specific to a particular system, to provide evaluation and support of the student. The fault effect data for a particular device model are produced automatically by a utility routine that inserts each possible object failure into the model and records the symptoms produced. These data allow the Profile reasoning process to consider possible causes of symptoms obtained by the student and to evaluate possible tests in terms of the inferences that could be drawn from their possible outcomes.

The diagnostic decisions made by Profile are sensitive to the symptom information already obtained by the student, the relative reliabilities of the replaceable parts, and the power of each test in discriminating the currently suspected system elements. The general formulation of this measure also considers the time required to perform each test in the real world.

Theoretical Basis of the RAPIDS Approach

RAPIDS has been designed to allow instructional planners to implement a wide range of instructional approaches to instruct in many technical areas and types of knowledge, thus there is no single theory underlying the RAPIDS instructional planning and delivery system. The design of RAPIDS has been determined by two main factors: (a) research findings in the areas of automated instruction and system simulation and (b) practical considerations in producing the highest possible ratio of instruction hours to development hours.

The first phase in developing RAPIDS (then called IMTS) was an explicit analysis of findings of previous research by others and ourselves in automated instruction. The resulting design review (Towne, Munro, Pizzini, & Surmon, 1985) yielded a set of principles that had direct implications for the design of RAPIDS. These instructional principles dealt with such areas as the timing, extent, and nature of feedback; techniques for providing expert advice; minimizing cognitive workload; and situating instruction within the context of tasks.

In addition, our earlier research had shown the feasibility of generating situation-specific instruction for specific devices, tasks, and students using a domain-independent instructional shell, while the STEAMER work proved the concept of employing behaviorally defined objects in simulations of devices. Thus RAPIDS has been designed to adhere to the available instructional principles offering an environment in which one can apply a customized instructional strategy.

Utility of Approach

Two types of data are required to evaluate the effectiveness of the RAPIDS approach: (a) instructional effectiveness data and (b) data concerning the effectiveness with which RAPIDS courseware can be developed. Although there are not yet any statistics available with which to measure the RAPIDS approach, there are findings that directly relate to the utility of the approach.

Instructional Effectiveness

The instructional effectiveness of a RAPIDS course will depend on two basic factors: (a) the inherent flexibility and power of the underlying RAPIDS resources and (b) the quality of the device simulation and captured expertise produced for a particular device.

Our experience with RAPIDS indicates that one could produce instruction with RAPIDS that appears similar to most existing instructional systems (with the exception of certain highly compute-bound and custom-programmed real-time flight simulators). A RAPIDS course, therefore, could range from a "page-turning" book-in-a-computer to a complex branching system to a highly animated exploration world. This is not to say that RAPIDS is all things to all people, but rather that its resulting forms of instruction and representation are relatively unbounded. The instructional effectiveness of a particular RAPIDS course, therefore, will be primarily a function of the instructional techniques employed in that application rather than of the underlying design of RAPIDS.

For the style of instruction most appropriate for delivery by RAPIDS, simulation-based technical instruction, research has shown rather clearly that cognitive skills can be trained effectively on simulations of the real device if (a) performance on the simulation requires virtually the same knowledge as does performance on the real device and (b) the simulated device responds to the learner's actions in a realistic manner. In one large study (Towne, Munro, & Johnson, 1983), 30 Navy technicians used a simulation-based trainer to practice fault diagnosis while 31 matched-ability students in the control group practiced using the real equipment, the AN/WSC-3 Satellite Communications System. All students then took a troubleshooting test on the real equipment. No significant differences were found between the ability of the two groups, either in time to isolate the failures or number of replacements (Table 5.1).

TABLE 5.1
Simulation-based Training Versus Conventional Training

| | Group | |
Measure	Experimental	Control
Practice problems		
Time required (min)	48.2	46.8
No. of replacements	10.3	10.6
Actual test problems		
Time required (min)	50.5	52.3
No. of replacements	8.6	8.7

Because these data were obtained using a much slower and less powerful system than RAPIDS, we can safely assume that RAPIDS instruction would be at least as effective. The results of this study speak to the effectiveness with which skills transfer from a simulation environment to the real equipment. Additional studies should now be undertaken to determine the skill levels achieved under the individualized instruction provided by RAPIDS.

Development Effectiveness

Extensive data are available concerning the time and costs of developing computer-based instruction. For conventional frame-based computer-aided instruction (CAI), development costs range from 100 to 500 of development for every hour of instruction. For custom-built simulation-based instructional systems the costs are rarely below several hundred thousand dollars and 6–12 months development time, and are often several times higher than this.

Although no quantitative studies have yet been conducted regarding development of RAPIDS instruction, we have developed several large device simulation using RAPIDS, and have taught others to develop RAPIDS instruction. Based on those experiences, we find that:

1. New users can learn to apply RAPIDS in about 1 week.
2. Small RAPIDS simulations (one-screen models, with 6–20 objects) can be developed in about 2–4 days.
3. Large simulations (2- to 10-screen models with 20–200 objects) can be developed in about 4–6 weeks.
4. The time to produce the expert instruction and instructional elaborations ranges between about 2–20 development hours per instruction hour.

Range of Applicability

RAPIDS has been developed to offer instruction related to understanding, operating, and maintaining complex systems that lend themselves to representation via interactive models. Its built-in instructional methods provide a mechanism for progressing from an instructional orientation to a guided practice orientation in an individualized fashion.

Instructional Range

RAPIDS attempts to support instruction ranging from highly guided and system-controlled to completely student-controlled exploration environments, with several options in the mid-range of shared responsibility between learner and instructional system (Fig. 5.9). One of the instructional methods in the mid-range, the monitored performance method, responds to student errors when

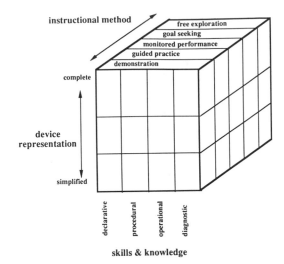

FIG. 5.9. Instructional applicability.

made; thus it offers an almost continuous bridge between guided practice and student-controlled practice.

Range of Devices and Processes

We know of no technical limitations in the applicability of RAPIDS to simulate devices. Of course there are those, such as computer central processing units (CPUs), whose internal composition and resulting behavior are so complex that they are not practical to simulate on computers employing comparable CPUs. Similarly, RAPIDS would not be an appropriate host for simulating a complex weather model involving millions of data points and equations.

For the purposes of instruction, however, RAPIDS appears capable of simulating a wide range of devices and processes. We know of no reason that RAPIDS applications would be confined to equipments and hardware systems. As long as the relationships among the parts were manageable, RAPIDS could simulate and instruct such topics as economic systems, complex scheduling problems, biological processes, and statistics.

In addition to the three example systems described earlier, these systems have been modeled in RAPIDS:

1. Ignition system of a dual-engine jet aircraft.
2. Blade-folding system of a helicopter.
3. Internal combustion engine.
4. Neural model of the human retina.
5. Jet engine diagnostic system.

6. "Pinball" example of binomial probability.

7. Programmable VCR.

Required Knowledge Engineering and Task Analysis Methods

The independence of the four elements of the system allows the generic instructional intelligence to be built in to RAPIDS, obviating a need for authoring it; it allows the domain expertise to be produced by a subject matter expert, even if he or she is not a skilled instructor; and it allows an instructional specialist to design the high-level instructional strategy independently of the low-level instructional interactions and content details. Thus the development of RAPIDS instruction can be carried out by instructional and domain experts directly, rather than through the involvement of intermediary knowledge engineers.

There is considerable leeway in the sequence in which various parts of a RAPIDS course can be developed. In some instances the instructional specialist will produce a preliminary instructional plan first, probably in concert with one or more domain experts. Then the domain experts can use the plan as their specification for the required device model and expert demonstrations and instruction. Alternatively, a new course might be built almost entirely of existing instructional units, for some device already modeled in RAPIDS. In this case, producing the instructional plan produces the course. Whatever the particular order in which the parts are produced, there will almost certainly be an iterative cycle in which the device model, the captured domain expertise, and the instructional plan are revised to take account of newly perceived needs, problems, or opportunities.

Producing a model of a complex system requires at least two types of knowledge: (a) an understanding of how the system behaves and (b) the ability to employ the RAPIDS tools to construct the model. If the subject matter expert has experience using the RAPIDS authoring tools, he or she can produce the model directly. Otherwise, the device expert would provide drawings or sketches of the system and descriptions of its behaviors to a second party for modeling. If the device model involves objects never before produced, the domain expert will also either produce the new objects in RAPIDS or provide sketches and operational descriptions to one versed in object building.

A device model for training of equipment operation can be built with "surface-oriented" rules: that is, the behavior rules express how each front panel element responds to changes in other front-panel elements without getting into the intermediary functions that cause the effects. A qualified equipment operator would possess the device knowledge to form these rules. The device model to support training of fault diagnosis must be substantially deeper, specifying how each replaceable part behaves. A qualified maintainer would have the knowledge to supply this information.

SUMMARY AND CONCLUSIONS

RAPIDS is currently operational on experimental AI computers (Xerox and Sun), running in InterLISP D. The only known limitations in the RAPIDS device modeling capabilities are related to (a) limitations in this hardware and (b) limitations in the primitive graphic elements provided to the RAPIDS simulation author. Lacking color, sound, and high-speed execution (interrupted at random intervals by a utility process known as a "garbage-collector"), the Lisp machines are not entirely effective at portraying such effects as flow through pipes and continuous rotations of complex graphics. In addition, their speed of operation and variable response times do not lend themselves to the instruction of such operations as high-speed tracking. Otherwise, the simulation speed and display resolution have been entirely satisfactory.

We are currently involved in implementing RAPIDS on PC-compatible platforms and will realize a significant improvement in processing speed along with color and sound options.

Potential for Research

The most recent development efforts have been aimed at making RAPIDS a complete system in which a wide range of topics can be taught, under a rich selection of instructional approaches. Having approached this objective, the system now stands as a potentially powerful research tool to investigate a number of crucial instructional issues.

The modular architecture of RAPIDS allows one to investigate the effectiveness of delivering well-controlled expertise under alternative instructional strategies. Alternative time-allocation strategies could easily be evaluated in this manner, as could alternative schemes for presenting a complex system in terms of its structure. In these cases only the instructional plan is changed.

Another area for study concerns the effectiveness of different types of instructional elaborations, holding the instructional strategy constant. Studies in this area could provide insights into the effectiveness of various amounts and forms of auxiliary textual information, graphical elaborations, video segments, and voice output.

Finally, the built-in instructional methods provide a convenient means for exploring learning effectiveness under different levels of learner control, especially as related to differing individual learning styles and aptitudes.

We are planning to conduct controlled studies in cooperation with Dr. Shute of AFHRL to explore some of these issues. In the process, we will obtain data concerning the time and cost to develop RAPIDS courses of various sizes.

REFERENCES

Hollan, J. D., Hutchins, E. L., & Weitzman, L. (1984). STEAMER: An interactive inspectable simulation-based training system. *The AI Magazine, 5* (2), 15–27.

Kieras, D. E. (1988). What mental model should be taught: Choosing instructional content for complex engineered systems. IN J. Psotka, L. D. Massey, & S. Mutter (Eds.), *Intelligent tutoring systems: Lessons learned,* (pp. 85–111). Hillsdale, NJ: Lawrence Erlbaum Associates.

Munro, A. (1990). *RAPIDS II authoring manual.* Los Angeles, CA: Behavioral Technology Laboratories, University of Southern California.

Norman, D. A. (1980). *Errors in human performance.* Center for Human Information Processing, Report No. 8004. University of California at San Diego.

Towne, D. M. (1969). Recursive functions for analysis of symbolic representations of task structure and human performance. Unpublished doctoral dissertation. University of Southern California.

Towne, D. M., Johnson, M. C., & Corwin, W. H. (1982). *A technique for projecting maintenance performance from design characteristics* (Report No. TR-100). Los Angeles, CA: Behavioral Technology Laboratories, University of Southern California.

Towne, D. M., Johnson, M. C., & Corwin, W. H. (1983). *A performance-based technique for assessing equipment maintainability* (Report No. TR-102). Los Angeles, CA: Behavioral Technology Laboratories, University of Southern California.

Towne, D. M., & Munro, A. (1989). *RAPIDS: A simulation-based instructional authoring system for technical training* (Report No. 112). Los Angeles, CA: Behavioral Technology Laboratories, University of Southern California.

Towne, D. M., Munro, A., & Johnson, M. C. (1983). *Generalized maintenance trainer simulator: Test and evaluation* (Report No. NPRDC-TR-83-28). Los Angeles, CA: Behavioral Technology Laboratories, University of Southern California.

Towne, D. M., Munro, A., Pizzini, Q. A., & Surmon, D. S. (1985). *Development of intelligent maintenance training technology: Design study* (Report No. ONR-106). Los Angeles, CA: Behavioral Technology Laboratories, University of Southern California.

White, B. Y., & Frederiksen, J. R. (1986). *Progressions of qualitative models as a foundation for intelligent learning environments* (Report No. 6277). Cambridge, MA: BBN Laboratories, Inc.

TRANSCRIPTION OF DISCUSSION

Alan Lesgold: I'm trying to understand what lives in the device model and what lives in the expert model, especially with the issue of things like goal states. Goal states can map onto levels of structure in a device or a process. And to some extent, there are really things that are totally on the expert side, things like goal structure for diagnosis or something like that. Do those two get highly coupled in your new architecture, or are they really both separate things?

Douglas Towne: I hope I am understanding your question properly. When I talk about a goal state, I'm talking about a state of the device that we want the learner to get it into. The expert authors the goal state simply by putting the simulated device into that configuration. Then an image of that is simply saved as a data structure. So that is the goal that you present to the student. You say "Get the device into that state."

Alan Lesgold: Are the goals hierarchically or empirically specified? What you have here is a simple model of that device that the test station has . . . it performs various tests.

Any goal state involves a test, there are some roles in the test and so on. Yes, and there are more specific definitions. There is also hardware doing all that stuff. So I guess the question is, can you model those goals?

Douglas Towne: Certainly, you could decide as an author that first you want to have a goal state of "energize." And you say, "Can you energize the thing?" Fine, he gets the thing energized. Then the next goal state would be, "Can you get it into a receive mode?" Yeah, fine, he accomplishes that. Now, "Can you get into receive mode in the single side band configuration?" and so on. In a tactical or in real problem-solving mode, you might have to say, "Can you get your cursor lined up with the bogie so that it is showing the proper course?" or something like that. It is very dependent upon what is going on in the time domain.

Alan Lesgold: In a behavioral kind of specification that says, "When you are in a power-on mode, these things are energized in this way," and we could go through all 1,200 parts and talk about what state each is in. There is also a number of higher-level views of that representing different kinds of goal structuring. For instance, "I'm doing a test and the stimulus I'm applying to the thing I'm testing is X, and the kind of measurement I'm making is Y." That is much different from saying, "This switch is set this way, and this switch is set that way." Are you able to capture these multiple views in the data structure or are they sort of appendages that are growing out of it?

Douglas Towne: No, the data structure would capture it for any one representation. This is achieved, in part, by stating which representation was used. So, if it was a highly simplified representation, we could say, "Look, all you are seeing here is this function, but here is how you get to it." So it is in the form of data that say exactly what is going on at different places.

Diane Barbee: Is your system written in an object-oriented programming language?

Douglas Towne: It's LISP. We wrote it directly in InterLISP-D, one of the good decisions we made rather than trying to take advantage of LOOPS and other intermediate systems, because we knew we were going to be up against a compute problem. LISP is a very good language to use. It had more than what we needed. We didn't need LISP's wonderful dynamic capabilities for changing data structures. I don't know any case where we really had to do that. Even the student model is dynamic—but the structure of the model is not changing over time, nor is the structure of the device changing over time. So we didn't need a lot of LISP's beauty and we paid a price for it, so we will be glad when we leave LISP. And we will clearly go to an object-oriented language when we say goodbye to LISP.

Diane Barbee: Do you have some goal of portability in that?

Douglas Towne: It's number one . . . and two. That is what it is all about is having a system that people can use and try. So that is top priority.

Diane Barbee: I'm curious, it sounds real whiz-bang to create your instructional parts and also to create new models. I'm wondering really what that entails? I know that you don't have time to teach me how to do it, but I'm curious about how complex it is.

Douglas Towne: There are some people here in this room that have been subjected to our treatment. We are still viewing it as about a week's effort to learn to use the system. We have had a number of people come in and learn to use the system and then produce simple simulations on the fifth day. And the simulations that I have showed you, the device models from Northrop, were done by two nonprogrammers that were not computer users. And they came in and learned how to do this. And they've been at it quite a few weeks now. So we feel good about the usability of the system. It is a lot easier to use now than it was a year ago, by a tremendous amount. I would say that anybody who can sit down and make up if-then statements and can think about a complex device, and understands the device . . . if he understands the device, he will be able to build a model of it, with some instruction.

Diane Barbee: And what about developing these instructional models?

Douglas Towne: If you know what you want to do, what you want to say, what you want to show, what you want to explain, that is easily done. Because it is done by doing it, the authoring is done by operating the device. Instead of talking to this student at your side, you type it in and point at things that you want highlighted and say look at that. We find that part to be pretty fun and the hours of instruction that you get for hours of authoring are very high, after you have done the one-time effort of building the device model.

Walt Schneider: Two things. One is, you say building a device model is easy, but this is exactly the same thing that the engineer had to do, in some sense.

Douglas Towne: No. Let me use an example. I don't want to minimize device modeling. I'm not going to say it is easy, but let's look at this one example. We read Kieras's description of how this thing works for the better part of the day, and drew it up on the board and tried to understand what was going on there. This thing is more complex than what it might appear. There is some very tricky business going on in this side of this relay. I'm not going to get into a lot of detail, but if you are up in the air and one engine goes out, it turns out that the power coming off of the other engine's generator is routed around to the other engine so that you can restart it. That is a nice feature, I think. The other nice thing is that if both engines go out, you can throw a switch here and this battery will give you enough power to start up one of the engines. It's tricky business. Now first of all, we didn't have to think of this. I could not have designed this and we don't have to deal with any quantitative matter at all. We would only have to say, "Look, this generator is putting out power to there, and you are either getting power from the generator or if you are on the ground, it is coming from over here." And you really only have to describe what each of these objects does. It is not really very quantitative. It's pretty much qualitative. Now, if Valerie Shute wanted to use it to for an Ohm's Law exercise, she could put Ohm's Law in there and it could become quantitative. But as model builders at high levels, there is no need for us to know how that generator works. I couldn't tell you how it works, I don't have to deal with this detail. As a model builder, I can go as detailed as I want to.

Walt Schneider: Do you have data about student acceptance?

Douglas Towne: That's a good question. Our experience so far only tells about the acceptance of authors and experts to build instruction. We don't yet have information of how students like it, except we have informal, anecdotal information from North Island

Naval Air Station in San Diego where they did use the blade-fold trainer. We don't have quantitative data but two things came out of the trial. One, the thing that students liked to do the most was set the system up and see if they could trick the device model and see if the model would work. Now this is anecdotal, I'm sorry, but that is what the students really enjoyed doing, saying, "Gee, I wonder if the model will do what it is supposed to do." They also liked to see if they could trick the diagnostic expert by putting in failures or making test readings and seeing if the diagnostic expert would follow correctly. We got very good feedback that they thought the logic used by the expert diagnostician was fine, but they disagreed with our assessment of reliabilities and so they would say, "It really shouldn't be suspecting this part because that thing never fails." Well, that simply meant our reliability data was not what it should have been. We are going to do an evaluation study in another month or two and we are going to get some data soon in Valerie's shop. We have none right now.

6

An Anchored Instruction Approach to Cognitive Skills Acquisition and Intelligent Tutoring

Cognition and Technology Group
Vanderbilt University

Like other authors in this volume, we are concerned with applications of cognitive theories of knowledge and skill acquisition to issues of instructional design. Our goal in this chapter is to discuss an approach to instruction and cognitive skill development that we have been developing at Vanderbilt's Learning Technology Center (e.g., Bransford, Sherwood, Hasselbring, Kinzer, & Williams, 1990; Cognition and Technology Group at Vanderbilt, 1990; Sherwood, Kinzer, Hasselbring, & Bransford, 1987). Our approach, called *anchored instruction,* represents an attempt to help students become actively engaged in learning by situating or anchoring instruction in interesting and realistic problem-solving environments. These environments are designed to invite the kinds of thinking that help students develop general skills and attitudes that contribute to effective problem solving, plus acquire specific concepts and principles that allow them to think effectively about particular domains (e.g., Bransford, Sherwood, Vye, & Rieser, 1986; Bransford, Vye, Kinzer, & Risko, in press).

Our work on anchored instruction is designed to be relevant to instruction in all content areas, including reading, writing, history, mathematics, and science (e.g., Bransford, Kinzer, Risko, Rowe, & Vye, 1989; Cognition and Technology Group at Vanderbilt, in press). We believe that there are some instructional problems that are common to all these areas, although each area also requires specific instructional techniques that mesh with domain-specific goals. In the initial parts of this chapter we discuss some of the general principles of anchored instruction and provide a specific example. Our discussion borrows heavily from a recently published paper by our group that appears in the *Educational Researcher* (Cognition and Technology Group at Vanderbilt, 1990). Our goal in that paper was to explain our concept of anchored instruction and to relate it to the work of Brown, Collins, and Duguid (1989) on situated cognition and authentic tasks.

Concepts such as situated cognition, task authenticity, and apprenticeships are relevant to normal classroom instruction as well as to intelligent tutoring environments. The present discussion of anchored instruction also presents a more detailed description of one example of anchored instruction—the Adventures of Jasper Woodbury mathematics problem-solving series. This discussion includes the design principles behind the materials and instructional model, as well as some initial results from classroom use.

In the final section of the present chapter we consider some implications of anchored instruction for intelligent tutoring systems. We specifically address the issue of what an anchored approach might contribute to the design of intelligent tutoring systems. In this context we also provide an example of work on a tutoring system that makes explicit use of the anchoring concept.

THE CONCEPT OF ANCHORED INSTRUCTION

Like many researchers (e.g., Brown et al., 1989; Porter, 1989; Scardamalia & Bereiter, 1985), our thoughts about problems with traditional approaches to instruction have been influenced by Whitehead's (1929) discussion of what he called the inert knowledge problem. Inert knowledge is knowledge that can usually be recalled when people are explicitly asked to do so but that is not used spontaneously in problem-solving contexts even though it is relevant. Whitehead was instrumental in calling attention to the phenomenon of inert knowledge. He also made the provocative claim that, in schools, information was particularly likely to be presented in ways that make it inert (see also Gragg, 1940; Simon, 1980).

Bereiter (1984) provided an informative illustration of the inert knowledge problem. He described a situation in which a teacher of educational psychology gave her students a long, difficult article and told them they had 10 minutes to learn as much as they could about it. Almost without exception, the students began with the first sentence of the article and read as far as they could until the time was up. Later, when discussing their strategies, the students acknowledged that they knew better than to simply begin reading. They had all had classes that taught them to skim for main ideas, consult section headings, and so forth. But they did not spontaneously use this knowledge when it would have helped.

In Sherwood, Kinzer, Bransford, and Franks (1987) we discussed an additional illustration of inert knowledge. We asked entering college students to explain how knowledge of logarithms might make it easier to solve problems. Why were they invented and what good do they do? The vast majority of the students had no idea of the uses for logarithms. They remembered learning them in school but they thought of them only as math exercises that one did in order to find answers to logarithm problems. They treated them as difficult ends to be tolerated rather than as exciting inventions (tools) that allowed a variety of problems to be solved. Imagine that our students had entered a contest that required them to multiply as many sets of large numbers as possible within 1 hr of time. The students could use anything they wanted to help them except a calculator or a computer. It is doubtful that they would have asked for tables of logarithms, even though the tables could serve as extremely helpful tools.[1]

It is useful to contrast the "mechanical procedure" knowledge of logarithms that we found with entering college students to the understanding suggested by the following quotation from Henry Briggs (1624), an astronomer who lived in the 1600s: "Logarithms are numbers invented for the more easy working of questions in arithmetic and geometry. By them all troublesome multiplications are avoided and performed only by addition. In a word, all questions not only in arithmetic and geometry but in astronomy also are thereby most plainly and easily answered." For Briggs and his fellow astronomers, logarithms were understood to be powerful tools that greatly simplified their lives.

We are indebted to theorists such as Dewey (1933) for helping us understand the importance of viewing knowledge as tools (e.g., see Bransford & McCarrell, 1974). As Dewey (1933) noted, when people learn about a tool they learn what it is and when and how to use it. When people learn new information in the context of meaningful activities (e.g., when Briggs and his colleagues learned how logarithms helped them do their astronomy better), they are more likely to perceive the new information as tools rather than as arbitrary sets of procedures or facts. In several demonstration studies, we have shown that one of the advantages of learning in problem-solving contexts is that students acquire information about the conditions under which it is useful to know various concepts and facts (e.g., Bransford et al., 1989). We also discuss how the learning successes of young children depend strongly on their opportunities to learn in meaningful, socially organized contexts (Bransford & Heldmeyer, 1983; Sherwood, Kinzer, Bransford, & Franks, 1987), and we discuss laboratory studies that indicate that meaningful, problem-oriented approaches to learning are more likely than fact-oriented approaches to overcome inert knowledge problems (e.g., see Adams et al., 1988; Lockhart, Lamon, & Gick, 1988).

Of course, the idea that one needs to "make information meaningful and useful to students" is hardly new. Teachers usually try to provide examples of how information is useful. When teaching logarithms, for example, a teacher or textbook author might discuss how logarithms make it easier to solve computa-

---

[1]Logarithm computations using tables and interpolation have been given less emphasis in recent years because of the availability of calculators. Logarithms, however, still serve useful computational purposes, such as calculation of an approximation of the factorial of large numbers, a calculation important in mathematical statistics. More importantly, they provide powerful tools for mathematical modeling. Students often do not understand these uses of logarithms.

tional problems. But statements about one or two potential applications of concepts are still a long way from the situation characteristic of the 17th century astronomers who were discussed earlier. The astronomers were intimately familiar with the kinds of problems that they confronted when trying to do their astronomy. They lived with these problems and had to spend a large portion of their time with tedious calculations. For them, logarithms did not represent a specialized tool that was useful for only one or two textbooklike problems. Logarithms represented a tool that could be used every day.

One of the major goals of anchored instruction is to create shared environments that permit sustained exploration by students and teachers (tutors) and to enable them to understand the kinds of problems and opportunities that experts in various areas encounter and the knowledge that these experts use as tools. A related goal is to help students experience the value of exploring the same setting from multiple perspectives (e.g., as a scientist, historian, etc.). The general principles of anchored instruction are discussed next.

ANCHORING INSTRUCTION IN MEANINGFUL CONTEXTS

As already discussed, a major goal of anchored instruction is to allow students and teachers to experience the kinds of problems and opportunities that experts in various areas encounter. Theorists such as Dewey (1933), Schwab (1960), and N. R. Hanson (1970) emphasized that experts in an area have been immersed in phenomena and are familiar with how they have been thinking about them. When introduced to new theories, concepts, and principles that are relevant to their areas of interest, the experts can experience the changes in their own thinking that these ideas afford. For novices, however, the introduction of concepts and theories often seems like the mere introduction of new facts or mechanical procedures to be memorized. Because the novices have not been immersed in the phenomena being investigated, they are unable to experience the effects of the new information on their own noticing and understanding.

The general idea of anchored instruction has a long history. Dewey (1933) discussed the advantages of theme-based learning. In the 1940s, Gragg (1940) argued for the advantages of case-based approaches to instruction—approaches that are currently used quite frequently in areas such as medicine, business, and law (Williams, 1991). One variation of case-based instruction is to use a variety of minicases that serve as microcontexts. Our contexts are usually complex and revisited from many perspectives over periods of weeks and months; hence we refer to them as macrocontexts. The purpose of these contexts is to serve as environments for cooperative learning and teacher-directed mediation (e.g., Feuerstein, Rand, Hoffman, & Miller, 1980: Vygotsky, 1978). Our contexts are meant to be explored and discussed, rather than simply read or watched.

Anchored instruction environments also share some of the characteristics of inquiry environments, which have been suggested as a model, especially for science instruction, since Schwab (1962). They are similar in that the anchored instruction environments, as well as inquiry environments, do not propose to "directly" instruct students but provide a situation where learning can take place. As will be noted in the descriptions of the development projects, the anchored instructional environments provide a context for other instructional environments, which many times will include inquiry activities.

We prefer our contexts to be in visual rather than text formats and to be on videodisc rather than videotape (see also Miller & Gildea, 1987; Spiro, Vispoel, Schmitz, Samarapungavan, & Boerger, 1987). We selected the videodisc medium for several reasons. One is that it allows students to develop pattern recognition skills. (A major disadvantage of text is that it represents the output of the writer's pattern recognition processes; see Bransford, Franks, Vye, & Sherwood, 1989.) Second, video allows a more veridical representation of events than text; it is dynamic, visual, and spatial. We think that one advantage of this is that students can more easily form rich mental models of the problem situations (e.g., Johnson-Laird, 1985; McNamara, Miller, & Bransford, 1991). The ease with which mental models can be formed from video is particularly important for lower-achieving students and for students with low knowledge in the domain of interest (Bransford, Kinzer et al., 1989; Johnson, 1987). A third reason for using videodisc technology is that it has random-access capabilities. Random-access is advantageous from an instructional viewpoint because it allows teachers to almost instantly access information for discussion (see Sherwood, Kinzer, Hasselbring, & Bransford, 1987). Because one of our primary goals is to help students explore the same domain from multiple perspectives, the random-access capabilities are particularly useful for our work.

An Example of Anchored Instruction: The Adventures of Jasper Woodbury Series

An example of anchored instruction is a project being conducted by the Learning Technology Center and sponsored by the James S. McDonnell Foundation and the National Science Foundation. It is designed to develop and evaluate a series of videodisc adventures whose primary focus is on mathematical problem formulation and problem solving. However, we are also developing secondary applications that will enable students to learn science, history, and literature concepts.

The videodiscs that we are developing involve the adventures of a person named Jasper Woodbury. We have completed four adventures, are currently working on two more, and envision a series comprised of 6–10 discs. The adventures are designed for use with middle-school students, although we have worked with students as young as fourth graders and as old as college freshmen.

TABLE 6.1
Seven Design Principles Underlying The Jasper Adventure Series

Design Principle	Hypothesized Benefits
Video-based format	A. More motivating B. Easier to search C. Supports complex comprehension D. Especially helpful for poor readers yet it can also support reading
Narrative with realistic problems (rather than a lecture on video)	A. Easier to remember B. More engaging C. Primes students to notice the relevance of mathematics and reasoning for everyday events
Generative format (i.e., the stories end and students must generate the problems to be solved)	A. Motivating to determine the ending B. Teaches students to find and define problems to be solved C. Provides enhanced opportunities for reasoning
Embedded data design (i.e., all the data needed to solve the problems are in the video)	A. Permits reasoned decision making B. Motivating to find C. Puts students on an "even keel" with respect to relevant knowledge D. Clarifies how relevance of data depends on specific goals
Problem complexity (i.e., each adventure involves a problem of at least 14 steps	A. Overcomes the tendency to try for a few minutes and then give up B. Introduces levels of complexity characteristic of real problems C. Helps students deal with complexity D. Develops confidence in abilities
Pairs of related adventures	A. Provides extra practice on core schema B. Helps clarify what can be transferred and what cannot C. Illustrates analogical thinking
Links across the curriculum	A. Helps extend mathematical thinking to other areas (e.g., history, science) B. Encourages the integration of knowledge C. Supports information finding and publishing

The adventures are designed in accord with a set of principles that are briefly considered next. The design principles and their particular advantages are summarized in Table 6.1.

Video-Based Presentation Format. Although some excellent work on applied problem solving has been conducted with materials that are supplied orally or in writing (e.g., Lesh, 1981), we decided to use the video medium for several reasons. One is that video allows characters, actions, and settings to all be depicted in a rich, vivid manner that text alone rarely matches. As a result, it is easier for us to make information interesting by embedding it in a video than it is for us to write equally interesting text.

A second reason for using the video medium is that students can comprehend much more complex and interconnected problems when they see the information in a video than when they read the information in a text—this is especially true for students who have difficulty with reading. Modern theories of reading comprehension view successful comprehension as the construction of mental models (McNamara et al., 1991). In many ways, these mental models resemble rich images, or even "movies-in-the-head," that capture the important information about the situations described by the text (Miller, 1989). The mental processes involved in translating a text to a mental model can be easily thwarted if readers are given large amounts of information that overtax the limitations of working memory. Moreover, there is a great deal of evidence that poor readers have even more limited memory resources available during comprehension than good readers do (e.g., Daneman & Carpenter, 1980).

Because video already depicts complex situations in an imagelike format, viewers of a video story should have fewer translations to make than readers when incorporating the story information into a mental model (Salomon & Perkins, 1989). Research shows that poor readers can be good television comprehenders (Pezdek, Lehrer, & Simon, 1984), and teachers who have worked with our pilot videos have consistently remarked that the video adventures are especially effective with students whose reading skills are subaverage.

Finally, because there is a great deal of rich background information on the video, there is much more of an opportunity to notice scenes and events that can lead to the construction of additional interesting problems in other context areas as well as in mathematics.

Narrative Format.   A second design principle is the use of a narrative format to present information. One purpose of using a well-formed story is to create a meaningful context for problem solving (for examples of other programs that use a narrative format, see Bank Street College, 1984; Lipman, 1985). Stories involve a text structure that is relatively well understood by middle-school students (Stein & Trabasso, 1982). Using a familiar text structure as the context for presentation of mathematical concepts helps students generate an overall mental model of the situation and lets them understand authentic uses of mathematical concepts (e.g., Brown et al., 1989).

Generative Learning Format.   The stories in the Jasper series are complete stories with one exception. As with most stories, there is setting information, a slate of characters, an initiating event, and consequent events. The way in which these stories differ is that the resolution of the story must be provided by students. (There is a resolution on each disc, but students see it only after attempting to resolve the story themselves.) In the process of reaching a resolution, students generate and solve a complex mathematical problem. One reason for having students generate the ending—instead of, for example, guiding them through a modeled solution—is that it is motivating: students like to determine for themselves what the outcome will be. A second reason is that it allows students to actively participate in the learning process. Research findings suggest that there are very important benefits from having students generate information (Belli, Soraci, & Purdon, 1989; Slameka & Graf, 1978; Soraci, Bransford, Franks, & Chechile, 1987).

Embedded Data Design.   An especially important design feature of the Jasper series—one that is unique to our series and is instrumental in making it possible for students to engage in generative problem solving—is what we have called "embedded data" design. All the data needed to solve the problems are embedded somewhere in the video story. The mathematics problems are not explicitly formulated at the beginning of the video, and the numerical information that is needed for the solutions is incidentally presented in the story. Students are then able to look back on the video and find all the data they need (this is very motivating). This design feature makes our problem-solving series analogous to good mystery stories. At the end of a good mystery, one can see that all the clues were provided, but they had to be noticed as being relevant and put together in just the right way.

Problem Complexity.   The Jasper videos pose very complex mathematical problems. For example, the first episode in the series contains a problem comprised of more than 15 interrelated steps. In the second episode, multiple solutions need to be considered by students in order to decide the optimum one. The complexity of the problems is intentional and is based on a very simple premise: Students cannot be expected to learn to deal with complexity unless they have the opportunity to do so (e.g., Schoenfeld, 1985). Students are not routinely provided with the opportunity to engage in the kind of sustained mathematical thinking necessary to solve the complex problem posed in each episode. The video makes the complexity manageable. We believe that a major reason for the lack of emphasis on complex problem solving (especially for lower achieving students) is the difficulties teachers face in communicating problem contexts that are motivating and complex yet ultimately solvable by students.

Pairs of Related Adventures.   All Jasper videos have been designed in pairs. One reason for pairs of videos stems from the cognitive science literature on learning and transfer. Concepts that are acquired in only one context tend to be welded to that context and hence are not likely to be spontaneously accessed and used in new settings (e.g., Bransford & Nitsch, 1978; Bransford et al., 1989; Bransford, Sherwood et al., 1986; Brown, Bransford, Ferrara, & Campione, 1983; Brown et al., 1989; Gick & Holyoak, 1980; Salomon & Perkins, 1989; Simon, 1980). By developing pairs of videos, students can be helped to analyze exactly what they are able to carry over from one context to another and what is specific to each context but not generalizable. For example, the first two episodes of the Adventures of Jasper Woodbury focus on the general issue of "trip planning." This pair of "trip planning" adventures allows students to learn to deal with the complexity in the first episode and then attempt to apply what they have learned in the second episode (plus learn some important additional information). Pairs of adventures provide students with the opportunity to use mathematical concepts in a variety of contexts, thus enhancing considerably their abilities to transfer these skills to new situations spontaneously.

Links Across the Curriculum.   Each narrative episode contains the data necessary to solve the specific complex problem posed at the end of the video story. The narration also provides many opportunities to introduce topics from other subject matters. For example, in the trip planning episodes, maps are used to help figure out the solutions. These provide a natural link to geography, navigation, and other famous trips in which route planning was involved; for example, Charles Lindbergh's solo flight.

One of the best ways to get a feel for the design principles is to "walk through" one of the episodes and see how the principles are instantiated. The first adventure in the series is titled "Journey to Cedar Creek." This episode opens with Jasper Woodbury practicing his golf swing. The newspaper is delivered and Jasper turns to the classified ads for boats. Jasper sees an ad for a 1956 ChrisCraft cruiser and decides to take a trip to Cedar Creek where it is docked. He rides his bicycle to the dock where his small rowboat, complete with outboard motor, is docked. We see Jasper as he prepares for the trip from his dock to Cedar Creek: He is shown consulting a map of the river route from his home dock to the dock at Cedar Creek, listening to reports of weather conditions on his marine radio, and checking the gas for his outboard. As the story continues, Jasper stops for gas at Larry's dock. Larry is a comical-looking character who knows lots of interesting information. For example, as he hands Jasper the hose on the gas pump, he just happens to mention all the major locations where oil is found. When Jasper pays for the gas, we discover the only cash he has is a $20 bill. As Jasper makes his way up river, he passes a paddle-wheeler, a barge, and a tugboat, and some information is provided about each of these. Next, Jasper runs into a bit of trouble when he hits something in the river and breaks his sheer pin. He has to row to a repair shop where he pays to have the pin fixed. Later, Jasper reaches the dock where the cruiser is located and meets Sal, the cruiser's owner. She tells him about the cruiser and they take the boat out for a spin. Along the way, Jasper learns about its cruising speed, fuel consumption, fuel capacity, and that the cruiser's temporary fuel tank only holds 12 gallons. He also learns that the boat's running lights don't work so the boat can't be out on the river after sunset. Jasper eventually decides to buy the old cruiser, and pays with a check. He then thinks about whether he can get to his home dock by sunset. The episode ends by turning the problem over to the students to solve.

It is at this point that students move from the passive televisionlike viewing to the active generation mode discussed earlier. They must solve Jasper's problem. Students have to generate the kinds of problems that Jasper has to consider in order to make the decision about whether he can get the boat home before dark without running out of fuel. The problem looks deceivingly simple; in reality it involves many subproblems. But all the data needed to solve the problem were presented in the video. For example, to determine whether Jasper can reach home before sunset, students must calculate the total time the trip will take. To determine total time, they need to know the distance between the cruiser's and Jasper's home dock and the boat's cruising speed. The distance information can be obtained by referring to the mile markers on the map Jasper consulted when he first began his trip. The time needed for the trip must be compared to the time available for the trip by considering current time and the time of sunset, information given over the marine radio. The problems associated with Jasper's decision about whether he has enough fuel to make it home are even more complex. As it turns out, he does not have enough gas and he must plan for where to purchase some—at this point money becomes a relevant issue. In this manner, students identify and work out the various interconnected subproblems that must be faced to solve Jasper's problem.

The second Jasper episode on trip planning is equally as complex as the first one, allows a number of possible solutions, and involves planning for a rescue. It is called "Rescue at Boone's Meadow," and revolves around Emily, a friend of Jasper and Larry. Emily is learning to fly an ultralight; her instructor is Larry. When the story begins, we see Larry describing the plane. He tells Emily about the weight limitations of the plane, its fuel consumption, fuel capacity, air speed, and so forth. Some days later, Emily makes her first solo flight, after which she, Jasper, and Larry celebrate over dinner. While eating, Jasper tells them of his plans to hike into the wilderness to go fishing. The next scene shows Jasper at this remote fishing area. The tranquility of the scene is disturbed by the sound of a gunshot. Upon investigating, Jasper finds that an eagle has been shot and wounded. Jasper immediately radios Emily for help.

Again, at this point in the story students move from passive televisionlike viewing to an active generation mode. They must decide the fastest way for Emily to get the eagle to a veterinarian. There are multiple vehicles, agents, and routes that can be used, subject to the constraints introduced by the terrain and capacities of the various vehicles and available agents. Like Jasper's river trip problem, the solution involves a multistep, distance-rate-time problem. It thus allows students to use the general schema of the Journey to Cedar Creek episode. In addition, the rescue problem involves generating multiple rescue plans and determining which is the quickest.

The third adventure is called "The Big Splash" and the fourth adventure is called "A Capital Idea." The content of this pair of adventures shifts from trip planning to using sample data to develop a business plan and then presenting an argument for someone else's support of that plan. Both stories take place in

Cumberland City. In the interest of space we will only provide a brief description of the plot in "The Big Splash." The principal character of this adventure is Chris, a young black male, approximately 15 years old. The story starts with Chris on his way to visit a fire station to get information for a school report he is writing. While there he sees a weird contraption that turns out to be a dunking machine. The dunking machine makes an impression on Chris and it inspires an idea for a booth at the upcoming school fun fair. The fair is designed to raise money for activities at the school. Chris thinks his idea of a booth where students can try to dunk a teacher is a potential money-maker, but first he must see Miss Stieger, the school principal, to find out what he needs to do to convince her about the payoff of his idea. Chris talks with Miss Stieger and she tells him exactly the kind of information she needs about costs, expected revenue, feasibility, etc. Chris then consults with his neighbor, Jasper, about how to get the information he needs to convince Miss Stieger about the economic viability of his idea. If he can do this, he can get a loan of $150 that he will need to make it all work. They decide to start by sampling the kids to see how much interest there is in the idea and how much they would be willing to pay to dunk a teacher. Chris finds out that most of the kids are interested. He and Jasper then set out to find out about the costs associated with other critical elements of the plan, such as rental of a pool. Finally, Chris thinks he has all the elements in place except one—what to do with the water once the fair is over. The final challenge for the viewer is to assemble all the elements of the plan that Chris will present to Miss Stieger.

INITIAL RESEARCH FINDINGS

As noted earlier, we designed the Jasper Adventures to provide students with the experience of formulating as well as solving problems. We also designed them to give students experience with very complex problems that involve a number of interdependent steps. Our assumption was that students cannot be expected to deal with complex problems unless they have the opportunity to work with complexity.

In our initial studies we collected baseline data on college students' ($N = 12$) abilities to formulate and solve Jasper's problem prior to instruction. We assumed that these students would be expert at the task and that their responses would serve as standards for comparison with the younger students. Students first viewed "Journey to Cedar Creek," after which they were individually interviewed. To assist in recall during problem solving, students were provided with still pictures summarizing the story. The interview consisted of three levels of questions of increasing specificity. These levels allowed us to assess problem formulation and problem solving under conditions of increased assistance. At the most general level (hereafter Level 1), no assistance was provided; students were asked to identify the problems that Jasper needed to consider to decide whether he could get the boat home and to solve these problems if they could. Students were asked to talk aloud as they solved the problem. Level 2 consisted of questions designed to cue students to consider each of the major subproblems comprising Jasper's problem, that is, (a) whether Jasper could reach home before sunset, (b) whether he could reach home without running out of fuel, and (c) whether he needed to be concerned about money. As with Level 1, at Level 2 students were asked to identify and solve the problems that Jasper would need to solve to make a decision about each of these subproblems. At Level 3, the subproblems were broken down further into simple word-problem-like questions. For example, students were asked to find the distance from Cedar Creek marina to Jasper's home dock.

Contrary to our original expectations, college students performed quite poorly on the task. At Level 1, students correctly formulated and solved a mere 28% of the problem. Level 2 prompting resulted in an improvement of students' performance; nevertheless, cumulative performance for Levels 1 and 2 was only about 38%. Level 3 prompting resulted in the greatest improvement in performance, with students correctly solving an additional 43% of the problem. Indeed, by Level 3, most students were at or near ceiling on the task.

The fact that Level 3 prompting produced the greatest effect on problem-solving performance suggests that students' poor performance on the task at Level 1 and 2 was a result of their having difficulty planning and formulating the multistep problem. The Level 3 data suggest that college students are quite good at formulating and solving the problem when it is presented as a series of one-step problems.

A second study was designed to collect data for comparison with the problem-solving data from the sample of college students. Our goal was to examine the relative abilities of the college and middle school groups to articulate a solution plan and to solve the problem in "Journey to Cedar Creek." Middle-school participants were sixth-grade students ($N = 12$) recruited from an above-average math achievement class. Students' mean score on the mathematics portion of the Stanford Achievement Test was 83%. Problem-solving performance was assessed through individual interviews with students. The same interview protocol and procedures were used with the sixth graders as were used in the initial baseline study with college undergraduates.

Students' overall problem-solving performance is summarized in Fig. 6.1. It is clear from the figure that even though the students were high achievers in mathematics, they performed very poorly, regardless of level of prompting. Less than a fifth of the students, even when prompted, correctly formulated and solved the problems. At Level 1, 73% of the students restated the major questions presented at the end of the video, but none of the students discussed Jasper's need to buy gasoline on the way home. Fewer than half of the students attempted to solve the problems they identified, and none of the students completely and

BASELINE PROBLEM SOLVING PERFORMANCE

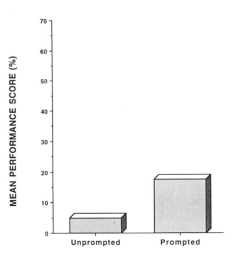

FIG. 6.1. Baseline problem solving performance of sixth-graders on the "Journey to Cedar Creek" adventure under prompted and unprompted conditions.

accurately solved a major problem. At Level 2, a greater proportion of students attempted to solve the problems they identified, but there was only one problem (i.e., does Jasper have enough time to get home before sunset?) for which a correct solution was produced and only 9% of the students generated correct solutions for this problem. Prompting at Level 3 resulted in greatly increased attempts to solve the identified problems and greater proportions of students who successfully completed solutions. However, on only one problem (i.e., does Jasper have enough gasoline to reach home?) did more than half of the students produce correct solutions.

The results indicated that the students were unsuccessful in planning a solution and solving the problems without assistance from the experimenter in identifying subproblems. Although students are relatively good at solving already-formulated single-step story problems of the same types as those contained in the "Journey to Cedar Creek" problem, the results indicate that students have great difficulty when these problems are part of a multistep problem that requires planning and formulation.

The sixth-grade results were not surprising in view of the data indicating that even college freshmen do relatively poorly on the "Journey to Cedar Creek" problem. Students rarely have the opportunity to attempt to solve complex problems like the one in "Journey to Cedar Creek" and hence cannot be expected to have developed these problem-solving skills.

Given that both college students and high-achieving sixth graders have difficulty with solving a problem like the one posed in "Journey to Cedar Creek," the obvious question is what happens to problem solving when instruction and opportunity to solve such problems are provided. We conducted a study to examine this issue. The overall goal of the study was to determine if anchored instruction with Jasper would produce learning and transfer of learning that were not experienced by students instructed in word-problem solving as presented in a traditional curriculum.

Participants were a fifth-grade class of above-average students. Based on students' scores on the mathematics section of the Stanford Achievement Test, a stratified random assignment was made of students to experimental or control group teaching conditions.

Students in the experimental group investigated the major questions Jasper had to answer. As each question (i.e., time, fuel, and money) was introduced in class, students were encouraged to generate subordinate questions of the stated question and to recall relevant facts from the video to answer the questions. This segment of instruction was designed to engage students in planning for problem solving and to focus their attention on gathering the needed information. Students were guided to generate complete solutions for all of the subproblems identified. Conversely, as subproblem solutions were generated, students were encouraged to relate the solutions to the overall problem. Students engaged in problem solving as a class, in small groups, and on an individual basis.

Control students viewed "Journey to Cedar Creek" along with experimental students the first day of the study. They did not, however, receive instruction in solving Jasper's problems. Traditional teaching methods—teacher lecture, question and answer, worksheets, and teacher and student presentations at the chalkboard—were used to instruct control students in traditional word problems. The problems involved distance, elapsed time, rates, fuel consumption, and money, topics around which the overall problem in Jasper was structured. The following example typifies problems solved by control students: Bill's car averages 25 miles per gallon of gas. At that rate, how many gallons of gas will Bill need to drive 480 miles? Control students also studied Polya's (1957) problem-solving model and were encouraged to apply the model during problem solving.

A pretest and two posttests were administered to experimental and control students. One of the posttests consisted of word problems of the type that students in the control group received during training. This measure allowed the comparison of performance of experimental students to that of control students who were instructed in solving these more routine problems. Somewhat surprisingly, experimental students were able to solve these problems as well as control students despite the fact that the control group had much more explicit practice on these types of problems. Both groups performed quite well on this measure, averaging 77% correct.

A paper-and-pencil pretest and an identical posttest were designed to assess how well students organized information in the Jasper video for problem solving before and after instruction. Students were asked to match factual information needed for solving Jasper's central problems with the appropriate problem. For example, the amount of money Jasper had left would be relevant to the problem of purchasing fuel needed to make the trip home. Experimental students showed significant gains from pretest to posttest, while control students showed no significant improvement.

The most dramatic finding involved student performance on "The Houseboat Adventure," a video transfer test. This measure was designed to allow assessment of students' abilities to identify, define, and solve problems similar to those posed in "Journey to Cedar Creek." Performance data were collected in individual interviews with children. Two levels of prompting were provided. These levels corresponded to Levels 1 and 2 described earlier for the "Journey to Cedar Creek" baseline study.

Scores assigned to the interview protocols reflected the completeness and accuracy of the student's problem solutions at each level of prompting. Figure 6.2 contains a summary of student's problem-solving performance on the transfer task. At each level of prompting, protocol scores of students in the experimental group were significantly higher than those of control students. It is evident that, following four sessions of instruction with "Journey to Cedar Creek," experimental students showed significant transfer of learning to a new, similarly complex problem compared to the control students. Several of the experimental students' scores were in the 75%–100% range. The maximum control student score was 51%. These results are quite different from those obtained in the baseline study involving students who received no problem-solving instruction.

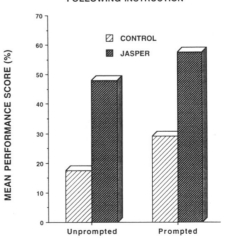

**TRANSFER PROBLEM SOLVING PERFORMANCE
FOLLOWING INSTRUCTION**

FIG. 6.2. Transfer problem solving performance under prompted and unprompted conditions for instructional control (word problem) and Jasper instructed students.

Experimental students showed great strength in identifying and solving the central distance-rate-time and fuel problems involved in the transfer video. Most of their difficulties seemed to stem from not considering carefully the subordinate problems relating to buying gasoline on the return trip. Several of the students appeared to assume that the character in the transfer story could "somehow" obtain the gasoline on the way home. Although most of the experimental students correctly determined the amount of money left after expenses, few related the result to decisions that needed to be made regarding quantity of gasoline that could be brought on the return trip.

Control students were generally unsuccessful in formulating and solving the video-based transfer problems. Control students, like experimental students, had particular difficulty with decision making relative to the problem of buying gasoline on the way home. One difficulty evident in control students' protocols that was not shown in the protocols of experimental students involved units of measurement. Some control students mixed units (e.g., added hours and miles) and seemed to make little distinction in rates (e.g., minutes per mile and miles per minute). This finding suggests that one benefit of the instruction anchored in the video context may have been clarification of units of measurement.

Earlier, we noted the need to provide experiences with complex examples of problem formulation. This need is well illustrated by our baseline data with both college students and sixth graders. Although the sixth-grade students had scored above average on standard mathematics achievement tests (Vye et al., 1989), they were extremely poor at problem identification and formulation (we expected these findings since students have few experiences like this). However, our instructional study data also indicate that fifth-grade students can become very good at complex problem formulation on tasks similar to Jasper after working with Jasper in cooperative learning groups for four to five class sessions (Van Haneghan et al., in press).[2] We are continuing to study the nature of the knowledge that children acquire after working in the Jasper Adventure context, including the effects of working with multiple episodes and adventures. Together with this work, we are examining issues regarding the optimal teaching and instructional conditions.

Finally, we should also note that teachers have been extremely enthusiastic about the Adventures of Jasper Woodbury series, mainly because their students seem to be challenged to solve the problems and because even students who normally are not good at math can contribute to problem solving; for example, they may have noticed information on the disc that is relevant for solving Jasper's problem.

---

[2]The following graduate students have been instrumental in our work on mathematics and anchored instruction: Paulo Alcantara, Brigid Barron, Laurie Furman, and Betsy Montavon.

FACILITATING BROAD TRANSFER

One of the design principles involves using pairs of related videos to facilitate transfer. We assume from the cognitive science literature on analogical transfer that spontaneous transfer would be limited if students worked on a complex trip planning problem only in one context (e.g., Bransford, Sherwood et al., 1986; Brown et al., 1983; Gick & Holyoak, 1980; Nitsch, 1977; Perkins & Salomon, 1989). It is for this reason, as well as the need to cover different types of content recommended by the National Council of Teachers of Mathematics (1989) that we are creating a series of 6–10 Jasper adventures that can provide the foundation for using key mathematics concepts in a variety of realistic settings.

The data we reported were for the first adventure, and we have described the second adventure, which involves an ultralight airplane flight in order to save a wounded eagle. In this adventure, students must determine the fastest way to get to the eagle and transport it to a veterinarian without running out of gasoline and without exceeding the weight limitations of the ultralight. The problems to be formulated and solved are similar to the basic problem in "Journey to Cedar Creek"; this allows students to discuss the analogies between the first and second episode and experience the fact that it becomes much easier to solve these types of problems the second time around. Evidence from other research projects suggests that an explicit emphasis on analyzing similarities and differences among problem situations, and on bridging to new areas of application, facilitates the degree to which spontaneous transfer occurs (e.g., Bransford, Stein, Delclos, & Littlefield, 1986; Littlefield et al., 1988; Perkins & Salomon, 1989). The types of transfer that children experience and the similarities and differences they note are objects of current investigation.

Our ultimate goal is to create an instructional environment that facilitates even broader transfer, transfer that extends into other domains of content and helps students appreciate the linkages among content and concepts from domains such as literature, history, geography, and science. To support this we are in the process of creating computer data bases and a multimedia publishing environment to accompany the discs in the Adventures of Jasper series. These "tools" for generative thinking provide an opportunity to create new problems that students can work on and to integrate subject matter areas. The publishing environment and database can help students learn history, science, geography, and other subject matter while also continuing to use quantitative reasoning in order to better understand the information being explored.

As a simple illustration, a database can be developed for "Journey to Cedar Creek" that includes historical information, including information relevant to life during the times of Mark Twain. When studying Mark Twain's world, it is very instructive for students to see how plans to go certain distances by water in "Journey to Cedar Creek' would have to be very different if the only mode of

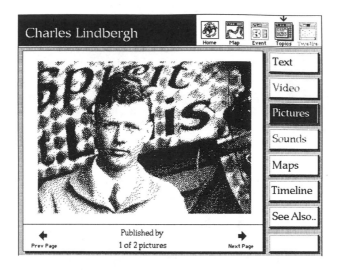

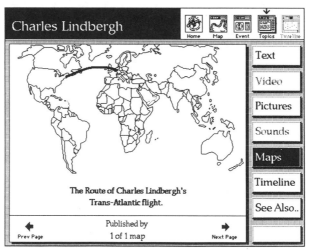

FIG. 6.3. Example screens on the topic of Lindbergh from the Jasper multimedia publishing environment.

travel were by raft. A 3-hr trip for Jasper by motorboat would have taken the better part of a day on Huckleberry's raft. This means that drinking water, food, and other necessities would need to be included in one's plans.

As another illustration of an extension problem that can be created in the multimedia publisher and database, consider water current problems for boats and headwind and tailwind problems for airplanes. We purposely keep details about these types of situations simple in the first two episodes of the Adventures of Jasper Woodbury series. Nevertheless, it is an easy matter to get students to imagine that weather or water conditions were slightly different than shown in the video. Instead of the calm day shown in "Rescue at Boone's Meadow," there could be a tailwind of 20 mph on a flight from A to B, which would become a headwind on the return flight. Does the wind's effect on flight time cancel itself out for the entire trip? With a light twist, winds can also be imagined as coming from an angle (rather than pure headwinds or tailwinds). This variation can help students understand the value of new types of mathematics such as trigonometry.[3]

Opportunities also exist for students to extend their knowledge about flight to topics such as aerodynamics and lift as well as to the history of flight. Figure 6.3 contains screens from the multimedia publisher and database showing a picture of Charles Lindbergh and a map indicating the route that he took for his historic flight. As can be seen from the screens, there are several options available in this environment, including linkage to other video, text, maps, timelines, sounds, and so on. Through this accompanying software environment we hope to have children develop topics of interest to them, topics that have been simulated by the content of one of more of the adventures. In this way, the adventures become anchoring contexts for cross-curricular discussions and projects. Currently, this software in being used by teachers and students in multiple classrooms

ANCHORED INSTRUCTION AND SITUATED COGNITION

An important set of principles that we believe should shape the development of anchored instruction environments derives from the situated cognition framework discussed by Brown and colleagues (1989). Brown and colleagues emphasize the importance of looking carefully at what we know about everyday cognition and of creating apprenticeships composed of authentic tasks. They note that authentic activities are most simply defined as the "ordinary practices of the culture" (p. 34).

Many school tasks lack genuine authenticity. This is often the case in "story problems" given to students in mathematics classes. Some problems contain settings that are authentic (going to a store, etc.) but the problems are often contrived and do not represent situations in which students would normally find themselves. One of our favorite examples comes from a commercial set of curriculum materials on word problems. One of them involved an interesting context: exploring a haunted house. However, the problem posed was "If there are 3 cobwebs on the first floor and 2 on the second, how many are there altogether?" This is hardly an issue that one would care about when exploring a haunted house.

---

[3]We thank Joe B. Wyatt for bringing these possibilities to our attention.

The situated cognition framework also reminds us that novices who enter into a particular apprenticeship have a reasonable chance to develop expertise. Apprentices have the opportunity for sustained thinking about specific sets of problem types over long periods of time. One of our goals in anchored instruction is to use "macrocontexts" (in contrast to "microcontexts") that can be explored for sustained periods of time.

Authenticity and Jasper.   Consider how the situated cognition framework relates to the Adventures of Jasper Woodbury series context. The degree to which our instruction involves authenticity can be analyzed from several points of view. A first level of authenticity involves the objects and data in the setting. We considered this factual level of authenticity when designing episodes of the Adventures of Jasper Woodbury series. For example, in the boat setting we had Jasper get a weather report from the marine radio (which is where boaters get such information), we used speeds and miles per gallon figures that were realistic for the boats in the video, we used formats for river maps that, though somewhat oversimplified compared to real boating charts, were true to life (e.g., they showed "mile markers" and other appropriate symbols). The airplane adventure is also factually authentic. Speeds, fuel consumption, required distances for takeoff of the ultralight, weight limits, and so forth are all very similar to actual values in everyday life.

A second level of authenticity—the one emphasized by Brown and colleagues (1989; R. D. Pea, personal communication, 1989)—involves the degree to which the tasks that students are asked to perform are authentic. Each of the details in a setting could be authentic but the tasks given to students could be contrived. For example, Jasper could pose arbitrary problems like, "If Jane had two marine radios and Mark had three, how many would they have altogether?"

In episodes of the Adventures of Jasper Woodbury series, the tasks to be performed require students to make and evaluate decisions that seem quite authentic, namely, decisions about when to leave in order to ensure getting somewhere before a specific deadline (Episode I) and decisions about the fastest way to get somewhere and return (Episode II). It is also authentic to be exposed to information (e.g., about weather predictions, gasoline consumption, etc.) and only later have it become relevant when specific needs arise and specific goals are formulated. And it is authentic to have to plan by generating sets of subproblems to be solved (e.g., "I have to see if I have enough money to buy gas") rather than simply having specific word problems presented by someone else (e.g., Lesh, 1985; Porter, 1989).

But for whom are these tasks authentic? We designed the Jasper discs to help students learn to "think mathematically", but our instruction does not focus on the kinds of experiences one might expect from the opportunity to be apprenticed to a true mathematician (indeed, many mathematicians we know would not be our first choice to model everyday planning tasks like those in the Adventures of

Jasper Woodbury series). The focus of Episodes I and II of Jasper is on the kinds of apprenticeship that one might hope to get from a well-informed parent or "mediator" (Feuerstein, Rand, & Hoffman, 1979; Feuerstein et al., 1980) who helps his or her children reflect on the types of skills and concepts necessary to deal with problems that can occur in everyday life.

A focus on everyday cognition also raises the question of whether it is reasonable to assume that novices who enter into a particular apprenticeship have a chance to develop expertise. In Jasper, the idea of a series of 6–10 discs makes it reasonable to believe that students will have the opportunity to develop expertise in solving a variety of planning problems. Without the opportunity for extended practice on a similar set of problem types, we would not expect the opportunity to work with Jasper to have much of an overall impact on students' knowledge and skills. Equally important, analyses of cognition in everyday settings reveal the use of a number of labor-saving inventions that reduce or eliminate the need for time-consuming computations and hence "distribute" intelligence across the environment (Bransford & Stein, 1984; Brown et al., 1989; Lave, 1988; R. D. Pea, personal communication, 1988; NCTM, 1989). For example, many cars now have trip-planning computers that make it easy to estimate fuel consumption and arrival time. Thanks to suggestions from the situated cognition perspective (especially R. D. Pea, personal communication, 1989), one of the major goals of Jasper series is to provide settings that motivate students to select and invent appropriate "intelligence-enhancing" tools.

A third level of authenticity regards the process of "doing" mathematics. What is the nature of mathematics for those in the mathematical community? In essence, what do "real" mathematicians do and how do these activities compare to what students do in classrooms? Lampert (1990) recently pointed out the disjuncture between authentic mathematics and school mathematics: Knowing mathematics in school therefore comes to mean having a set of unexamined beliefs, whereas Lakatos and Polya suggest that the knower of mathematics needs to be able to stand back from his or her own knowledge, evaluate its antecedent assumptions, argue about the foundations of its legitimacy, and be willing to have others do the same (p. 32). Furthermore, the process by which mathematicians come to "know" mathematics is masked to the outsider. Lampert (1990) summarized Lakatos's argument on this point: "mathematics develops as process of 'conscious guessing' about relationships among quantities and shapes, with proof following a 'zig-zag' path starting from conjectures and moving to the examination of premises through the use of counterexamples or 'refutations.' . . . Naive conjecture and counterexamples do not appear in the fully fledged deductive structure: The zig-zag of discovery cannot be discerned in the end product" (Lakatos, 1976, pp. 42 and 30). In exemplary work, Lampert has demonstrated that it is indeed possible to establish classroom contexts in which authentic mathematical discourse occurs among students. Such contexts involve students in arguing from data, in proposing, testing, and revising hypotheses, and in accepting criticisms and counterarguments from their peers (Lampert, 1990). As we extend the Jasper series into content areas such as geometry, statistics, and probability, the adventures will provide opportunities for students to engage in authentic mathematical discourse.

AN ANCHORED INSTRUCTION APPROACH
TO INTELLIGENT TUTORING

Our goal in this section of the chapter is to consider some of the ways in which the general concept of anchored instruction, including the emphasis on authenticity and apprenticeships found in the situated cognition perspective (e.g., Brown et al., 1989), might be used to guide the design of intelligent tutoring. To do so requires that we consider some of the issues that have arisen from others' experiences in designing such systems.

At a general level, intelligent tutoring or training systems are designed with several integrated components. These include a model of domain-specific expertise, a model of tutoring, and a student model. The goal is to use the tutoring strategies to move the student along a path to expertise; that is, to bring the student model in congruence with the expert model. The problem for the tutoring system is determining what is the current state of the student's model and then what that implies for next steps. Because the space of possibilities is quite large, the teaching strategy is often used to tightly constrain the space of possibilities. As such it can lead to highly scripted modes of tutoring.

Several authors have considered the role of teaching on the evolution of student knowledge and the constraints that this evolutionary model places on the task of identifying student procedures (e.g., Anderson, 1984; Van Lehn, 1983). Van Lehn's SIERRA makes a number of assumptions about the teaching strategy used to guide the student, including the idea that problem solving by the teacher be transparent (i.e., all steps are observable) and that one procedure is taught per lesson. These assumptions considerably constrain the space of student procedures that are likely to emerge after each lesson. Thus, SIERRA considers only buggy procedures that are one-step modifications of existing procedures. A similar benefit/limitation stems from Anderson's (1984) model-tracing approach: each step of a student's behavior is monitored and matched against the simulated results of plausible student rules; the best matching rule is taken to be the one used by the student and if necessary it may be remediated immediately. Similar strategies are taken by White and Frederiksen (1990a, 1990b), who carefully direct a student along a path of systematically more complex mental models. In contrast, Langley, Wogulis, and Ohlsson's (1987) ACM makes no assumptions about the training strategy to which a student is subjected. Thus, it searches more extensively for procedure sequences that are consistent with a student's final answer.

In general, it would appear that there is a trade-off between the directedness of the training strategy and the effort required to identify probable student procedures. Van Lehn, Anderson, and their colleagues assume highly directed training, making the student modeling task relatively simple. In contrast, Langley et al. (1987) make no assumptions about training; they have noted that their modeling procedure is too expensive and have suggested the automatic formation of macroprocedures to shortcut simulations of student behavior.

Unfortunately, overdirection and tight scripting can be problematic; students at intermediate levels of skill acquisition often find it undesirable. In addition, it may overly constrain the space of procedures that are exercised by students, and for this reason it may reinforce behavior that focuses on specific skills, in contrast to the exploratory behaviors of creative experts. Lesgold's MHO system for learning principles of electricity supports some free exploration on the part of students, along with the guided problem-solving activity of other tutors, but there needs to be a continuum between these extremes.

A primary issue is whether there are hidden, and perhaps unfortunate, implications that can result from the way that training and student diagnosis are typically linked in intelligent tutoring systems. Specifically, directedness of training covaries with the effort required to model student procedures for further "intelligent" training. Many systems opt for highly directed and circumscribed training schemes and thereby limit the search space of possibilities with respect to modeling student knowledge. Such an approach is consistent with the assumption that there is a single asymptotic state defining expertise and a single trajectory, with an identifiable set of sequenced subskills or knowledge components, for reaching that endstate. An unfortunate consequence of such "intelligent" training systems designs is that they may severely restrict the types of expertise that can be developed by individuals who have the capacity to move beyond mere competence in skill execution to more abstract levels of knowledge and task mastery.

With respect to the latter, it would appear essential that some basis be established for discriminating different types of proficiency, all of which can be considered to exemplify high levels of expertise. Consider that in many domains there are those who are technically skilled but not spontaneously inventive and exploratory, as well as those who are similarly skilled but continue to learn and innovate throughout their careers (Miller, 1978). For example, a skilled electronic troubleshooter may correctly find the problem in a circuit and be content to stop and wait for the next assignment. In contrast, another may think about ways that the circuit might be redesigned to make troubleshooting easier, and so forth. Differences such as these in the area of information systems design are described by Miller (1978) and are analogous, in part, to differences in how students attempt to learn from worked-out examples (Chi, Bassok, Lewis, Reimann, & Glaser, 1989) and to differences among people that have been revealed in the literature on practical intelligence (Sternberg & Wagner, 1986). Ultimately, it is important to design integrated training-assessment packages that promote the development of the highest and most flexible levels of expertise.

We believe that it is important to recognize the differences among experts because this implies very different asymptotic states that can result from different training histories and training trajectories. This knowledge should be critical to any training/assessment system. We also believe that it is possible to design intelligent training systems that help people become creative experts rather than mere skilled performers.

Given the instructional design issues we have just presented, the question is, how might an anchored instruction approach be profitably used in future design and implementation cases? It is sometimes less than obvious that the process of materials selection and design and selection of a tutoring approach are intimately related. If the tutoring strategy is to be highly scripted and linked to performance with small units of information, then the design, selection, and sequencing of materials must accommodate such a strategy. If, however, the tutoring strategy is designed to encourage more generative processing activities and the pursuit of a topic from multiple perspectives, then the materials and instructional environment must afford the use of such strategies. The real issue is not to pose the problem as an either/or situation, because different forms of instruction may be needed to accomplish varying levels of instructional outcomes. The real issue is whether the context provided for the presentation of materials and tutoring is "rich" enough to afford multiple approaches and activities.

In this volume there are numerous examples of instructional and tutoring environments that share design principles in common with an anchored instruction approach and/or situated cognition perspective. For example, there is an emphasis on authenticity of tasks, whether it be electronics troubleshooting, nuclear powerplant operation, or aircraft device control. To the extent possible, the learning environment or simulation should not be so abstract as to lose all contact with the physical reality it is designed to represent. Thus, the environments are designed to afford opportunities to solve real problems as they might appear in the actual field environment. What is less clear is how the problems are posed, whether the learner is aware of the reality base, and whether the individual is actively engaged in the learning activity and problem-solving process.

Using rich, multimedia contexts to embed content and instruction should be seen as part of an overall strategy for instructional design and delivery, irrespective of whether the context for presentation is a traditional classroom or a computer-based tutoring system. For example, the effective use of a given type of tutoring environment or microworld may depend on how the student views the content to be learned. One such example is the Smithtown microworld developed for economics tutoring (Shute & Glaser, 1990, 1991). This environment allows students to explore different components of basic economics and simulate the outcomes in a mythical world that adheres to basic economic "laws." In many ways this world emulates an inquiry environment, and thus it affords the learning of basic concepts as well as general planning and problem-solving skills. However, what makes for effective use of the environment and for effective learning outcomes remains somewhat unclear. Consider what might happen when a realistic macrocontext is used to establish a problem (or problems) in need of solution. The environment and tools embedded in Smithtown might be very profitably used to solve the problem. In this way the concepts become embedded or situated in real problems and environments. If students fail to perceive the knowledge provided by a tutoring environment as tools for solving real problems, then it is highly likely that the knowledge will remain inert. Thus, the effective use of a rich environment such as Smithtown may hinge on anchoring its use to larger, more meaningful macrocontexts and problems that students can share in common and want to (rather than need to) solve.

AN ENVIRONMENT FOR TUTORING
OF ADULT LITERACY

The majority of our discussion regarding anchored instruction has focused on problem-solving activities. A reasonable question is whether the approach has relevance to instruction in "basic skills." We feel that much of basic skills instruction often lacks the contextualization that is needed to both motivate the practice needed for proceduralization of skills and to ensure that the skills are encoded for use in the contexts where they are appropriate. For these reasons it is especially important that tutoring environments for basic skills situate the training in meaningful contexts.

We have been involved in development of a computer-based tutor for developing adult literacy. There are far too many adults who lack basic reading skills, and this severely impedes their capacity to perform many jobs and many everyday tasks associated with basic living. The focus of this tutoring project is the development of basic literacy skills by embedding training in interesting and meaningful contexts. The adult literacy project employs a variety of tutoring strategies and materials in a program that develops fluency with many of the most frequently occurring words in the English language.

The tutoring environment has a number of general and specific design characteristics. First the foremost, it uses high-interest videos as anchors for all the basic instruction. These videos are used to sustain integrated training procedures that support both a code emphasis and a meaning emphasis approach to reading. Since this is a program focused on adults, it includes a set of video-based anchors selected by adults as being high-interest topics. As shown by the still pictures in Fig. 6.4, these include a report on cholesterol, consumer reports information on products, videotaping your children for safety, and one on workplace safety. All of the video segments are ones developed for television viewing, and thus they are professionally done and intended to be highly comprehensible. Each video

Contemporary Topics as
Video-based Anchors

Cholesterol

Consumer Reports

Literacy

Videotaping your children
for safety

FIG. 6.4. Examples of the video program content used for the adult literacy tutoring environment.

contains a wealth of information that serves as a context for the reading instruction and tutoring environment.

The tutoring environment includes fluency training on single-word decoding, as well as comprehension training, both of which are tied to the content of the videos. The fluency training employs a voice recognition system that trains as sight words the 400 most frequently used words in the English language. A number of research-based training principles are incorporated into the fluency training, such as (a) a small instruction set, (b) assessment prior to instruction, (c) systematic presentation of new information, (d) guided practice, and (e) independent practice.

The comprehension training also involves a number of strategies. Perhaps the critical one of interest is the use of discrepancy passages. The student is presented with sets of passages that are tied to a particular video program. The passages vary in their consistency with the information contained in the video. The goal of using these passages is to get the student to read for meaning so that discrepancies between the content extracted from the passage and the content of the video can be recognized. In the course of this training, the student also has access to a

Decoding and Comprehension Tools

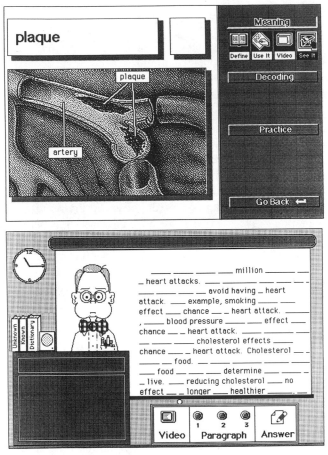

FIG. 6.5. Example screens to support comprehension and skill development in the adult literacy tutoring program.

variety of resources including a video dictionary. Figure 6.5 illustrates some of the decoding and comprehension tools available to the student in the interactive tutoring environment.

The ideas behind the design structure of the adult literacy tutor are not "radical," but what is important is the realization of the anchored instruction concept. By selecting anchors that are of high interest and that are rich in information, the instruction is situated in a meaningful context. Furthermore, the tutoring need not be rigidly scripted since the inferences about what the student knows are much easier given that a context has been established prior to beginning the formal instruction. As we noted earlier, a major difficulty in tutor design and implementation is diagnosing the student's model at any point in time. By using rich and comprehensible materials to set a context, one is "controlling" the nature of the knowledge base and thereby the student model prior to instruction. This avoids some of the indeterminacy that often plagues tutoring or teaching environments and allows for more flexible instructional strategies. An obvious issue is how to employ this same principle of context setting for other instructional domains and skill areas. We believe that it can be done by a careful, reflective analysis of not just what we want people to know but how and where we intend them to use that knowledge.

At this point we must be cautious about claims and indicate two important caveats. First, a true "intelligent" tutor has yet to be implemented for the adult literacy environment. The current tutor is much more student-driven and reactive. A context-sensitive student model does not exist, nor is it used to guide the tutoring exchanges. Such a model and tutoring package could be developed, and we feel that it would be quite flexible, given the anchoring context of the video. The second important caveat is that knowledge engineering is not a trivial issue and the selection/design of video-based anchors requires extensive work. Nevertheless, we feel that it is important that individuals involved in tutor development consider the critical role that a broad, well-selected anchoring context or set of contexts can play in designing flexible tutors that achieve the necessary range of reactive responding.

SUMMARY

Our goal in this chapter was twofold. In the first part we borrowed from our article in the *Educational Researcher* in order to discuss our general approach to instruction-anchored instruction. We illustrated this by our mathematical problem-solving series and some initial results obtained within that context. In the second part of this chapter we discussed how our approach to anchored instruction relates to issues of intelligent tutoring and provided one example of an "anchored tutor." The goal of our approach is to anchor or situate instruction in semantically rich and interesting environments that invite and permit sustained thinking on the part of students. Students explore the environments from their current perspectives (complete with their current preconceptions) and are then able to experience changes in their own noticing and understanding as they are introduced to new information generated by peers, experts, and others. By situating instruction in meaningful contexts, we hope to help students acquire specific skills and knowledge as well as knowledge of general strategies and theories that are noninert. Cognitive skills are more than the nuts and bolts and girders of an intellectual erector set. How they work together depends on the object we wish to design. The problem for any teacher or tutor is to help students acquire the basics without losing sight of why and how they might be useful. A good teacher or tutor never loses sight of the need to establish a shared context for the discourse and apprenticeship that are to be transacted.

ACKNOWLEDGMENTS

Preparation of this chapter was supported in part by a grant from the James S. McDonnell Foundation and a grant from the National Science Foundation.

This chapter is based in part on an article in the *Educational Researcher*. Contributors to this chapter are Linda Barron, Gautam Biswas, John Bransford, Olin Campbell, Bill Corbin, Doug Fisher, Laura Goin, Elizabeth Goldman, Susan Goldman, Ted Hasselbring, Charles Kinzer, Jim Pellegrino, Kirsten Rewey, Vicki Risko, Robert Sherwood, James Van Haneghan, Nancy Vye, Susan Williams, and Michael Young.

REFERENCES

Adams, L., Kasserman, J., Yearwood, A., Perfetto, G., Bransford, J., & Franks, J. (1988). The effects of facts versus problem-oriented acquisition. *Memory & Cognition, 16,* 167–175.

Anderson, J. (1984). Cognitive psychology and intelligent tutoring. *Proceedings of the Sixth International Conference of the Cognitive Science Society.* Boulder, CO, pp. 2–8.

Bank Street College of Education. (1984). *Voyage of the Mimi.* Scotts Valley, CA: Wings for Learning, Inc., Sunburst Co.

Belli, R., Soraci, S., & Purdon, S. (1989). *The generation effect in learning and memory: Implications for theory and practice.* Unpublished manuscript, Vanderbilt University, Learning Technology Center, TN.

Bereiter, C. (1984). How to keep thinking skills from going the way of all frills. *Educational Leadership, 42,* 75–77.

Bransford, J. D., Franks, J. J., Vye, N. J., & Sherwood, R. D. (1989). New approaches to instruction: Because wisdom can't be told. In S. Vosniadou & A. Ortony (Eds.), *Similarity and analogical reasoning* (pp. 470–497). New York: Cambridge University Press.

Bransford, J. D., & Heldmeyer, K. (1983). Learning from children learning. In J. Bisanz, G. Bisanz, & R. Kail (Eds.), *Learning in children: Progress in cognitive development research* (pp. 171–190). New York: Springer-Verlag.

Bransford, J., Kinzer, C., Risko, V., Rowe, D., & Vye, N. (1989). Designing invitations to thinking: Some initial thoughts. In S. McCormick & J. Zutell (Eds.), *Cognitive and social perspectives for literacy research and instruction* (pp. 35–54). Chicago: The National Reading Conference, Inc.

Bransford, J. D., & McCarrell, N. S. (1974). A sketch of cognitive approach to comprehension. In W. B. Weiner & D. S. Palermo (Eds.), *Cognition and the symbolic processes* (pp. 299–303). Hillsdale, NJ: Lawrence Erlbaum Associates.

Bransford, J. D., & Nitsch, K. E. (1978). Coming to understand things we could not previously understand. In J. F. Kavanaugh & W. Strange (Eds.), *Speech and language in the laboratory, school, and clinic* (pp. 267–307). Cambridge, MA: MIT Press.

Bransford, J. D., Sherwood, R. S., Hasselbring, T. S., Kinzer, C. K., & Williams, S. M. (1990). Anchored instruction: Why we need it and how technology can help. In D. Nix & R. Spiro (Eds.), *Advances in computer-video technology, computers, cognition, and multi-media: Explorations in high technology* (pp. 115–142). Hillsdale, Lawrence Erlbaum Associates.

Bransford, J. D., Sherwood, R., Vye, N. J., & Rieser, J. (1986). Teaching thinking and problem solving: Research foundations. *American Psychologist, 41*(10), 1078–1089.

Bransford, J. D., & Stein, B. S. (1984). *The IDEAL problem solver.* New York: Freeman.

Bransford, J. D., Stein, B. S., Delclos, V., & Littlefield, J. (1986). Computers and problem solving. In C. Kinzer, R. Sherwood, & J. Bransford (Eds.), *Computers strategies for education: Foundations and content-area applications* (pp. 147–180). Columbus, OH: Merrill.

Bransford, J. D., Vye, N. J., Kinzer, C., & Risko, V. (1990). Teaching thinking and content knowledge: Toward an integrated approach. In B. F. Jones & L. Idol (Eds.), *Dimensions of thinking and cognitive instruction* (pp. 381–413). Hillsdale, NJ: Lawrence Erlbaum Associates.

Briggs, H. (1624). *Arithmetica logarithmica.* Londini: Excudebat Gulielmus Iones.

Brown, A. L., Bransford, J. D., Ferrara, R. A., & Campione, J. C. (1983). Learning, remembering and understanding. In J. H. Flavell & E. M. Markman (Eds.), *Carmichael's manual of child psychology* (Vol. 1, pp. 77–166). New York: Wiley.

Brown, J. S., Collins, A., & Duguid, P. (1989). Situated cognition and the culture of learning. *Educational Researcher, 17,* 32–41.

Chi, M. T. H., Bassok, M., Lewis, M. W., Reimann, P., & Glaser, R. (1989). Self-explanations: How students study and use examples in learning to solve problems. *Cognitive Science, 13,* 145–182.

Cognition and Technology Group at Vanderbilt. (1990). Anchored instruction and its relationship to situated cognition. *Educational Researcher, 19* (6), 2–10.

Cognition and Technology Group at Vanderbilt. (in press). Anchored instruction and science education. In R. Duschl & R. Hamilton (Eds.), *Philosophy of science, cognitive psychology and educational theory and practice* New York: SUNY Press.

Daneman, M., & Carpenter, P. (1980). Individual differences in working memory and reading. *Journal of Verbal Learning and Verbal Behavior, 19,* 450–466.

Dewey, J. (1933). *How we think* (rev. ed.). Boston: Heath.

Feuerstein, R., Rand, Y., & Hoffman, M. (1979). *The dynamic assessment of retarded performers: The learning potential assessment device: Theory, instruments, and techniques.* Baltimore, MD: University Park Press.

Feuerstein, R., Rand, Y., Hoffman, M. B., & Miller, R. (1980). *Instrumental enrichment.* Baltimore, MD: University Park Press.

Gick, M. L., & Holyoak, K. J. (1980). Analogical problem solving. *Cognitive Psychology, 12,* 306–365.

Gragg, C. I. (1940). Because wisdom can't be told. *Harvard Alumni Bulletin,* October 19, 78–84.

Hanson, N. R. (1970). A picture theory of theory meaning. In R. G. Colodny (Ed.), *The nature and function of scientific theories* (pp. 233–274). Pittsburgh: University of Pittsburgh Press.

Johnson, R. (1987). *The ability to retell a story: Effects of adult mediation in a videodisc context on children's story recall and comprehension.* Unpublished doctoral thesis, Vanderbilt University, Nashville, TN.

Johnson-Laird, P. N. (1985). Deductive reasoning ability. In R. J. Sternberg (Ed.), *Human abilities: An information-processing approach* (pp. 173–194). New York: Freeman.

Lakatos, I. (1976). *Proofs and refutations: Logic of mathematical discovery.* New York: Cambridge University Press.

Lampert, M. (1990). When the problem is not the question and the solution is not the answer: Mathematical knowing and teaching. *American Educational Research Journal, 27,* 29–63.

Langley, P., Wogulis, J., & Ohlsson, S. (1990). Rules and principles in cognitive diagnosis. In N. Frederickson, R. Glaser, A. Lesgold, & M. Shafto, (Eds.), *Diagnostic monitoring skill and knowledge acquisition* (pp. 217–250). Hillsdale, NJ: Lawrence Erlbaum Associates.

Lave, J. (1988). *Cognition in practice.* Boston: Cambridge University Press.

Lesh, R. (1981). Applied mathematical problem solving. *Educational Studies in Mathematics, 12,* 235–264.

Lesh, R. (1985). Processes and abilities needed to use mathematics in everyday situations. *Education and Urban Society, 17,* 330–336.

Lipman, M. (1985). Thinking skills fostered by philosophy for children. In J. Segal, S. Chipman, & R. Glaser (Eds.), *Thinking and learning skills: Relating instruction to basic research* (Vol. 1, pp. 83–108). Hillsdale, NJ: Lawrence Erlbaum Associates.

Littlefield, J., Delclos, V., Lever, S., Clayton, K., Bransford, J., & Franks, J. (1988). Learning logo: Method of teaching, transfer of general skills and attitudes toward school and computers. In R. E. Mayer (Ed.), *Teaching and learning computer programming* (pp. 111–135). Hillsdale, NJ: Lawrence Erlbaum Associates.

Lockhart, R. S., Lamon, M., & Gick, M. L. (1988). Conceptual transfer in simple insight problems. *Memory & Cognition, 16,* 36–44.

McNamara, T. P., Miller, D. L., & Bransford, J. D. (1991). Mental models and reading comprehension. In T. D. Pearson, R. Barr, M. Kamil, & P. Mosenthal (Eds.), *Handbook of reading research* (Vol. 2, pp. 490–511). New York: Longman.

Miller, D. L. (1989). *Characterizing mental models in narrative comprehension.* Unpublished doctoral dissertation, Vanderbilt University, Nashville, TN.

Miller, G. A., & Gildea, P. M. (1987). How children learn words. *Scientific American, 275*(3), 94–99.

Miller, R. B. (1978). The information system designer. In W. T. Singleton (Ed.), *The analysis of practical skills* (pp. 278–291). Baltimore: University Park Press.

National Council of Teachers of Mathematics. (1989). *Curriculum and evaluation standards for school mathematics.* Reston, VA: Author.

Nitsch, K. E. (1977). Structuring decontextualized forms of knowledge. Doctoral dissertation, Vanderbilt University. *Dissertation Abstracts International, 38B,* 3935.

Perkins, D. N., & Salomon, G. (1989). Are cognitive skills context-bound? *Educational Researcher, 18*(1), 16-25.

Pezdek, K., Lehrer, A., & Simon, S. (1984). The relationship between reading and cognitive processing of television and radio. *Child Development, 55,* 2072–2082.

Polya, G. (1957). *How to solve it.* Garden City, NY: Doubleday Anchor.

Porter, A. (1989). A curriculum out of balance: The case of elementary school mathematics. *Educational Researcher, 18*(5), 9–15.

Salomon, G., & Perkins, D. (1989). Rocky road to transfer: Rethinking mechanisms of a neglected phenomenon. *Educational Psychologist, 24*(2), 113–142.

Scardamalia, M., & Bereiter, C. (1985). Fostering the development of self-regulation in children's knowledge processing. In S. F. Chipman, J. W. Segal, & R. Glaser (Eds.), *Thinking and learning skills: Research and open questions* (Vol. 2, pp. 563–578). Hillsdale, NJ: Lawrence Erlbaum Associates.

Schoenfeld, A. (1985). *Mathematical problem solving.* Orlando, FL: Academic Press.

Schwab, J. J. (1960). What do scientists do? *Behavioral Science, 5,* 1–27.

Schwab, J. J. (1962). The teaching of science as enquiry. In J. Schwab & P. Brandwein (Eds.), *The teaching of science* (pp. 3–103). Cambridge, MA: Harvard University Press.

Sherwood, R. D., Kinzer, C. K., Bransford, J. D., & Franks, J. J. (1987). Some benefits of creating macro-contexts for science instruction: Initial findings. *Journal of Research in Science Teaching, 24*(5), 417–435.

Sherwood, R., Kinzer, C., Hasselbring, T., & Bransford, J. (1987). Macro-contexts for learning: Initial findings and issues. *Journal of Applied Cognition, 1,* 93–108.

Shute, V. J., & Glaser, R. (1990). Large-scale evaluation of an intelligent tutoring system: Smithtown. *Interactive Learning Environments, 1,* 51–76.

Shute, V. J., & Glaser, R. (1991). An intelligent tutoring system for exploring principles of economics. In R. E. Snow & D. Wiley (Eds.), *Improving inquiry in social science: A volume in honor of Lee J. Cronbach* (pp. 333–360). Hillsdale, NJ: Lawrence Erlbaum Associates.

Simon, H. A. (1980). Problem solving and education. In D. T. Tuma & R. Reif (Eds.), *Problem solving and education: Issues in teaching and research* (pp. 81–96). Hillsdale, NJ: Lawrence Erlbaum Associates.

Slamecka, N. J., & Graf, P. (1978). The generation effect: Delineation of a phenomenon. *Journal of Experimental Psychology: Human Learning and Memory, 4,* 592–604.

Soraci, S. A., Jr., Bransford, J. D., Franks, J. J., & Chechile, R. (1987). A multiple-cue model of generation activity. *Proceedings of the 1987 Psychonomics Society,* New Orleans.

Spiro, R. J., Vispoel, W. L., Schmitz, J., Samarapungavan, A., & Boerger, A. (1987). Knowledge acquisition for application: Cognitive flexibility and transfer in complex content domains. In B. C. Britton & S. Glynn (Eds.), *Executive control processes in reading* (pp. 177–199). Hillsdale, NJ: Lawrence Erlbaum Associates.

Stein, N. L., & Trabasso, T. (1982). What's in a story: An approach to comprehension and instruction. In R. Glaser (Ed.), *Advances in instructional psychology* (Vol. 2, pp. 213–267). Hillsdale, NJ: Lawrence Erlbaum Associates.

Sternberg, R. J., & Wagner, R. K. (1986). *Practical intelligence.* Cambridge: Cambridge University Press.

Van Haneghan, J., Barron, L., Young, M., Williams, S., Vye, N., & Bransford, J. (in press). The Jasper Series: An experiment with new ways to enhance mathematical thinking. In D. Halpern (Ed.), *Concerning: The development of thinking skills in the sciences and mathematics.* Hillsdale, NJ: Lawrence Erlbaum Associates.

Van Lehn, K. (1983). *Felicity conditions for human skill acquisition: Validating an AI-based theory.* Unpublished doctoral dissertation, Massachusetts Institute of Technology, Cambridge.

Vye, N., Bransford, J., Furman, L., Baron, B., Montavon, E., Young, M., Van Haneghan, J., & Baron, L. (1989, April). *An analysis of students' mathematical problem solving in real world settings.* Paper presented at the meeting of the American Educational Research Association, San Francisco, CA.

Vygotsky, L. S. (1978). *Mind in society.* Cambridge, MA: Harvard University Press.

White, B. Y., & Frederiksen, J. R. (1990a). Causal model progressions as a foundation for intelligent learning environments. *Artificial Intelligence, 42,* 99–157.

White, B. Y., & Frederiksen, J. R. (1990b). Intelligent tutors as intelligent testers. In N. Frederiksen, R. Glaser, A. Lesgold, & M. G. Shafto (Eds.), *Diagnostic monitoring of skill and knowledge acquisition* (pp. 1–26). Hillsdale, NJ: Lawrence Erlbaum Associates.

Whitehead, A. N. (1929). *The aims of education.* New York: Macmillan.

Williams, S. M. (1991). *Case-based approaches to instruction in medicine and law.* Unpublished manuscript, Vanderbilt University, Nashville, TN.

TRANSCRIPT OF DISCUSSION

Val Shute: What transfer types were used in the evaluations you described?

James Pellegrino: What we did was construct another story. It was similar to the first in terms of having a general theme of "trip planning." It was another adventure, which did not have exactly the same structure as the Jasper adventure, but which involved multiple stages of problem solving with goals and subgoals. The task was for students to set up the goal structure and figure out what information was needed to solve the various goals and subgoals.

Wes Regian: The term *anchoring* implies that what's happening here is that you are tying new knowledge to existing knowledge and that is the key point. But some of your words sound like its more a motivational effect, that it is more motivating for the students.

James Pellegrino: I think that it does both. I indicated early on, one of the problems of instruction is that often, the teacher and students don't have a shared context. So one of the things that the anchor does is create a context that everybody has seen and is rich enough for them to explore. The other thing, is to motivate students. Not only to motivate, but to help them understand where the skills are needed, where the components come in. By creating an environment that is rich enough and realistic enough, individuals can become interested in working in that environment. Kids *like* to work in "Young Sherlock" dealing with the life of young Sherlock Holmes. One question that is often asked is, "Well, this is all video, what about reading?" It turns out that kids read more to solve problems or to find information, and that behavior is motivated by questions that come out of the video. It motivates the kids to go find out information and read various sources to address questions that they can generate themselves about the context.

Dan Fisk: I think this is a wonderful approach. It is certainly something I'd like to do in my classroom myself, at the college level. This notion of shared context sets the right context for me. You said that you were going to mention something about cognitive analysis. Could you set the stage of how one might do this in an environment where the people are somewhat motivated to learn things in the first place, areas like air traffic control?

James Pellegrino: In all honesty, I have not thought about it in those kinds of task environments because I am not familiar enough with some of them to know the way with which the training is done and whether the context is set or not, irrespective of whether the individuals are motivated. I suspect that you can decouple the issue of motivation from the issue of context setting. The implication I draw from hearing you, Walt Schneider, and others talk about the way in which training is often done is that individuals are thrown into the training situations. But they are not allowed the opportunity to explore the context in which they are going to be solving the problem. They are given sets of problems to start solving without fully understanding where they are going or why they are doing what they are doing, other than, "This is an intercept task," or whatever. I don't know how well the context is established.

Dan Fisk: What is the cognitive analysis that we would use to allow us to independently develop these anchors? Is there transfer to something else?

James Pellegrino: We don't have a set of rules in common that we can use at this point. Basically, what we are trying to do is ask what are the high-level goals and subgoals of the domain that you want to study. In your case, you would ask, "What is the environment all about? What are the high-level goals and subskills that the individual needs to master?" And then you should try to focus the anchor around getting them to appreciate what the high-level goals actually are. So when we are working on statistics, we are trying to get them to understand the process of collecting data to structure an argument, and then sampling is part of a process by which to do that, rather than sampling being the specific goal itself. The same thing applies with certain components in geometry—the concept is one of using data to structure an argument. If you look at Greeno's analysis in geometry, one of the things that is not taught is the strategic knowledge. His argument was that in geometry, proving something means that you're trying to find a measure of something or prove that something equals something else. Basically, you are trying to fill in a pattern, and kids don't often see that this what the goal is. So what you are trying to do is take the facts and create an argument. The argument often is not at all transparent. So what we try to do is create a situation where the anchor focuses on the high-level notion of using data to construct an argument. I think that you may need multiple anchors and contexts as you get into some domains which are extremely rich. We are not making the claim that you can do everything with just one anchor or one context.

Wes Regian: I like the approach and when I worked for you at UCSB, I tutored statistics on the side. I got better and better at it, and what I noticed was I would give people examples that hit home for them. For example, trying to explain a distribution to somebody that happens to be in bicycling, you could say: "Suppose you're riding your bike over a four mile course, twenty times . . . ," so I embedded it into something they knew about and were interested in. My idea is that maybe in the context of intelligent tutoring, you could start by asking people a few questions. What are your hobbies? What part of the country are you from? Just a few pieces of information that you could later use to generate canned examples for stuff. So if I found out a guy's hobby was bicycling, I could use that in an ITS on statistics as an example, rather than another example on fishing or something.

Dan Fisk: Isn't that what the challenge is, because what you have done is developed a coach, in a sense, that is allowing active involvement in what are important underlying skills.

James Pellegrino: One of the problems with what Wes is saying is that people come from so many different backgrounds that one of the difficulties for a teacher or coach is finding or tailoring things to a person's background. What we are trying to do is to say, "Hey, wait a minute, we realize that it is important to make this stuff meaningful. Let's try to create a context that is rich enough and interesting enough so that lots of people want to explore it." So we can work with that for developing the tutoring strategies. Then I as tutor and you as the person to be coached have the same context that we are working from. When I know what is in that context and so do you, we can go back and explore it again, and we can use that as a basis for doing an analysis of whether you really understand how to generate the goals and subgoals or the specific details.

Doug Towne: What are you finding when you teach the teachers? Are they receptive and does it take more or less skill to support this? How much variance is there in their abilities?

James Pellegrino: The real interesting thing with the teachers is that teachers almost universally like this idea. They say, "This is great; this is what I'm looking for." But then their next issue is, "How am I going to teach all the objectives that the tests specify?" One of the things that we are doing to respond to that is showing them the mapping between the content of the video and the objectives of the standard math curriculum. Then they can use the video as a vehicle to teach decimals and fractions because the content is embedded within it. The other thing that I mentioned at lunch today is that for teachers to use this, they have to go through the experience of solving the problem and feeling as if they know it inside out. It is hard to get some of them to not treat this as a glorified word problem. Some teachers, if you give them the material, will have kids watch the video and then say, "Okay, now we're going back to it a second time. Write down every fact that you see." This is exactly what we *don't* want. Because that is essentially an extension of the "key word" approach that they are using in teaching simple word problems. Getting them to restructure their way of thinking about teaching problem solving is hard. . . . A lot of them don't understand very much about problem solving. They need to get comfortable with this. In fact, one of the things that we are doing now is running an institute in which we are bringing teachers in and exposing them to this approach to instruction. We are going to be doing a test this next year on the materials that will be implemented in about 10 or 15 different schools throughout the country, including a couple of schools here in Texas. We will see what the issues are in terms of implementation and the effects that it has on the instructional process.

Walt Schneider: I want to take the devil's advocate position. If it is the case that we at this point have students that will only look at something that comes out of a box, then that's okay, if boxes are cheaper than teachers, let's buy more boxes. The issue that I don't understand is this: I'm having trouble separating the use of video as a *motivating issue* from the aspect of the approach which is what you're providing, I think, sort of a long-term context that you can recycle. Sort of "spin-off" teaching as opposed to Fact A, Fact B, Fact C. The question, particularly in terms of the assessments, is to try and separate out just what is it? For example, if you had a mechanism, let's say in the Sherlock case, how does somebody read a story to be a good spin-off teacher or an anchor teacher? And you could take something that is of greater interest to this group. Or you also have the flexibility of now teaching the teachers so they can do it themselves. They can't pay $60,000 for a video tape every time they want to do a different lesson. Are there tests planned in the system to try and identify what is it? Can you do the technique without this specific technology? And how do you structure that approach?

James Pellegrino: First let me respond to the issue of why the video is more powerful than the text. For example, a lot of concepts imply action, and so they are dynamic. Suppose I wanted a kid to learn the meaning of the term *pretentious*. If you actually saw the Young Sherlock video, there is a wonderful set of scenes where pretentious behavior is remarkably well illustrated by the characters' actions. When we get away from noun concepts, or simple static images to more dynamic events, the videos are a much more natural vehicle in which you can begin to understand them rather than simply reading text. As far as using anchors and developing anchors, I think good teachers try to do this all the time. What we are trying to do is (a) get teachers to understand the utility of doing that and (b) give them ways in which they can develop anchors by using existing material. We also would like to get them into the habit of using materials on more than just a one-shot basis. Too much in the curriculum, even in the literacy classes, is looked at once and only once.

Alan Lesgold: Building further on what you just said. . . . Good students have the opportunity to some extent to participate in, or even make their own anchors. I wonder whether more of the things that go on when students put on a play, or do "Students of the United Nations," or something like that, where there are real interactions and where the problem-solving is more given than interactive, isn't necessary. And whether the video anchor isn't a first step around which much more interstudent interactions is important. The best of the teachers, including some of your colleagues who have taught classes using the Jasper video, get the students to interact with each other and trying to understand what they are saying to each other, and each student tries to understand what the other student thinks the problem really is. I suspect that is a very big piece of where the real action is.

James Pellegrino: A lot of this has been done in a group context. There have been cases in which we have done small groups as well as whole-group instruction. I think that you are right about that, particularly when it comes to involving the at-risk or low-achieving kid who is in the typical classroom. The way in which it is currently structured, there are usually questions that are posed in which there is only a single answer. These kids seldom, if ever, have the opportunity to contribute anything because some other kid knows the answer already. And so, a lot is achieved by this dynamic situation of allowing kids to share and exchange information with each other.

Alan Lesgold: If you look at what is really being said in reports like the newspaper article you cited, business people are saying that among other things, the skills that are missing in students and the people in the workplace are the skills of listening and understanding somebody else's problem and trying to figure out what that problem is. I'm responding to a memo from the boss by actually doing what I think he actually needs, as opposed to minimally satisfying the direct commands. So I try to figure out what the customer's problem really is, as opposed to how to get him to stop complaining. These kinds of things are really the core of the problem.

James Pellegrino: I think that this is part of it as far as group problem solving.

Sharvari Dixit: How are these anchoring videos used in a typical middle-school class? Is it about a half hour class in which one of your films are shown? Would it be shown full-length and so on?

James Pellegrino: The way that it's used is that the video is shown once, and typically the instructional activity surrounding the video is extended over several days. They may start out the first day trying to figure out what the larger problems are that need to be solved. Then they try to get to the point of figuring out "Where is the information?" So the next day they might go back and explore certain cases and they will construct the solution over time that way. So it is not done in all one shot. It may actually be done over the course of one to two weeks.

7

The Application
of Consistency Principles
for the Assessment
of Skill Development

Arthur D. Fisk
Georgia Institute of Technology

Wendy A. Rogers
Memphis State University

Our goal for this chapter is to outline recent research that may aid in the ultimate understanding of how to develop guidelines for real-time monitoring of skill development. The theoretical underpinnings of our research are based on a general theory of skill acquisition that assumes that as an individual undergoes transition from a novice to an expert, information-processing requirements change across identifiable phases or stages of skill development. Our approach to skill acquisition is not new; rather, it is based on models proposed by Fitts (1964, 1965/1990), Shiffrin and Schneider (1977), and Anderson (1982, 1983). Like other theorists, we refer to these phases as controlled, associative, and automatic.

The first phase, controlled processing, seems required for performance of novel tasks. During this early stage of skill acquisition, the individual must interpret task instructions and goals, as well as develop strategies for task-appropriate behavior. The performance of individual task components requires attention, and it is necessary to monitor each step of the task.

After some practice, with the amount of practice generally being task specific, the information processing requirements of the task change. Performance can be described as transitioning to the associative phase. This phase involves forming task-specific associations and learning to attend and respond to specific cues. Because task-dependent context activates information in long-term memory, the load in working memory is reduced. Goal state information (i.e., task-specific rules) becomes well learned and no longer needs to be actively rehearsed in working memory.

The final phase of skill acquisition is referred to as the automatic phase because the requirements for attention are greatly reduced. Task requirements are modified such that a given stimulus or pattern of stimuli evokes a particular response or a behavioral sequence.

It is important to note that these stages are not discrete: they have "fuzzy boundaries" (as day vs. night has a fuzzy boundary) and should be thought of as more gradual shifts in the underlying processes required for task performance. This caveat notwithstanding, in one form or another, these phases of skill development are well documented from a nomethetic perspective. As important, differential studies provide converging evidence for these stages (e.g., Ackerman, 1988). The individual differences studies clearly demarcate changing information processing requirements by demonstrating different performance/ability functions across task practice.

SIMPLIFICATION OF THE PROBLEM

Our approach to the problem of real-time diagnosis of skill acquisition is to focus on what we believe to be fundamental building blocks of skill—automatic component processes. Although it is clear that skill and automaticity are not synonymous terms, our basic premise is that most complex skills are tasks that are dominated by automatic component process. Indeed, we take the position argued by Logan (1985) that automaticity refers to components of tasks while skill refers to a collection of automatic processes that drives skilled performance. We further take the position that only consistent task components result in automatic component processes; hence, real-time diagnostic monitoring of skill acquisition requires understanding, isolating, and monitoring the consistent components of the to-be-learned task.

To more fully describe our approach to the problem of real-time diagnosis of skill development, we first discuss basic principles of consistency and then outline research that expands these basic principles. We discuss processing principles that can be used to predict performance limits as well as to aid in the specification of training program designs. A brief discussion of a theoretically driven task-analytic methodology for identification of consistent trainable components is presented followed by a discussion of issues of real-time diagnosis of skill acquisition.

PRINCIPLE OF CONSISTENCY

"Never suffer an exception to occur 'til the new habit is securely rooted in your life. . . . Continuity of training is the general means of making the nervous system act infallibly right" (James, 1890). James' quote describes the criticality of consistency (i.e., continuity) for the acquisition of habits. Much work since the time of James has been devoted to understanding the many facets of consistency that must be considered for optimization of habit, or skill, acquisition (see Shiffrin, 1988, for a review).

The purpose of the present chapter is to present a selective review of some recent laboratory work investigating consistency from simple, stimulus-based consistency to higher-order, rule-based, and contextually defined consistencies. Issues of degree of consistency, benefits accrued from consistent practice, and the transfer and retention of consistent task components are also discussed. The review culminates in a collection of principles of consistency.

The principles of consistency are based on laboratory work that has primarily been focused on perceptual skills. However, we also describe situations in which more complex, cognitive skills have been shown to reap similar benefits from consistent practice and yield similar patterns of performance. For example, we describe a classroom scenario in which base-5 arithmetic skills were taught according to the principles of consistency. Furthermore, the results of experimentation with a simulated "dispatching" task are presented to demonstrate the application of these principles in another domain.

Our inherent message is that in order for practice improvements to occur, some modicum of consistent practice must be provided. The principles of consistency are applicable in perceptual domains as well as more complex cognitive skill domains. Importantly, these principles also provide guidelines for the development of computer-based programs of instruction.

EMPIRICAL INVESTIGATIONS EXTENDING THE PRINCIPLE OF CONSISTENCY

In the following sections, we outline several recent empirical investigations. These experiments have been conducted to provide a more complete understanding of factors important in skill development. Taken as a whole these data, combined with previous research (for a review see Fisk, Ackerman, & Schneider, 1987), provide for a principled approach to task decomposition.

Higher-Order, Rule-Based Consistency

The concept of consistency is an important cornerstone of the theory of automatic and controlled processing.[1] Think back for a moment about learning to drive a manual shift automobile. Imagine how difficult learning how to shift would have been if the location of each gear changed every time you drove the car. This would necessitate the continuous devotion of attention to remembering where the

---

[1]For a more detailed analysis of the characteristics of automatic and controlled processing see Fisk et al. (1987), Logan (1985), Posner and Snyder (1975), Schneider, Dumais, and Shiffrin (1984), Shiffrin (1988), and Shiffrin and Dumais (1981).

gears were; the task of shifting gears would never become automatic. This example illustrates the importance of consistency for the development of automatic processing, namely, if a task is inconsistent, or varied, automatic processing will not develop.

In their seminal series investigating controlled search and automatic detection, Schneider and Shiffrin (1977; Shiffrin & Schneider, 1977) demonstrated differences in performance that varied according to whether training was consistent or variable. This has been referred to as training that is consistently or variably "mapped." More precisely, in a consistent mapping (CM) situation, the individual always deals with (i.e., attends to, responds to, or utilizes information from) a stimulus, or class of stimuli, in the same manner. CM training conditions result in dramatic performance improvements (see Schneider & Shiffrin, 1977), and the eventual development of performance characteristics indicative of automatic processing. Varied mapping (VM) training situations are those in which the practice is inconsistent; that is, the response or degree of attention devoted to the stimulus changes from one stimulus exposure to another. VM training conditions result in little performance improvement.

The research conducted by Shiffrin and Schneider (1977; Shiffrin & Schneider, 1977) always employed a one-to-one stimulus-to-response mapping. However, consistency need not occur at the individual stimulus level to benefit performance. For example, Durso, Cooke, Breen, and Schvanaveldt (1987) demonstrated the importance of relational consistencies for the development of automatic processing. Durso et al. compared performance improvement with practice on a traditional CM letter-search task to improvements on a "digit detection" task. Their digit task differed from both traditional CM and VM search tasks. In the digit task, subjects were asked to respond to the largest digit in a display (largest in terms of ordinal property, that is, 9 is larger than 8, 8 is larger than 7, etc.). This task was not consistently mapped in the traditional sense because a given digit was not always responded to when it appeared on the screen. For example, the digit 7 would be the largest, and responded to, when digits 6 and below are on the screen. However, the digit 7 would be ignored, and thus not responded to, when the digits 8 or 9 are in the display. Durso et al. found that performance on the digit task was comparable to the CM letter search task; that is, there was an overall reduction in reaction time and an attenuation of comparison load effects with practice.

At first glance, the Durso et al. (1987) research calls into question the need for consistency in training. However, Fisk, Oransky, and Skedsvold (1988; also Fisk & Eboch, 1989: Kramer, Strayer, & Buckley, 1990) explored whether relationships among stimuli might generate task-relevant consistencies. Their experiments demonstrated the facilitating role of "higher-order" or "global" consistency in developing skill-like performance. Higher-order consistency in this case was the relationship among the numerical stimuli. Fisk et al. replicated the Durso et al. findings even when response learning was controlled for. That replication provided a clear example of a situation where the individual stimulus was not driving performance. Instead, the higher-order knowledge of "numerical orders" served to activate and cue the correct response. In follow-on experiments, Fisk et al. showed that in a minimal amount of training time (approximately 30 hr) similar higher-order representations could be developed for novel stimuli. In summary, these studies furthered the understanding of consistency in complex tasks by demonstrating that in conditions where subjects could utilize higher-order consistencies (relationships), normal CM practice effects occurred even when the individual stimuli were not always mapped to a particular response.

Fisk and Lloyd (1988) extended our understanding of higher-order consistency using a spatial, rule-governed task. They examined the role of consistency of stimulus-to-rule relationships in the facilitation of learning and performance of a rule-based task. They used chesslike tasks that required the development of a complex, multicomponent skill conceptually similar to a component of a chess game. Fisk and Lloyd conducted a series of experiments designed to investigate the development of perceptual/rule-based processes. The subjects were required to learn to distinguish the game pieces, understand their legal moves, and also determine the source of the "threat-of-capture" on a simulated game board. The stimulus-to-rule mappings were either consistent or varied.

The Fisk and Lloyd (1988) spatial learning data are remarkably similar to previous perceptual learning results from studies using more traditional visual search tasks (e.g., Fisk & Schneider, 1983; Schneider & Shiffrin, 1977). There were dramatic decreases in reaction time (RT), comparison slopes, response variability, and attention demands for the consistently mapped version of the task. These performance changes are all demonstrated markers for the development of automatic processing (see Ackerman, 1988; Schneider & Fisk, 1982; Schneider & Shiffrin, 1977). Consequently, the Fisk and Lloyd results support the relevance of consistent mapping in the training of patterns of information in complex tasks. Importantly, the use of external stimulus patterns to determine response actions maps on to other real-world tasks such as computer programming (Jeffries, Turner, Polson, & Atwood, 1981), electronic troubleshooting (Egan & Schwartz, 1979), interpreting x-rays and medical diagnoses (Parasuraman, 1985), and in-flight refueling (Eggemeier, Fisk, Robbins, Lawless, & Spaeth, 1988).

Contextually Defined Consistency

An understanding of the facilitative effects of contextual cues is critical for any training program developed to facilitate skill acquisition. A real-world example of the importance of context comes from observation of skilled air-intercept controllers. Responses made to pilots in one context (an intercept with the goal simply to identify) are different from those made in other contexts (e.g., if the goal is defense against hostile intruders).

Fisk and Rogers (1988) investigated the issue of situation-specific context using a search/detection task in which context was defined as the combination of target and distractor sets. That is, a given category was the target set only in the context of another particular category as the distractor set. For example, "Animal" words might be the target set if "Weapons" are the distractors; however, if "Animal" words are paired with "Vegetables," the "Animal" words are distractor items. Thus, the experimental context defines whether a particular set of items is attended to or ignored. Fisk and Rogers found that, in the absence of traditional consistency, context can play an important role in facilitating performance. In addition, their data support the suggestion that context can also be important for completely consistent tasks (e.g., see Schneider & Fisk, 1984). The results from their experiment revealed that performance in the context conditions improved more than performance in the VM condition, although not as much as in the traditional CM condition (where a particular set serves as the target set or the distractor set but not both).

Subsequent analyses of the Fisk and Rogers data suggested that the context effect seemed to occur within five exposures to the context situation; that is, the temporary "salience" biasing built up very quickly and overrode previous contextual cues. Lee, Rogers, and Fisk (1991) investigated this issue in more detail. They varied the number of trials per context condition in order to directly assess the temporal buildup of context effects. In their experiment, context was modified either every trial, every 5 trials, every 10 trials, or every 50 trials; hence, the temporal nature of the acquisition of contextual benefits could be assessed. The data showed that, for this class of tasks at least, temporary salience-biasing (context effects) can be seen within five exposures to the context situation. Importantly, when context was shifted every trial the benefits of context were minimized. Furthermore, the pure CM condition, which was embedded within this one trial cycle, shown a reduction in performance improvement.

The Fisk and Rogers (1988) and Lee et al. (1991) results suggest that contextual cues may be used to bias performance and mimic the effects of consistency. In other words, in some situations, consistencies may be context-dependent and the trainee must be made aware of the critical contextual cues. This "situation awareness" may be trained by making the appropriate contextual cues most salient. After training, these cues may serve to activate particular "automatized" sequences of behavior.

Degree of Consistency

Performance principles based on an understanding of consistent practice have been applied to designing training programs for a variety of domains including map reading skills (Fisk & Eboch, 1989), instructional system design (Fisk & Gallini, 1989), in-flight refueling (Eggemeier, Fisk, Robbins, Lawless, & Spaeth, 1988), and air traffic control (Kanfer & Ackerman, 1989), However, the majority of applications-oriented research has been based on an assumption that the stimuli are always attended to, responded to, or classified in exactly the same manner in all situations. Unfortunately, in real-world settings perfect consistency may be unattainable.

Degrees of Between-Category Consistency. The issue of degree of consistency was investigated in the laboratory by Schneider and Fisk (1982) using a relatively simple letter-search task. Subjects were required to search for a single letter in a series of displays, each of which contained four letters. The degree of consistency was manipulated to be 100% (traditional CM task), 67%, 50%, 33%, or 13% (traditional VM task). With extensive training (6,720 trials), there was a functional relationship between degree of consistency and accuracy rate. The 100% and 67% consistent conditions showed the greatest improvements in performance across practice, while the 50% condition showed a moderate level of improvement. The 33% and 13% conditions showed the least improvement and did not differ from each other. In the second experiment in this series, Schneider and Fisk demonstrated that there was also a functional relationship between degree of consistency of training and dual-task performance; that is, as the degree of consistency increased, dual-task performance improved.

Fisk and Rogers (1990) replicated and extended the Schneider and Fisk results. They used a multiple-frame, word-search task that increased the depth of processing required of the stimuli. Furthermore, the timing of the stimulus presentation was adapted to each individual's perceptual ability level. A fairly low criterion was used (75% correct detection within a group of trials) for increasing the presentation rate. As a result, the subjects were challenged to perform at their perceptual limits. This design has obvious implications for training situations that involve high-speed tasks and require processing at a level higher than the "featural" level of briefly presented stimuli.

The issue of interest was whether the subjects would be able to take advantage of the consistency levels present in the task even under time-stress situations requiring semantic processing. The data suggest that there was in fact a functional relationship between degree of consistency and accuracy performance. These data suggest that even in a high-speed, perceptually demanding task the subjects were able to benefit in terms of performance improvement as a function of the degree of consistency present in the task. These results are important because they extend what was previously known about automatic process development in situations with less than perfect consistency in a conceptual analog of a real-world, high-performance, perceptual processing task. Furthermore, this paradigm required automatic detection at a more global level than an individual stimulus feature.

Degree of Within-Category Consistency. An experiment recently conducted by Fisk and Jones (in press) was designed to assess the effect of the degree of within-category consistency on performance and learning in a semantic-category search task. Within-category consistency was manipulated by varying the ratio of consistent to inconsistent words within a category. The ratios of consistent to inconsistent words (CM:VM) within a category were 8:0, 6:2, 2:6, and 0:8. To illustrate, the category for condition 6:2 might be Animals. Six exemplars of this category would appear only as targets and two different exemplars would serve as both targets and distractors. Consequently, the higher-order category of animals was not consistent because some of the words served as both targets and distractors. However, six of the exemplars were consistently mapped as targets. After 12 days of practice, performance was tested on new exemplars of the trained categories (e.g., animal words that had not been used during training).

The results of the Fisk and Jones experiment suggested that performance improved as a function of within-category consistency. More detailed analyses revealed that individual stimulus items were not affected by higher-order consistency. That is, CM words were responded to the fastest, irrespective of whether they were in the completely consistent (8:0) category or the generally inconsistent (2:6) category. However, category learning, as assessed by transfer to untrained elements of the trained categories, was a direct function of the previous degree of within-category consistency. The transfer results of that experiment provide an estimate of learning at the category level (see Schneider & Fisk, 1984). Transfer to the untrained exemplars increased as a function of increasing within-category consistency; that is, RT decreased for untrained exemplars from the trained categories as within-category consistency increased.

The Fisk and Jones data provide several pieces of information. First of all, learning at the word level can occur, even if the higher-level category is not completely consistent. Second, some learning at the category level also occurs, and it is a direct function of the degree of category consistency encountered during training. However, even a small amount of inconsistency at the category level greatly attenuates the learning at that more global level. These results suggest that specific item-based learning (i.e., target strengthening and distractor weakening) is unaffected by higher-order inconsistencies. However, transfer to related situations is greatly disrupted by higher-order inconsistencies.

The implication of the Fisk and Jones study is that learning will occur at the level of the highest-order consistency. If consistency is at the item level, learning will be for the most part stimulus-bound. If, however, consistency is at the higher-order rule or category level, more general and transferable learning will occur. The training implications are paramount. Rich, real-world tasks may be composed of different levels of consistency. Training should be geared toward the level at which learning should occur: that is, if the higher-order consistencies are most critical, then they should be made salient to the learner and the lower-level consistencies should be deemphasized.

Benefits of Consistency as a Function of Amount of Practice

Optimization of final-level performance is the goal of most training programs designed to aid the acquisition of skilled behavior. An issue relevant to this goal involves the amount of practice provided on a task. How much practice is enough? Is more practice always better? Is there a point at which more practice will not yield substantial performance improvements (i.e., diminishing returns)? Fisk, Lee, and Rogers (1990) have conducted a series of experiments designed to address these questions (see also Fisk, Hodge, Lee, & Rogers, 1990).

Using a visual search paradigm, Fisk, Lee, and Rogers (1990) investigated the difference between consistent and inconsistent practice in terms of the amount of overall training both between and within subjects, as well as between and within blocks. In their first experiment, Fisk et al. compared the performance levels of subjects who had received 3,528 trials, 2,352 trials, 1,176 trials, or 588 trials on both a CM and a VM version of a semantic category visual search task. At the end of training, there was a greater improvement in CM relative to VM performance for the first three groups but not for the 588-trial group. This result suggest that the major qualitative changes that accrue from consistent mapping practice may take nearly 1,000 trials to develop (but see results below). The second general pattern of training results demonstrated that more practice is beneficial, to some degree. The 3,528-trials, 2,352-trials, and 1,176-trials training groups were all superior (i.e., faster RTs) to the 588-trials group; however, they were not significantly different from each other. In order to assess learning and not just performance improvement, subjects were tested in a task that assessed the degree to which stimuli "capture" attention (referred to as a reversal task by Shiffrin & Schneider, 1977). This sensitive measure of stimulus-based learning revealed significantly greater attention-attraction strength for the 3,528-trials and 2,532-trials groups compared to the 1,176-trials and 588-trials groups.

The experiment just described did not separate the amount of time on task from stimulus specific practice. It is conceivable that this between-subjects design may have masked some potential benefits from general training on the search task. In two follow-on experiments, Fisk, Lee, and Rogers (1990) manipulated the amount of training provided for a condition within-subjects, but in Experiment 2 the training was provided with all conditions intermixed within a block whereas in Experiment 3 the training of each condition was separated by blocks. In Experiment 2, it was proposed that the subjects might benefit from the within-block training by forming a superordinate category containing all of the CM categories.

In Experiment 2, conditions were compared that had received 3,150 CM trials, 1,575 CM trials, or 525 CM trials. As in Experiment 1, more practice did yield greater performance benefits: the 3,150-trials and 1,575-trials conditions were both faster than the 525-trials condition but not different from each other. However, assessment of learning using the reversal procedure, to assess attention "capture," revealed similar learning for all three conditions. This result suggested that perhaps there was some benefit from training all conditions within-blocks to facilitate the forming of a superset. This possibility was explored in Experiment 3, which removed the opportunity for forming a superset but was a within-subject design, thus equating time on task.

The results from Experiment 3 were essentially the same as found in Experiment 2. These data suggest that fewer trials of practice than previously suggested in the literature may be needed for performance to reach some level of proficiency. Performance may not be automatic in the sense that it may still be resource sensitive, may still be under the control of the subject, and so on. However, performance was certainly within the late phases of the associative phase of skill development (intermediate phase of skill development; see Ackerman, 1988; Anderson, 1982, 1983; Fitts, 1964, 1965/1990).

The data reported by Fisk, Lee, and Rogers (1990) may have substantive implications for understanding the focus of CM performance improvements. The fact that, when amount of training is manipulated between subjects, 3,000 trials of practice leads to performance superior to 2,000 practice trials and that 1,000 trials of practice leads to performance superior to 500 practice trials clearly argues that at least a partial focus of CM practice is stimulus based. However, the experiment which manipulated practice within-subjects and within blocks of trials demonstrated that 3,000 practice trials did not result in performance that was superior to 1,500 trials of practice (performance improvement measured in terms of asymptotic reaction time, accuracy, power function fit, etc.). The final experiment replicated that latter finding using a within-subjects, between-block manipulation, thus ruling out the possibility of memory-set unitization as the major cause of that within-subjects training effect.

Those data suggest that CM practice is clearly important for stimulus-based strengthening; however, CM practice seems to facilitate performance in another important manner. That data seem to support and extend the context activation hypothesis proposed by Schneider and Fisk (1984) as an important focus of CM training. That framework assumes that consistent exposure to the training context is a critical factor leading to performance improvement. This line of reasoning suggests that neither stimulus-based target strengthening nor consistent training context is sufficient (within the number of training trials presently provided) to lead to automatic target detection. Both are necessary for observed qualitative performance changes to be observed with CM practice.

These statements must be tempered somewhat because Fisk, Lee, and Rogers (1990) did not examine performance after tens of thousands of practice trials. After such extensive practice, stimulus-based processing may supersede the training context. (For example, Schneider and Shiffrin 1977, reported subjects experiencing trouble reading subsequent to CM CRT-based letter detection training because the trained letters "popped out" of the page. Clearly, this demonstrates stimulus-based processing superseding training context; however, those subjects had received thousands of trials of practice.)

Component Recombination

The utility of part-task training methods has been extensively investigated for skills training (e.g., see Wightman & Lintern, 1985). Part-task training, as the name implies, includes methods such as breaking tasks down into components through segmentation or chaining or simplifying the task for training. Most relevant to the current discussion is the strategy of training consistent component parts of a task. A critical consideration of this strategy involves the ultimate combination of the components into the whole task. Fisk, Lee, and Rogers (1991) describe an experiment designed to systematically assess the effects of component recombination. Subjects were training for 8,400 trials of CM practice to automatize detection in a semantic category search task. The components of the task (i.e., the target sets and distractor sets) were then recombined in a variety of situations. The results revealed that if the components were reused in a compatible manner there was positive transfer. That is, in the target transfer condition a specific CM-trained target set maintained its role as a target set but was paired with a new distractor set; this transfer situation yielded positive transfer. Distractor transfer was based on the same principle, and it too revealed positive transfer. However, if the role of the component process was reversed (e.g., a target set became a distractor set) there was significant negative transfer. Both target reversal and distractor reversal resulted in severe performance disruption. In "conflict" situations, a previously trained target was paired with another previously trained target set, which was changed to a distractor set. In this case, both stimulus sets had been trained to attract attention and were thus in conflict. This situation also resulted in severe performance disruption. Finally, a distractor conflict situation (both sets had previously been trained to be ignored) showed less disruptive effects on performance. These "conflict" situations require the inhibition of one automatized task component and the reuse of another. The Fisk et al. data suggest that the amount of disruption will be a function of the type of competing component, namely, target conflict yielded greater and longer-lasting disruption than distractor conflict.

From a pragmatic perspective, understanding high-performance skills training must include assessments of potentially deleterious effects of incompatible automatic components on learning new skills. It is a rarity that trainees are completely naive; hence, it is of interest to know what the effects of "old habits" will be on new skill development. These issues will also be of concern for the redesign of systems; the extent to which a new design will result in competing automatic process components should be minimized. Thus, when planning part-task training of automatic components, it will be important to identify situations in which the automatic components ultimately could be incongruous with whole-task demands or with other related tasks.

Retention of Consistent Components

The retention of skills is an issue of interest in a variety of domains. For example, there is a range of situations in which personnel are trained to perform actions that are necessary only in emergency situations and hence are infrequently used (e.g., cardiopulmonary resuscitation training). Knowledge of the characteristics of retention will enable the most appropriate scheduling of refresher training.

Fisk and Hodge (in press) have recently conducted an investigation of the retention of memory and visual search components of detection tasks. They conducted a series of experiments to examine retention of detection performance in memory scanning and visual search approximately 1 month after training. They further explored the issue of retention in pure visual and hybrid memory/visual search tasks[2] at intervals of 1, 30, 90, 180, and 365 days following training. Across experiments their results revealed no decay in CM trained memory search and minimal decay in CM visual search. The declines in visual search, although minimal (8%), seemed to be related to the perceptual tuning required to perform their task (see Fisk & Hodge for details). The significant decline in CM performance (18%) was largely due to performance in the hybrid memory/visual search conditions. This suggests that there was some degree of complexity in the hybrid tasks that was not present in either the pure memory of the pure visual search tasks. The Fisk and Hodge (in press) data further suggested that declines in performance stabilized at approximately 30 days following training. In fact, performance at the 30-day retention interval was predictive of skill decay for retention intervals of up to 1 year.

Complex, Real-World Activities

Learning Base-5 Arithmetic. Fisk and Gallini (1989) investigated the relative effectiveness of two common approaches to classroom instruction: structural and single-step approaches. The structural approach is primarily rule-based in nature and the focus is on teaching consistent, generalizable rules. The single-step approach is the more traditional, microlevel method in which a task is decomposed into individual steps and those steps are practiced separately. Fisk and Gallini utilized these two approaches to train subjects in a classroom situation on base-5 arithmetic skills of addition and multiplication. The students had been previously exposed only to the base-10 number system.

The rule-based instruction consisted of presenting integrated schemas of procedural and declarative knowledge. For example, concept maps were used to

---

[2]In a hybrid memory/visual search task, both memory scanning and visual search are required.

demonstrate relationships among concepts and processes. Subjects were taught how to recognize common problem structures and how to apply rules to solving those problem types.

The single-step training consisted of providing step-by-step instructions for the completion of individual problems. For example, steps for solving addition problems might be explained and then the subjects would practice many additional problems. Thus distinct examples were provided from different problem types and the more general, consistent rules were not emphasized.

Fisk and Gallini found that there were clear differences in performance as a function of the different types of instruction. Their results suggest that rule-based instruction that focuses on the consistencies of a domain will be superior to a single-step drill-and-practice approach primarily for more complex tasks (e.g., multiplication in base 5). However, simpler tasks such as counting and addition in base 5 might be learned more readily with the single-step approach (given comparable amounts of practice). These results suggest that benefits from rule-based instruction will accrue with increasing task complexity. However, tests of automaticity using a Stroop-like task demonstrated that for both addition and multiplication the rule-based training group showed greater component automaticity. Thus, while the single-step approach may yield improved performance on simple tasks, the underlying learning may be reduced relative to the rule-based instructional approach. Importantly, the Fisk and Gallini findings suggest that principles of consistency can be beneficial in at least some domains of complex academic tasks.

Dispatching Task.   The dispatching task developed by Fisk and Hodge (1990) is a conceptual analog of the resource allocation required in real-world, battle management, or dispatching tasks. The task has several procedural components, requires learning a substantial amount of declarative knowledge, and is very heavily rule-based. Subjects are required to choose the optimum "driver" for a given "delivery." The choice of driver is based on rules associated with how to determine load level, load type, and delivery location characteristics. In addition, the subject must learn to associative 27 drivers to various "license classes," which determine who is qualified to make particular deliveries.

The dispatching task also has memory scanning components (e.g., maintaining in working memory the specifications of a particular job or the personnel qualified to carry it out). Visual search components include searching through help screens for relevant information, and decision components involve choosing the "best" driver for the job (there may be several who are qualified but some may be overqualified and thus not cost-effective).

Although the task is quite complex, there is a host of consistent elements. For example, the assignment of driver to license classification is consistently mapped. Similarly, the characteristics of deliveries which require certain license classifications is consistent (e.g., flammable liquids require a Level-3 driver).

Consequently, these consistencies allow for improvements in performance as a function of practice. Fisk and Hodge (1990) trained subjects for 10 hr to investigate skill development in this dispatching task. All subjects showed increased accuracy and increased decision speed, as well as reduced use of help screens and redundant keystrokes. Importantly, all aspects of performance improvement followed a "power law" of practice (Newell & Rosenbloom, 1981) Furthermore, individual differences in performance decreased as a function of task practice, which is another indicator of skill development (e.g., Ackerman, 1988; Fisk, McGee, & Giambra, 1988). The Fisk and Hodge study demonstrates that consistency plays a critical role in learning and performance of complex tasks. Improvements in performance on the complex dispatching task show striking similarities to improvements observed in simpler search tasks (as discussed earlier).

Processing Principles

One important outcome of the research described above is the opportunity to specify what we refer to as "processing principles." Such processing principles illustrate human performance guidelines that have been shown to be important for the development of "knowledge engineering" for understanding and developing training programs for complex, operational tasks. General principles based on research conducted prior to the work discussed above were well described by Fisk et al. (1987). Those early principles of human performance can be summarized as follows:

1. Performance improvements will occur only for situations where stimuli (or information) can be dealt with the same way from trial to trial.
2. The human operator is limited, not by the number of mental operations he/she is required to perform, but by the number of inconsistent or novel cognitive or psychomotor operations.
3. In order to alleviate high-workload situations, consistent task components must be identified and then trained to levels of automaticity.
4. Similar to number 3, to make performance reliable under environmental stressors (e.g., alcohol, fatigue, heat, noise, etc.), training should be conducted to develop automatic task components.
5. For tasks requiring sustained attention (i.e., vigilance), automatic target detection should be developed prior to participation in the vigilance task; also, variably mapped information should not be presented in a continual and redundant pattern.
6. When preparing training programs, instructional designers should consider the nature of the underlying processing modes (automatic or controlled) when choosing part-task training strategies.

The research discussed throughout this chapter provides an empirical basis for augmenting these performance guidelines. Our approach has been not only to specify the boundary conditions under which the principles of consistency operate, but also to demonstrate situations in which consistency may be "mimicked" through context, or even detrimental in transfer situations. Listed below is a summary of the augmented processing principles gleaned from the research presented within the chapter.

Higher-Order, Rule-Based Consistency. Consistency need not be related to the individual stimulus level. Consistent relationships among stimuli, rules, and context should be identified when considering part-task training strategies (Fisk & Lloyd, 1988; Fisk & Rogers, 1988; Fisk, Oransky, & Skedsvold, 1988; Myers & Fisk, 1987).

Contextually Defined Consistency. Context affects performance in two major ways. Contextual cues may (a) be used to bias performance and mimic the effects of consistency; however, performance in this situation remains resource sensitive and (b) may activate automatic sequences of behavior. Context activation follows lawful temporal development (Fisk & Rogers, 1988; Lee, Rogers, & Fisk, 1991).

Degree of Consistency. Performance improvements will occur only for consistent elements of a task and the degree of improvement is directly related to the degree of consistency (Fisk & Rogers, 1990; Schneider & Fisk, 1982).

Performance is limited by the number of inconsistent cognitive operations; however, performance may also be limited by the type of task structure (e.g., memory vs. visual vs. hybrid memory/visual search) (Fisk & Rogers, 1991).

Global consistency can dominate performance improvement if lower-level consistency is absent. Instructional designers should locate, understand, and capitalize on global consistencies (Fisk & Eboch, 1989; Fisk, Oransky, & Skedsvold, 1988).

Performance improvement occurs for lower-level, stimulus-based, consistencies regardless of higher-order inconsistency. However, learning at the higher-order relational level is greatly attenuated by any degree of global inconsistency (Fisk & Jones, in press; Fisk & Thigpen, 1986).

Benefits of Consistency as a Function of Amount of Practice. A direct relationship exists between amount of consistent practice and stimulus activation strength. However, the functional relationship may be superseded by other variables. For example, the opportunity to form a "superset of memory-set elements or general task training to improve the motor components of the task may mask the performance benefits resulting from stimulus activation strength (Fisk, Lee, & Rogers, 1990).

Component Recombination. Disruption due to recombination of automatized task components is directly related to the "priority strength" of competing components (Fisk, Lee, & Rogers, 1991).

Part-task training can result in efficient associative learning, at least for semantic-based processing. Target strengthening (priority learning) benefits most from part-task training (see Fisk & Whaley, 1990).

Retention of Performance for Consistent Components. Long-term retention of automatized task components is related to the type of task-specific processing: memory access shows no decay for at least 1 year and visual search shows statistically nonsignificant (8%) decay after a year. Maximum decay (18%) is related to the coordination of component information, not component activation (Fisk & Hodge, in press).

TASK ANALYTIC METHODOLOGY

Successful utilization of the processing principles, as they relate to training consistent task components, relies on successful identification of the consistent elements of complex tasks. Such task elements represent candidates for various forms of part-task training. Therefore, application of automatic/control processing theory to training program development requires a task-analytic methodology that is capable of identifying consistent trainable components of complex tasks. Recently, we (Eggemeier, Fisk, Robbins, & Lawless, 1988; Fisk & Eggemeier, 1988) explored the direct application of the consistent component training concept to rich, real-world tasks performed as part of the U.S. Air Force Tactical Command and Control Mission. A brief description of the task-analytic methodology used to identify consistent trainable components in that operational environment is provided next. The actual application of that methodology is described in Eggemeier, Fisk, Robbins, and Lawless, (1988).

The methodology is based on systematic interviewing techniques (McMillen & Fisk, 1983, 1984) and is designed for application with novice to experienced operators of complex systems. Essentially, the technique involves identification of the major steps and components of the targeted skill through interviews and observation. This identification stage is followed by an iterative interview process that results in the development of detailed specifications of the component skills required for performing each step, including the sources of information and the responses required to perform the task. These detailed specifications are further analyzed in order to identify consistent elements of the skill.

Eggemeier, Fisk, Robbins, and Lawless (1988) recommended small-group and individual interviews. Several individuals who perform the same functional activities should be interviews by one or two interviewers. In addition, a subject-matter expert (SME) should be present during the interviews to provide feedback and maintain the scope of the analysis. Both the SME and the interviewer(s) should be familiar with the concepts of automatic and controlled processing, as well as the principles of consistency.

The initial interview should generally be conducted to gather sufficient information from the SME to drive further interviews and analysis. The goal of these early interviews is to narrow down the range of possibilities for candidate consistent task components. Subsequent interviews should be conducted to further specify the stimuli or classes of stimuli that lead to specifiable responses. In addition to the interviews, the task analysis should include on-site observation of the activities of interest. Such observations can provide useful insight into how activities are actually performed under different situations of time-stress or fatigue, as well as differences between novices and experts.

Following the interview and observation stages of the task analysis, the consistent components must be precisely identified. Initially, more general questions may be used to begin focusing on particular task components. For example, sample questions include: (a) What is the initial step of the particular activity? What inputs are presented, how and from what sources are they presented? What is the frequency of this kind of information? (b) What is your output or product of this particular activity and how often is the output produced? (c) Are there any on-the-job resources available to help you perform the activity (job aids, instructions, checklists, etc.)? (d) What type of training did you receive for this activity (classroom, self-paced instruction, on-the-job, etc.) and what additional training do you think would be beneficial? (e) Under what situations is it difficult to perform this activity? and (f) How do you get feedback concerning your performance?

Identifying Consistent Components

The following are guidelines to use when performing the task analysis, reviewing task activities with a SME, documenting results of the task analysis, etc. The guidelines are based, in part, on suggestions presented by Fisk, Scerbo, and Schneider (1983; see also Schneider, 1985). The guidelines are:

1. Break the task into high-level component skills such as vocabulary, rule application, perceptual-motor, etc.
2. Differentiate between declarative and procedural knowledge. Declarative knowledge is characterized by fact information or "knowing what" to do. Procedural knowledge is that knowledge that allows a task to be completed ("knowing how") using the declarative knowledge.
3. Determine decision points in the task and determine the differential decision points used by novices versus experts (and vice versa). Decision points may signal the requirement for controlled processing and/or potential component boundaries. Easily identifiable decision points in

novice task performance, points that are not recognizable when experts perform the task, may signal an automatized component or task unitization/compilation.

4. Determine where task performance difficulty arises for novice performers but not for the expert. Where and when is the novice qualitatively different (overloaded, time pressured, error prone) from the expert?

5. Identify where performance of the novice is different under those extremes. Also look for where there are qualitative differences among novice and expert performers under other exceptional situations, such as stress caused by sleep loss, illness, etc.

6. Identify where consistent categories of information exist or where higher-level rules supersede element-level variability. Similarly, note where performance is context dependent. Identify where and how task goals consistently change as a function of specifiable characteristics of given situations.

7. Find consistent mapping components of the task that are at "perceptual threshold," which may be candidates for non-real-time training (e.g., slowing task down, speeding task up, enhanced signals, etc.). Tasks may be at perceptual threshold if (a) signals are initially too weak for consistencies to be noticed; (b) the task is too slow for immediate feedback of some given input (such as roll out headings); or (c) the task is too fast to allow for consistent correct execution of component (e.g., identifying cues to provide pilot with "situational awareness" and the required voice communication to actually transmit it.)

8. Related to 7, find consistent mapping situations where high precision is required. Specialized guided training may be used here to aid in task training.

9. Determine where expert performance difficulty arises even when tasks are well practiced. These difficulties may indicate the presence of controlled processing requirements.

10. Determine where expert performance is different under low and high workload. Again, this may indicate controlled processing requirements.

11. Identify expert decision points. As in 9 and 10, decision points in expert task performance may indicate the presence of task components dominated by the requirement for controlled processing.

Computer-Based Instruction

Much has been written about the value of computer-aided instruction for training complex skills (e.g., see Eberts & Brock, 1984; Tennyson, Christenson, & Park, 1984), and its potential as an instructional aid has been considered to be enormous (e.g., Salomon, 1984; Williges & Williges, 1980). Given current technology, desktop computer-aided instruction is a feasible alternative for a variety of situations and may be most beneficial in part-task training situations. Several examples include training the components of air intercept control to air weapons controllers (Eggemeier, Fisk, Robbins, & Lawless, 1988), training fault diagnosis when teaching maintenance skills (Johnson & Rouse, 1982), as well as training the complex components required of a Navy Surface Warfare Officer (Holland, Stevens, & Williams, 1981).

A computer-based training program can allow for many correct executions of component skills within a given time frame, and it can be used to facilitate the understanding of consistent relationships within the task components. As discussed by Schneider (1985), providing many training trials and highlighting the consistencies within a task are two important training guidelines for facilitating the development of high-performance skills.

Most importantly, any computer-based training program should be theory-based. As with any piece of hardware used in training, its use must be principled and guided by appropriate instructional design. A profitable first step in the design process might be an application of the consistent component task-analytic methodology described above.

The principles of consistency discussed above provide a rich source of information for the design of computer-aided instruction. Programs may be designed that vary the degree of consistency at stimulus levels and/or higher, more global levels; training can be time-compressed to increase the number of trials for critical components of tasks; components can be trained and recombined in a variety of configurations to allow assessment of component compatibility; refresher training may be based on only those components that have been shown to decay with time, and so on (see Cream, Eggemeier, & Klein, 1978; Fisk, Scerbo, & Schneider, 1983; Schneider, 1985).

Future Efforts

Another aspect of computer-based training that may benefit from the principles of consistency involves the inclusion of markers to assess performance improvements and readiness of the trainee to advance to the next level of training. Clearly, phases of skill development (and automatism) have fuzzy boundaries. This is because performance in each phase is dominated by a particular set of information-processing requirements that are characteristic of each phase. It is difficult to find tasks that require one and only one set of information processing requirements. Rather, performance improves as the dominating information-processing requirements shift across stages of practice. Hence in order to specify markers of phase of skill development one would need to incorporate (a) amount of practice at the time a given assessment is made, (b) qualitative performance characteristics, and (c) ability/performance correlates.

Obviously, however, a single number will not provide the qualitative information utilized by a good "coach." Hence, a taxonomy of performance characteristics as related to "promotability" should be developed. Although it has been well documented that no single criterion is necessary and sufficient for determining automatism (Schneider, Dumais, & Shiffrin, 1984; Shiffrin, 1988), a "factoranalytic" approach to defining promotability could yield promising results. The approach would be to determine the "automaticity characteristics" structure for individuals at different levels of performance. Ideally, if the "automaticity characteristics" structure, derived on-line during training, were to meet given criteria, then the individual would be a candidate for promotion. The feasibility of the approach from a generalizable perspective remains an open question. However, the idea is appealing and exciting.

REFERENCES

Ackerman, P. L. (1988). Determinants of individual differences during skill acquisition: Cognitive abilities and information processing. *Journal of Experimental Psychology: General, 117,* 288–318.

Anderson, J. R. (1982). Acquisition of cognitive skill. *Psychological Review, 89,* 369–406.

Anderson, J. R. (1983). *The architecture of cognition.* Cambridge, MA: Harvard University Press.

Cream, B. W., Eggemeier, F. T., & Klein, G. A. (1978). A strategy for the development of training devices. *Human Factors, 20,* 145–158.

Durso, F. T., Cooke, N. M., Breen, T. J., & Schvanaveldt, R. W. (1987). Is consistent mapping necessary for high speed search? *Journal of Experimental Psychology: Learning, Memory, and Cognition, 13,* 223–229.

Eberts, R. E., & Brock, J. F. (1984). Computer applications to instruction. In F. A. Muckler (Ed.), *Human factors review* (pp. 239–284). Santa Monica, CA: Human Factors Society.

Egan, D., & Schwartz, B. (1979). Chunking in recall of symbolic drawings. *Memory & Cognition, 7,* 148–158.

Eggemeier, F. T., Fisk, A. D., Robbins, R. J., & Lawless, M. T. (1988). Application of automatic/controlled processing theory to training tactical command and control skills: II. Evaluation of a task analytic methodology. *Proceedings of the Human Factors Society 32nd Annual Meeting* (pp. 1232–1236). Santa Monica, CA: Human Factors Society.

Eggemeier, F. T., Fisk, A. D., Robbins, R. J., Lawless, M. T., & Spaeth, R. (1988). *Task analysis of selected Air Force jobs requiring high-performance skills. Final report* (AFHRL-TP-88-32). Dayton, OH: Systems Exploration, Inc.

Fisk, A. D., Ackerman, P. L., & Schneider, W. (1987). Automatic and controlled processing theory and its applications to human factors problems. In P. A. Hancock (Ed.), *Human factors psychology* (pp. 159–197). Amsterdam: North Holland.

Fisk, A. D., & Eboch, M. (1989). Application of automatic/controlled processing theory to training component map reading skills. *Applied Ergonomics, 20,* 2–8.

Fisk, A. D., & Eggemeier, F. T. (1988). Application of automatic/controlled processing theory to training tactical command and control skills: I. Background and task analytic methodology. *Proceedings of the Human Factors Society 32nd Annual Meeting* (pp. 1227–1231). Santa Monica, CA: Human Factors Society.

Fisk, A. D., & Gallini, J. K. (1989). Training consistent components of tasks: Developing an instructional system based on automatic/controlled processing principles. *Human Factors, 31,* 453–463.

Fisk, A. D., & Hodge, K. A. (1990). *Learning and performance retention in a high-performance skill-based problem solving task*. Unpublished manuscript.

Fisk, A. D., & Hodge, K. A. (in press). *Retention of trained performance in consistent mapping search after extended delay. Human Factors*.

Fisk, A. D., Hodge, K. A., Lee, M. D., & Rogers, W. A. (1990). *Automatic information processing and high performance skills: Acquisition, transfer, and retention* (AFHRL-TR-89-69). Brooks Air Force Base, TX: AFHRL/SCV.

Fisk, A. D., & Jones, C. D. (in press). *Global versus local consistency: Effects of degree of within-category consistency on learning and performance. Human Factors*.

Fisk, A. D., Lee, M. D., & Rogers, W. A. (1990). *Effects of amount of consistent practice*. Unpublished manuscript.

Fisk, A. D., Lee, M. D., & Rogers, W. A. (1991). Recombination of automatic processing components: The effects of transfer, reversal, and conflict situations. *Human Factors, 33*, 267–280.

Fisk, A. D., & Lloyd, S. J. (1988). The role of stimulus-to-rule consistency in learning rapid application of spatial rules. *Human Factors, 30*, 35–49.

Fisk, A. D., McGee, N. D., & Giambra, L. M. (1988). The influence of age on consistent and varied semantic category search performance. *Psychology and Aging, 3*, 323–333.

Fisk, A. D., Oransky, N. A., & Skedsvold, P. R. (1988). Examination of the role of "higher-order" consistency in skill development. *Human Factors, 30*, 567–581.

Fisk, A. D., & Rogers, W. A. (1988). The role of situational context in the development of high-performance skills. *Human Factors, 30*, 703–712.

Fisk, A. D., & Rogers, W. A. (1990). *Performance improvement as a function of degree of between semantic-category consistency*. Unpublished manuscript.

Fisk, A. D., & Rogers, W. A. (1991). Toward an understanding of age-related memory and visual search effects. *Journal of Experimental Psychology: General, 120*, 131–149.

Fisk, A. D., Rogers, W. A., Lee, M. D., Hodge, K. A., & Whaley, C. J. (1990). *Automatic information processing and high performance skills: 2. Principles of consistency, part-task training, context, retention, and complex task performance* (AFHRL-TR-90-XX). Brooks Air Force Base, TX: AFHRL/SCV.

Fisk, A. D., Scerbo, M. W., & Schneider, W. (1983). Issues in training for skilled performance. In A. T. Pope & L. D. Haugh (Eds.), *Proceedings of the Human Factors Society, 12*, 392–396.

Fisk, A. D., & Schneider, W. (1983). Category and word search: Generalizing search principles to complex processing. *Journal of Experimental Psychology: Learning, Memory, and Cognition, 9*, 177–195.

Fisk, A. D., & Thigpen, M. (1986). *The effect of amount to be learned on consistent mapping training effects in visual search* (HAPL-AFHRL-8605). Columbia, SC: University of South Carolina, Human Attention and Performance Laboratory.

Fisk, A. D., & Whaley, C. J. (1990). *The effects of part-task training on memory-set unitization: Learning and retention*. Unpublished manuscript.

Fitts, P. M. (1964). Perceptual-motor skill learning. In A. W. Melton (Ed.), *Categories of human learning* (pp. 243–285). New York: Academic Press.

Fitts, P. M. (1965/1990). Factors in complex skill training. In M. Venturino (Ed.), *Selected Readings in Human Factors* (pp. 275–295). Santa Monica: Human Factors Society.

Holland, J., Stevens, A., & Williams, N. (1981). *STEAMER: Computer assisted instruction for learning population engineering concepts*. Paper presented at the Annual Meeting of the Psychonomic Society, Philadelphia, PA.

James, W. (1890). *Principles of psychology* (Vol. 1). New York: Holt.

Jeffries, R., Turner, A., Polson, P., & Atwood, M. (1981). Processes involved in designing software. In J. R. Anderson (Ed.), *Cognitive skills and their acquisition* (pp. 111–141). Hillsdale, NJ: Lawrence Erlbaum Associates.

Johnson, W. B., & Rouse, W. B. (1982). Training maintenance technicians for troubleshooting: Two experiments with computer simulation. *Human Factors, 24,* 271–276.

Kanfer, R., & Ackerman, P. L. (1989). Dynamics of skill acquisition: Building a bridge between abilities and motivation. In R. J. Sternberg (Ed.), *Advances in the psychology of human intelligence* (Vol. 5, pp. 83–134). Hillsdale, NJ: Lawrence Erlbaum Associates.

Kramer, A. F., Strayer, D. L., & Buckley, J. (1990). Development and transfer of automatic processing. *Journal of Experimental Psychology: Human Perception and Performance, 16,* 505–522.

Lee, M. D., Rogers, W. A., & Fisk, A. D. (1991). Contextual change and skill acquisition in visual search: Does the rate of change affect performance? *Proceedings of the Human Factors Society 35th Annual Meeting* (pp. 1377–1381) Santa Monica, CA: Human Factors Society.

Logan, G. D. (1985). Skill and automaticity: Relations, implications, and future directions. *Canadian Journal of Psychology, 39,* 367–386.

McMillen, L. D., & Fisk, A. D. (1983). SIT: A systematic interviewing technique. In A. T. Pope & L. D. Haugh (Eds.), *Proceedings of the Human Factors Society, 12,* 437–440.

McMillen, L. D., & Fisk, A. D. (1984). Designing for change: Dynamic communications using a logical model. *Proceedings of the Human Factors Society, 13,* 53.

Myers, G. L., & Fisk, A. D. (1987). Training consistent task components: Application of automatic & controlled processing theory to industrial task training. *Human Factors, 29,* 255–268.

Newell, A., & Rosenbloom, P. S. (1981). Mechanisms of skill acquisition and the law of practice. In J. R. Anderson (Ed.), *Cognitive skills and their acquisition* (pp. 1–55). Hillsdale, NJ: Lawrence Erlbaum Associates.

Parasuraman, R. (1985). Detection and identification of abnormalities in chest x-rays: Effects of reader skill, disease prevalence, and reporting standards. In R. E. Eberts & C. G. Eberts (Eds.), *Trends in ergonomics/human factors II* (pp. 59–66). Amsterdam: Elsevier.

Posner, M. I., & Snyder, C. R. R. (1975). Attention and cognitive control. In R. L. Solso (Ed.), *Information processing and cognition* (pp. 55–85). Hillsdale, NJ: Lawrence Erlbaum Associates.

Salomon, G. (1984). Computers in education: Setting a research agenda. *Educational Technology, 22,* 7–11.

Schneider, W. (1985). Training high-performance skills: Fallacies and guidelines. *Human Factors, 27,* 285–300.

Schneider, W., Dumais, S. T., & Shiffrin, R. M. (1984). Automatic and control processing and attention. In R. Parasuraman & R. Davies (Eds.), *Varieties of attention* (pp. 1–27). New York: Academic Press.

Schneider, W., & Fisk, A. D. (1982). Degree of consistent training: Improvements in search performance and automatic process development. *Perception and Psychophysics, 31,* 160–166.

Schneider, W., & Fisk, A. D. (1984). Automatic category search and its transfer. *Journal of Experimental Psychology: Learning, Memory, and Cognition, 10,* 1–15.

Schneider, W., & Shiffrin, R. M. (1977). Controlled and automatic human information processing: I. Detection, search and attention. *Psychological Review, 84,* 1–66.

Shiffrin, R. M. (1988). Attention. In R. C. Atkinson, R. J. Herrnstein, G. Linzey, & R. D. Luce (Eds.), *Stevens' handbook of experimental psychology* (pp. 739–811). New York: Wiley.

Shiffrin, R. M., & Dumais, S. T. (1981). The development of automatism. In J. R. Anderson (Ed.), *Cognitive skills and their acquisition* (pp. 111–140). Hillsdale, NJ: Lawrence Erlbaum Associates.

Shiffrin, R. M., & Schneider, W. (1977). Controlled and automatic human information processing: II. Perceptual learning, automatic attending, and a general theory. *Psychological Review, 84,* 127–190.

Tennyson, R. D., Christenson, D. L., & Park, S. I. (1984). The Minnesota Adaptive Instructional System. *Journal of Computer-Based Instruction, 11,* 2–13.

Wightman, D. C., & Lintern, G. (1985). Part-task training for tracking and manual control. *Human Factors, 27,* 267–283.

Williges, R. C., & Williges, B. H. (1980). Critical issues in enhancing team performance in computer-based systems. *Proceedings of the Human Factors Society 24th Annual Meeting* (Abstract 536). Santa Monica, CA: Human Factors Society.

TRANSCRIPT OF DISCUSSION

Alan Lesgold: You made the comment that automated skill dominates complex performance. I was thinking of Allen Newell's problem of a collection of performance. It more or less argues that impasses and partial lapses of automaticity dominate complex performance. Is it because you are studying different things than he looks at or is there an interesting empirically testable question?

Arthur Fisk: I don't know if I'm necessarily going to answer this question right or if this is the direction you want to go in, but I think one of the more interesting questions is: "When does performance fail in complex environments?" I think it becomes very obvious when someone is failing in a complex task. What we might think about is why and when there are failures of automatic processing.

Alan Lesgold: I guess because he looks at different tasks, Newell would probably argue that the rate of impasses is more or less constant, that all complex situations generate lots of needs to generate new subgoals to go to new problem spaces. Some portion of that may not be entirely automated. It may just be that you're dealing with tasks that you've looked at which have a high component of automaticity.

Arthur Fisk: I am not sure that I want to argue with Newell, but again I do think that component-task automaticity defines certain limits to complex performance. However, our differences in opinions probably relate largely to the level of task detail we examine.

Walt Schneider: Also, a lot of what Allen, I think, would concede is happening at these impasses is that you are applying these chunk production rules which would map into some of our automatic components. That system sort of spins along and all of a sudden comes up with an impasse and then it is "How you deal with that impasse." In my view, that would be very much where you would see the interaction between control models. You need to have those chunk components to operate within the memory constraints of the system it's operating in and to identify likely subgoals to operate at the next stage. When you go into an applied setting, what happens in terms of the reaction by the experts once you've come back with this set of components to train?

Arthur Fisk: Well, Mike can speak for that. Sometimes they want to apply it right away.

Mike Young: The task we're working is an early warning task. I can't go into great detail, but basically you are looking at a screen and the screen contains random dots. The dots are scanned by some type of system. Some of the dots will potentially build into a pattern. Your problem is to detect when the dots are becoming a pattern as quickly as possible. A lot of noise is coming back to you, but there might be a pattern of dots that will build up. The system is currently being trained by 3 months of on-the-job-training with real operational equipment, where we have to take one of the systems off-line to train people. We built a part-task training approach based on automatic processing theory for this detection skill. And the people are extremely excited. One of the unusual things for us is that they offered to modify their curriculum to take away simulator time and put it in part-task training time so that we would have good control groups. They got very excited about this approach.

Arthur Fisk: What should be obvious to the people that are dealing with educational environments is that if you don't approach these individuals properly and give these individuals the kind of perspective they deserve, that it is not going to go anywhere. I think that the kind of reaction that we have received has been "My gosh, this is what we've been looking for." Of course, this is what we want to train—the notions of training in non-real time. I think that being able to speed up and give extensive practice on these components (where consistencies are very salient) is what the trainers are looking for.

Wes Regian: I've seen this situation a lot where academicians will go out to applied science. And it is not just a function of having the right approach and having them recognize it. You have to overcome something before that. And personality is real critical that you don't turn those people off initially. You have that skill of putting people at ease and that, coupled with a good approach that they can recognize, is what I suspect works for you.

Arthur Fisk: I think that we have a good team . . . and you have to do that but you also have to have the right approach. What is exciting is that we were able to convey to two of these trainers who have been in business for twenty or so years what this approach was and they would come back to us in our follow up visit and say "What about this and what about that?" And so on.

Val Shute: I need some clarification. The arithmetic study that you mentioned involved two different instructional approaches: ruled-based and single-step. I think that you concluded that for the more complex tasks, the ruled-based approach would be better, and you showed these differences in bar charts. I wrote down, maybe erroneously, that you concluded: simple tasks are better suited for the single-step approach, but I didn't see that in your data.

Arthur Fisk: You're right, you didn't see it in the data. It wasn't statistically different. In some of the measures, when you give someone a very simple step-by-step procedure and they don't have to apply it to other problems, that's learned much more quickly in drill and practice. It wasn't until there were applications of rules that we saw the differences. I was excited about it because I thought it related to what you were talking about yesterday, except that we obviously can't talk about ability levels.

8 Modeling Student Performance in Diagnostic Tasks: A Decade of Evolution

William B. Johnson
Jeffrey E. Norton
Galaxy Scientific Corporation, Atlanta, Georgia

Since 1976, the authors have been involved in an evolving research and development program focusing on the application of computer-based simulation to diagnostic training in technical environments. Eight simulation-oriented training systems were used to describe the authors' understanding of and approach to student diagnosis. Each of the systems described capitalized on experimental and/or empirical findings from the previous experiences. This chapter describes how design decisions were driven, first by research findings, and then by the reality of building effective, computer-based training systems within the constraints of operational environments.

Fault diagnosis, troubleshooting, or similar technical problem solving is difficult for humans. This statement is true across a variety of applications from electronics to mechanics, from computer program debugging to medical diagnosis. Design and delivery of training for such problem solving are also a very difficult challenge.

Conventional wisdom holds that trial and error is, perhaps, the best method to become a competent troubleshooter/problem solver. If this wisdom is correct, then training systems must permit the learner to undergo trial (i.e., practice problem solving) and error. Designing systems that permit trial is a relatively straightforward engineering task. Simulators exist to emulate a variety of domains, ranging from flight to nuclear power plant control. However, building systems that recognize and remediate error is more difficult. This chapter reviews over a decade of research and development (R&D), by the authors and their colleagues, on the design and development of computer-based systems for diagnostic training. It also reviews the development and evaluation of eight diagnostic training systems in an attempt to determine the appropriate level of student modeling needed for technical training.

AN EMPIRICAL PERSPECTIVE

Much can be learned by observing troubleshooters. The trained observer notices the subtle actions that characterize the quality of diagnostic performance. For over 20 years, we have studied troubleshooters working on real equipment, as well as on computer simulations. The first 10 of these 20 years, in technical training environments, permitted hundreds of hours of empirical and experimental analysis of human troubleshooting performance on automobile and aircraft systems (Johnson, 1980, 1986). During the second 10 years, we studied the effects of simulation-based training on diagnostic performance (Johnson, 1987).

These technical training experiences form the foundation for this chapter. From this empirical and practical perspective, this chapter describes a series of evolving computer-based simulations that experimented with numerous variables to improve training for troubleshooters in a variety of technical domains. The evolution discussed here goes beyond basic research issues of student modeling. The laboratory experiments underwent transition to development and implementation of training systems for operational environments. The discussion includes changes in interface design, displays, and system architecture that have been afforded by increased hardware and software capability. The chapter also discusses the complexity and the importance of the knowledge engineering task.

CONTENT-FREE TROUBLESHOOTING

From 1976 through 1978, Rouse (1979a, 1979b) conducted research to better understand how humans collect and process information during problem solving. He developed a computer-based problem-solving game called Troubleshooting by Application of Structural Knowledge (TASK). The troubleshooting problem presented a graphically displayed network with a single failed component, as represented in Fig. 8.1.

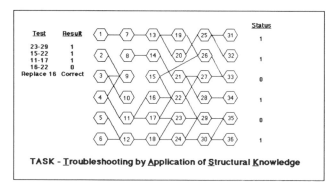

FIG. 8.1.   Troubleshooting by application of structural knowledge.

TABLE 8.1
TASK Student Information

Number of actions per problem

Number of problems solved

Number of errors per problem

Time to solution

Each node in the network represented a component in the system. Each line represented a relationship between the nodes. A "0" meant a bad relationship; a "1" was a good relationship. Given the system "Status," the problem solver tried to identify the failed node by testing between nodes. The "Tests" and "Results" are shown on the left side of Fig. 8.1. Rouse and Hunt (1984) described a series of five experiments conducted with TASK from 1976 to 1978.

The TASK software, in an attempt to model student performance, kept a record of the actions shown in Table 8.1. Errors were based on illogical and/or redundant actions ("tests"). Problem-solving time was recorded in seconds.

The information in the TASK student model was sufficient to detect performance changes and to differentiate quality of performance among various experimental groups. The student model also provided the necessary data to help the experimenter to adjust problem complexity based on performance (i.e., if good performance, then increase difficulty).

Variations of the TASK problems experimented with the use of computer aiding, forced pacing, and various feedback approaches. Many of Rouse's findings contributed to the design of subsequent diagnostic training software. For example, computer aiding seemed to work best when the learner understood what the aiding was doing. If aiding eliminated a component from the feasible set, it had to show elimination was derived. Rouse did this by graphically "Xing" out the components eliminated with each test. Thus, the TASK user could see what the computer was doing after each test.

In another example, Pellegrino (1979) found that unexplained feedback during problem solving can have a negative effect on performance. These two examples present a strong argument for an explanation capability in an intelligent training system. Just like a human tutor, a computer-based tutor must be able to

TABLE 8.2
TASK Research Findings Applicable to Student Modeling

Computer aiding must be explained to the learner.

Forcing a learner to solve problems faster does not improve learning.

Positive and negative feedback should be explained to the learner.

explain how the remediation is derived and why a specific student action is appropriate or inappropriate.

The experiments with TASK provided valuable insights on context-free problem solving and provided direction regarding the nature of the data that should be used for student modeling. Table 8.2 contains a summary of the important findings from Rouse's research with context-free problem solving.

TASK Knowledge Engineering

"Knowledge engineering" was not necessary for TASK. The problems were computer-generated and based only on a connectivity matrix. Knowledge engineering assumes knowledge and/or data related to the technical domain. Being context-free, TASK had no technical domain.

CONTEXT-SPECIFIC PROBLEM SOLVING

All problem solving is not context-free. Therefore, the Rouse research team added context to subsequent diagnostic training research. The Framework for Aiding the Understanding of Logical Troubleshooting (FAULT) became the simulation software for the study of context-specific problem solving. The FAULT software was designed to provide a low-fidelity simulation of real-world technical troubleshooting. The system was designed to promote an understanding of how system components were functionally connected. For example, a fuel pump has the function of providing fuel to the fuel metering device to which it is connected.

FAULT also provided the learner with on-demand declarative information about each system component. FAULT is described extensively (Johnson, 1980, 1987; Rouse & Hunt, 1984). Figure 8.2 shows a functional flow diagram that can

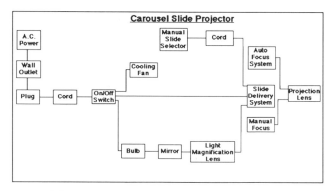

FIG. 8.2.   A functional flow diagram for FAULT.

TABLE 8.3
FAULT Student Information

Number of actions per problem

Number of errors by category

Number of problems solved

Number of requests for advice

Total dollar and time cost of diagnostic actions

Time to solution

be used with FAULT. The example functional flow diagram is for troubleshooting a slide projector.

The FAULT system permits the user to obtain information about parts, learn how to perform tests, and then perform the necessary actions to diagnose a malfunction within a system. The FAULT approach has been used for such domains as auto mechanics, aircraft mechanics, military electronics, nuclear power safety systems, space shuttle electrical power systems, and other domains (Johnson, 1987; Johnson, Norton, Duncan, & Hunt, 1988).

The FAULT system modeled the student by recording the information shown in Table 8.3. In the period between 1978 and 1980, FAULT was used for two expensive experiments with technical trainees (Johnson, 1980; Johnson & Rouse, 1982a, 1982b)

The two major experiments with FAULT were structured to compare a simulation-based training with traditional instruction (via instructional television) (Johnson & Rouse, 1982a, 1982b). The posttraining troubleshooting performance results of the first experiment favored traditional instruction (control group) over the FAULT computer simulation. The primary performance difference between the groups was that the experimental group committed significantly more procedural errors than the control group when transferred to live equipment. In the second experiment, FAULT was modified to provide more procedural information during the simulation-based training. This change resulted in equal performance between the experimental group and the control group.

The results of the two experiments with FAULT had significant implications for the design of subsequent computer-based simulation. The experiments showed that the simulation should not change concrete, real-word diagnostic procedures to abstract, simple, "0" and "1" kinds of tests (Johnson & Rouse, 1982a, 1982b). Of greater significance was the finding that global measures such as "number of problems solved" or "time to solution" are, in themselves, not sufficient to differentiate performance between groups. The research generated a significant off-line error classification scheme that promoted a higher bandwidth

TABLE 8.4
FAULT Findings Applicable to Student Modeling

Diagnostic training must provide procedural information.

Low-fidelity simulation for training can affect diagnostic performance

Low-fidelity simulation can provide realistic and challenging diagnostic
practice for training, but can benefit more from exposure to real equipment.

of student diagnostic performance. The experiments also suggested that the
FAULT simulation could benefit from increased physical fidelity and perhaps
should be combined with the use of real equipment for improved diagnostic
training. Table 8.4 summarizes the FAULT experimental findings that contributed to subsequent development.

FAULT Knowledge Engineering

Knowledge engineering for FAULT was comprised of two steps: (a) development
of the functional connectivity matrix, and then (b) database development. The
functional connectivity matrix, also called the functional flow diagram, is the
basis for all FAULT feedback. Development of the diagram is often a difficult
task because it forces the subject matter expert (SME) to depict the technical
system in a new format. The FAULT flow diagram requires a depiction of how
parts are functionally connected rather than how they are physically connected.

Once the FAULT functional flow diagram is constructed, knowledge engineering becomes a database completion task. The database requires part descriptions, information about tests, and all data related to each failure.

For the version of FAULT described here, the knowledge engineering was
done by the FAULT system developers, based on their extensive subject matter
experience with automobile and aircraft systems. In this case, the tough tasks of
accessing and communicating with an SME were not necessary. In subsequent
developments, described later, knowledge engineering was not as straightforward.

Moving to "Real World" Training Environments

The next stage in the evolution took place from 1982 through 1986. During this
4-year period, the research transitioned from the "laboratory" into the "real
world." The FAULT simulation was modified, first to provide training for Army
communications technicians and then for operators and maintainers of safety-
related systems in nuclear power plants. The R&D sought solutions on issues
related to design, development, implementation, and evaluation of simulation-
oriented training in operational training environments. The development in ap-

plied training environments shifted the laboratory focus on experimental evaluation to a focus on delivery issues such as hardware, interface, knowledge-base development, and so on. This transition made the research team acutely aware that software design is often driven not solely by scientific findings, but also by such constraints as resources, existing computer hardware, organizational politics, and preconceived opinions of managers, instructors, and students. Knowledge engineering in operational environments is also very different than building "proof of concept" systems in the laboratory. The remainder of the systems described herein were developed and implemented into a variety of environments with such constraints/opportunities.

Simulation-Based Training for Army Communications (SB-3614)

The majority of the TASK and FAULT research was sponsored by the U.S. Army Research Institute for Behavioral and Social Sciences (ARI). The laboratory research provided ARI with basic scientific findings about human problem solving in simulated technical environments. However, ARI wanted to determine if the TASK and FAULT simulation-based training could be effective and efficient for Army communications training.

The ARI identified a training environment, at the Army Signal Center at Fort Gordon, conducive to the development and evaluation of computer-based training. The Army communications hardware was a tactical switchboard (designated SB-3614). The domain was selected because the system was relatively modern and because the training had a very high annual student population. ARI was particularly interested in the feasibility of using off-the-shelf microcomputer-based training in the Army school environment. Thus, the system was developed on an Apple II computer configured with 64K of memory, two floppy drives, and a monochrome display. This hardware redefines the word "constrained," at least by today's standards.

One of the findings of the early FAULT experiments concluded that a low-fidelity training simulation should be combined with practice on the real equipment and/or high-fidelity simulation. The Army SB-3614 Tactical Switchboard training system attempted to bridge the gap between low-fidelity simulation and the real equipment. The system was designed to permit the Army student to see graphic depictions of the switchboard. The graphical depictions raised the fidelity of the simulation so the student would understand that the simulation-based training had a reasonable expectation of transfer to the real equipment. It was clear from the beginning that the Army instructors and students would not accept an abstract simulation that seemed to work for the proverbial "college sophomore" in the laboratory environment of the university.

The SB-3614 simulation had two main sections: (a) a "symptom-finding" section using graphical depictions of the system and (b) a troubleshooting section based on FAULT. The representation of the switchboard provided a visual link between the simulation and the real equipment. FAULT provided training on logical troubleshooting and helped the student to learn the functional connectivity of the various components within the system. A more detailed description of the SB-3614 software can be found elsewhere (Johnson & Fath, 1983, 1984).

The SB-3614 simulation's student model was identical to the FAULT system's student model. The system tracked and remediated logical errors. It kept a record of the time to solution and the number of problems solved. The student modeling was not necessarily sophisticated, but it did advise the student of errors and explained why a particular action was an error.

The SB-3614 was experimentally evaluated in the training environment at Fort Gordon (Johnson & Fath, 1984). In summary, the evaluation showed that the computer-simulation training fared as well as the use of real equipment for training. Posttraining evaluation forms from nearly 400 soldiers showed a high acceptance of the simulation-based training. Perhaps the most important statement about the value of the training was its longevity after the ARI research was completed. The simulation-based training was adopted into the Army program of instruction and was used from 1984 until 1988, when the SB-3614 equipment was retired from the Army inventory.

The R&D at the Signal School showed that microcomputer-based, low-fidelity, simulation-oriented training is a reasonable complement to Army communication training. The level of fidelity was acceptable because it provided both reasonable feedback and a stimulating diagnostic challenge. The research also showed that novice military trainees need a sufficient level of fidelity for the individual to be able to conceptually link the simulation to the real equipment. This is best achieved by mixing the use of simulation with the use of real equipment. Table 8.5 summarizes the SB-3614 experimental findings.

SB-3614 Knowledge Engineering

Knowledge engineering for the SB-3614 training system was a new experience for the research team. The knowledge engineering required the developers to become familiar with the training curricula and the SB-3614 switchboard. This was accomplished by participating in the course as a student for approximately 2

TABLE 8.5
SB 3614 Research Findings

Novice trainees need reasonable physical fidelity to be able to associate the simulation with the real equipment.

Feedback should provide explanation.

Sophisticated computing hardware is not necessarily a requirement for simulation-based training.

weeks. This initial investment permitted the knowledge engineer to build "straw man" functional flow diagrams and system displays for review by the SMEs. This development showed SMEs are much better at reviewing or modifying a "straw man" than at attempting the initial development themselves.

Knowledge engineering can be considered an "art." It is much more than merely eliciting technical information from the head of the SME. If done properly, the knowledge-base development process permits the SME to "buy in" to the new system.

Good instructors usually develop or modify their lecture materials. In the same way, good instructors want to drive portions of the system design for computer-based training. A good knowledge engineer must be able to understand the hardware and software constraints as the SME becomes involved in the system design and development. The knowledge engineer must work with the SME during system design to ensure that the SME does not attempt to force design changes that exceed the resources of the project. The experience at the Signal School demonstrated that proper involvement of technical instructors as SMEs and codesigners is critical to adoption and acceptance of the system upon completion.

Evaluating Results Within a Nuclear Utility

The Electric Power Research Institute (EPRI) became interested in FAULT because of the potential to provide diagnostic training that might generalize to a variety of technical systems throughout a nuclear utility. Further, EPRI was interested in offering their member utilities a low-cost, simulation-based training alternative.

The demonstration system for the project was the diesel-powered emergency generator. This unit provides standby power to operate cooling pumps, computers, and other critical safety equipment in the event of loss of power from a nuclear station's steam turbines. The diesel generator system was chosen because it was a critical safety system that has been problematic for many utilities. In addition, the system was selected for the research because the finished training product was potentially generalizable to many utilities.

The diesel generator simulation (DGSIM) continued with the context-specific diagnostic practice, as in the SB-3614 simulation, but increased the physical fidelity of the displays. The DGSIM displays were accessed by the student as "symptom-finding" tools. Figure 8.3 shows one of the informational displays. Once again, the student diagnosis was based on FAULT: counting logical errors, time to solution, and number of problems solved. The DGSIM training also kept track of simulated time to problem solution. This was important since equipment downtime in the nuclear plant is very expensive (e.g., estimated $1 million/day) and could have safety repercussions. The DGSIM software is described extensively elsewhere (Johnson, Maddox, & Kiel, 1984; Johnson, Maddox, Rouse, & Kiel, 1985; Maddox, Johnson, & Frey, 1986).

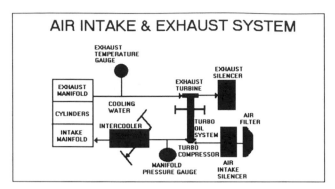

FIG. 8.3.   A system schematic in DGSIM.

EPRI was committed to the evaluation of the simulation-oriented, computer-based training (Maddox, Johnson, & Frey, 1985, 1986). The DGSIM evaluations involved both nonlicensed operators and technicians. Twenty operators/technicians were trained using real equipment and 20 operators/technicians were trained with DGSIM. One day after the training, both groups performed equally well troubleshooting problems with live, in-plant diesel generator equipment. However, 140 days after training, the experimental group (DGSIM) performed better than the control group.

The DGSIM software contained some additions requested by the nuclear utility instructional personnel. An example of such a modification was the addition of extensive declarative information about the diesel generator. Another example was a record-keeping system that recorded, for replay, student performance in a problem. During the experimental evaluation, it was observed that students seldom accessed declarative information. Instead, students always gravitated toward the simulation to practice troubleshooting. The diagnostic practice, with feedback and explanation, seems to hold the most training potential for technical training environments. Perhaps declarative information can be best delivered via books or instructor presentations.

The nuclear training example also suggested that extensive, computer-based record keeping of student actions, for human analysis, is unnecessary. Human instructors engaged in the conceptual design of training software often want to "keep all student data." However, human instructors seldom have the time/ability to review transaction files of student performance. Unless the transaction files are used by the automated, intelligent tutoring system they should not be saved. Table 8.6 lists the experimental findings for DGSIM.

DGSIM Knowledge Engineering.   Knowledge engineering for DGSIM involved extensive interaction with technical instructors and plant engineers. Again, the developer/knowledge engineer enrolled in a short course to be able to

TABLE 8.6
DGSIM Research Findings

Increased fidelity enhanced initial user acceptance.
Initially, users gravitate toward flashy graphics, then toward displays that provide maximum feedback and information.
Users access declarative information minimally.
Extensive problem-specific student data files are seldom used by human instructors.

develop "straw man" examples of functional flow diagrams and displays. At the same time, the SMEs referred to examples of the FAULT system developed for other domains. The SMEs' use of FAULT made it clear what the system could do and what information would be necessary for system development. This continued interactive development of the DGSIM knowledge base assured technical accuracy as well as ultimate user acceptance.

The DGSIM software was widely distributed throughout the nuclear power industry. Operating on an IBM PC, DGSIM has been providing diesel generator diagnostic training since 1987.

Microcomputer Intelligence for Technical Training (MITT)

The Air Force Human Resources Laboratory (AFHRL) has been conducting basic research on intelligent tutoring systems (ITS), but wanted to demonstrate that ITS technology could be applied on low-cost microcomputers in a relatively short period of time.

MITT provided a system that combined the logical troubleshooting of FAULT with a diagnostic, procedural expert. This combination allowed the student to receive feedback based on either the appropriate diagnostic procedure or the functional connectivity of the system.

MITT has been used to develop training systems for troubleshooting the fuel cell on the space shuttle (Johnson et al., 1988) and for the message processing system for the Minuteman missile (see Fig. 8.4). The procedural troubleshooting advice was incorporated into rule bases of an expert system. These rules were fired when the user requested procedural advice on the current malfunction.

For the first time, MITT provided dynamic data values to the simulation. In previous software, every display was merely a snapshot of the system at a given time. MITT allowed the data values to change over time. This permitted degradation of the system and provided the user with a more "realistic" training environment.

MITT also increased the fidelity of the displays. The displays became more

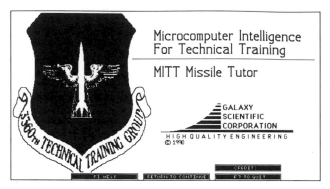

FIG. 8.4. MITT missile message processing system.

interactive. Knobs and controls were added to displays to give the student "hands-on" experience with some of the equipment. As controls changed positions, the corresponding data values also changed. Figure 8.5 shows a manipulatable display from the fuel-cell tutor.

MITT Knowledge Engineering. The MITT tutor knowledge engineering must be described for each of the knowledge bases developed: the space shuttle fuel cell and the missile message processing system. Each development was unique.

The original MITT fuel-cell tutor was designed and completed, as contracted, in 6 calendar months for less than 1 person-year of effort. As a result, the technical domain was to be selected early in the project and false starts had to be minimized. However, there were a few false starts before the appropriate group at NASA Johnson Space Center became involved in the project. Since the shuttle's electrical power distribution and fuel-cell system were so complex (and time was so limited), it was not feasible for the knowledge engineer to become a

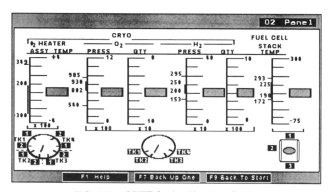

FIG. 8.5. MITT fuel-cell tutor display.

pseudo-expert on the hardware. Instead, responsibility for the FAULT system knowledge was transferred to the SME. This was accomplished by permitting the SME to use DGSIM and other FAULT-based software to understand what the finished product would look like. This approach worked fine. Due to changing work assignments of NASA personnel, two SMEs were involved, independently, as the fuel-cell tutor was developed.

MITT was the first time the research team required the development of production rules by the SME. The team worked closely with the SME to transfer NASA cockpit procedures to CLIPS rules. Further, the SME assisted in database changes to mitigate discrepancies between the FAULT expert and the new CLIPS-based procedural expert.

Knowledge engineering for the second MITT tutor, in the missile domain, involved SMEs from the Air Training Command (ATC). The goal of the project was to show that the MITT software could be generalized to a second domain. The approach was to teach the SMEs how MITT worked by permitting them to use the NASA fuel-cell tutor. The SMEs became proficient with the fuel-cell tutor, thus permitting them to create a missile tutor in the MITT likeness. The missile SMEs chose to deemphasize the FAULT system and force the user to follow procedures directly from technical orders. The SMEs also wanted the user to decompose a component down to the wire and pine level. This design required more graphical displays than the previous MITT system, thus prompting memory optimization and a slight redesign of MITT.

The MITT missile tutor taught the research team an important lesson about training system development. The missile domain was selected out of convenience and politics, rather than out of training need. The approach forced a technology-based solution where there was not a dire need for a new training system. While this development was a successful test of the generality of the MITT software, it may not result in the adoption of the MITT missile tutor into the training courseware.

The MITT fuel-cell tutor was completed in 1988 and 1989 and the MITT missile tutor was completed in 1990. MITT was well received by astronauts, flight controllers, and instructors at NASA Johnson Space Center. User acceptance tests at NASA indicated that additional failure scenarios were needed to lengthen each training session. ATC user evaluation indicated that MITT tutors had potential value for colateral and periodic training rather than primary instruction. ATC personnel referred to the MITT approach as "scenario-style" training. ATC recommended that MITT should be tested in a variety of additional environments such as airfield management and air traffic control. Table 8.7 summarizes the research findings for MITT.

MITT Writer. The MITT systems developed for NASA Johnson Space Center and for the U.S. Air Force ATC at Chanute Technical Training Center demonstrated that the approach was effective, yet generic enough to support varied

TABLE 8.7
MITT Research Findings

NASA users demanded high physical fidelity.

The combination of logical and procedural advice is acceptable to the population of users at NASA

ATC felt that MITT tutors are best for periodic training.

MITT tutors are applicable to a variety of domains.

---

domains. It has become increasingly clear that the feasibility of the application of intelligent tutoring systems for technical training will be cost driven. To maintain a reasonable development cost, the system development and knowledge engineering must be accomplished by training system developers and/or SMEs. Further, such systems must be developed and delivered on affordable off-the-shelf microcomputers. The goals of low-cost development of MITT Writer, an authoring system for MITT (see Fig. 8.6).

MITT Writer allows the author to design and edit domain-specific files for use by MITT. MITT Writer is designed for use by government training developers and SMEs. Technical instructors are also likely users of such development tools (Johnson, 1988). MITT Writer allows the author to develop new domain-specific information for use by the MITT tutor without having to know how to program a computer. This is both convenient and cost-effective for the developer.

MITT Writer contains an embedded, advisory, expert system to support the developers with their design. This advisory system compares the state of the current database to the "expert" authoring procedure. The "expert" authoring procedure evolved from over 5 years of experience in developing MITT tutors.

MITT Writer also contains a "consistency checker" that ensures that the files that are written will be readable by the MITT tutor. Any inconsistencies are classified as either errors or warnings. Warnings are minor inconsistencies that

FIG. 8.6.   MITT Writer authoring system.

TABLE 8.8
MITT Writer Development Guidelines

Provide graphical interface

Minimize the need for hard-copy documentation

Provide advisory system to aid author

Keep it simple

would result in an incomplete MITT Writer database, but the database could still be run with MITT. Errors, on the other hand, are not compatible with MITT and would have to be corrected before attempting to run MITT.

MITT Writer was scheduled to be tested and fielded during 1991. Therefore, it is too soon to report on the system's success. The system has been designed with the novice user in mind, but also includes transitionally for the experienced user. Table 8.8 shows the guidelines that were adhered to during MITT Writer design and development.

Advanced Learning for Mobile (ALM) Subscriber Equipment: A Hypermedia Approach

The ARI, Fort Gordon Field Unit, conducts R&D in support of the Army Signal School for the operational Army Signal Corps. ARI supports the active Army as well as the Army Reserve. ALM Subscriber Equipment capitalizes on hypermedia with extensive computer graphics to build a training system for the ALM Subscriber Equipment for the Army National Guard (see Fig. 8.7).

ALM provides an environment in which to build, operate, and troubleshoot an Army communication system. ALM departs from the logical diagnosis tech-

FIG. 8.7.   Advanced learning for MSE system.

TABLE 8.9
ALM Research Findings

The Army sees ALM as a potential solution to their current CBT shortage.

Knowledge-base development requires a stable personnel pool.

---

niques incorporated in FAULT. ALM uses a hypermedia approach for system design (Coonan et al., 1990). The diagnosis is limited to established troubleshooting procedures.

The student model tracks the information seen by the student and the actions taken by the student. The amount of information logged by the student model depends on the user-designated level of problem difficulty. Problems are considered "easy" if detailed advice is available to the student. The "harder" problems provide less detailed advice and impose a time limit on the student. The problem difficulty level for each problem can be changed at any time. There is also a "browse" level that allows the student to look around and see how the system operates under normal operating conditions. The "browse" mode does not provide any remediation.

ALM was fielded in early 1991. Therefore, it is too soon to report on user's reactions. However, early reactions indicate that the Army user population is eager to evaluate the system and that they would like to see more training like ALM (Table 8.9).

ALM Knowledge Engineering. The ALM knowledge engineering experience was plagued with multiple changes in SMEs. As a result, much of the ALM system knowledge was derived from technical manuals. This knowledge was correct, but the knowledge engineering effort did not attract a cadre of SMEs who considered ALM to be theirs. Experience has shown that SME investment and acceptance is critical. This pride of ownership by the SMEs would have been helpful as the system was transferred from ARI to the operational training environments.

Advanced Technology for Aviation Technician Training

The Federal Aviation Administration (FAA) Office of Aviation Medicine, as part of the National Aging Aircraft Research Program, sponsors a number of projects related to Human Factors in aircraft maintenance. The Advanced Technology for Aviation Technician Training research is investigating the use of ITS technology for maintenance training (Johnson, 1990).

The current research is a three-year effort as shown in Table 8.10. The first year of the project assesses the current training technology used by aircraft

TABLE 8.10
FAA Advanced Technology Research Phases

Phase 1	1990	Technology assessment and Prototype
Phase 2	1991	Build complete Intelligent tutoring system
Phase 3	1992	Conduct system evaluation

maintenance technicians and develops a prototype training system. The second year of the project builds a complete training system based on feedback on the prototype developed during the first year. The third year will conduct formal user-acceptance, training-effectiveness, and cost-effectiveness evaluations.

During the first phase of this project, the aviation training audience required constant definition of the term *ITS*. After a while, it became obvious that, for most systems developed and planned by this research team, the term *intelligent simulation* is more appropriate. Intelligent simulation is more easily understood by most audiences, even though it is equivalent to the term intelligent tutoring systems. The term intelligent simulation will be used for the remainder of the FAA project.

The system involves the Environmental Control System on the Boeing 767-300 aircraft. The project involves both industry (Delta Airlines) and academia (Clayton State College) (see Fig. 8.8). The project is currently in the prototype phase of development. The prototype relies heavily upon established troubleshooting procedures to provide student diagnosis. It tracks the actions taken and the information seen by the student. Part of the troubleshooting also involves the use of a troubleshooting fault tree. The student model includes a mechanism to provide feedback based on any of these fault trees. The system will react when the student chooses an incorrect path in the tree.

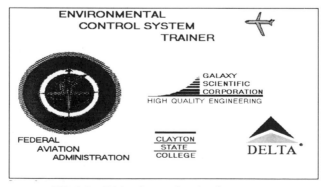

FIG. 8.8.   FAA advanced technology system.

Since the evaluation is scheduled for 1992, it is premature to predict user acceptance. However, the authors continue to interact with the SMEs at Delta as the prototype nears completion. The reactions of the Delta and Clayton State instructors, who will be intimately involved with the system and knowledgebase development, are crucial to success and acceptance of the system in 1992.

EIGHT TRAINING SYSTEMS LATER: A SUMMARY OF FINDINGS ABOUT STUDENT MODELING

Since 1976, the authors have been involved in the development of eight training systems that have been described herein. In that time period, the authors have seen significant changes in hardware, software, and user expectations. We have seen the diagnostic training software transition from the laboratory into the "real" world. We know that intelligent tutoring systems (a.k.a. intelligent simulation) can be developed at a reasonable cost and delivered outside the laboratory. We have shown that intelligent tutoring systems can have a positive effect on posttraining performance Concisely, the summary findings follow.

Training systems must be designed and developed with and/or by training personnel. The eight projects have shown that the larger the role of training personnel in design and development, the greater the likelihood of user acceptance. The MITT Writer authoring system promises to involve training personnel in system design and modification.

The various evaluations have shown that users prefer advice, explanation, and meaningful feedback over "pretty" pictures. The authors believe that current hardware and software will permit both. However, compromises, if necessary, should be made on the displays rather than on the student modeling and subsequent feedback routines.

This chapter has shown that basic research can evolve into operational training systems. Once the tough scientific issues have been solved, the ideas can be transitioned from the laboratory to the field. This transition must consider the realities of the operational environment, which include people, politics, dollars, hardware, and software. These realities are the components that drive the disappointments and fuel the successes in the development of advanced technology training for today and the future.

REFERENCES

Coonan, T. A., Johnson, W. B., Norton, J. E., & Sanders, M. G. (1990). An hypermedia approach to technical training for the electronic information delivery system. *Proceedings of the Eighth Conference on Instruction Delivery*. Warrenton, VA: Society for Applied Learning Technology.

Johnson, W. B. (1980). Computer simulations for fault diagnosis training: An empirical study of learning transfer from simulation to live system performance. *Dissertation Abstracts International, 1981, 41* (11): 4625-A (University Microfilms No. 8108555).

Johnson, W. B. (1986). Transfer of training in technical training research. In V. E. Holt (Ed.),

Issues in psychological research and application in transfer of training. Washington, DC: American Psychological Association.

Johnson, W. B. (1987). Development and evaluation of simulation-oriented computer-based instruction for diagnostic training. In W. B. Rouse (Ed.), *Advances in man-machine systems research* (vol. 3, pp. 99–127). Greenwich, CT: JAI Press.

Johnson, W. B. (1988). Developing expert system knowledge bases for technical training. In L. D. Massey, J. Psotka, & S. A. Mutter (Eds.), *Intelligent tutoring systems: Lessons learned* (pp. 83–92). Hillsdale, NJ: Lawrence Erlbaum Associates.

Johnson, W. B. (1990). Advanced technology for aviation maintenance. *Proceedings of Human Factors in Aviation Maintenance and Inspection.* Washington, DC: Federal Aviation Administration Office of Aviation Medicine.

Johnson, W. B., & Fath, J. L. (1983). Design and initial evaluation of the mixed-fidelity courseware for maintenance training. *Proceedings of the 27th Annual Meeting of the Human Factors Society* (pp. 1017–1021). Norfolk, VA: Human Factors Society.

Johnson, W. B., & Fath, J. L. (1984). *Implementation of a mixed fidelity approach to maintenance training* (TR-661). Alexandria: VA: U.S. Army Research Institute for the Behavioral and Social Sciences.

Johnson, W. B., Maddox, M. E., & Kiel, G. C. (1984). Simulation-oriented computer-based instruction for training nuclear plant personnel. *Proceedings of the 28th Annual Meeting of the Human Factors Society* (pp. 1008–1012). San Antonio, TX: Human Factors Society.

Johnson, W. B., Maddox, M. E., Rouse, W. B., & Kiel, G. C. (1985). *Diagnostic training for nuclear plant personnel, I: Course development* (EPRI NP-3829). Palo Alto, CA: Electric Power Research Institute.

Johnson, W. B., Norton, J. E., Duncan, P. C., & Hunt, R. M. (1988). *Development and demonstration of microcomputer intelligence for technical training (MITT)* (AFHRL-TP-88-8). Brooks Air Force Base, TX: Air Force Human Resources Laboratory.

Johnson, W. B., & Rouse, W. B. (1982a). Analysis and classification of human errors in troubleshooting live aircraft powerplants. *IEEE Transactions on Systems, Man, and Cybernetics, SMC-12*(3), 289–393.

Johnson, W. B, & Rouse, W. B. (1982b). Training maintenance technicians for troubleshooting: two experiments with computer simulations. *Human Factors, 24*(3), 271–276.

Maddox, M. E., Johnson, W. B., & Frey, P. R. (1985). *Diagnostic training for nuclear power plant personnel, 2: Implementation and evaluation* (EPRI NP-3829-II). Palo Alto, CA: Electric Power Research Institute.

Maddox, M. E., Johnson, W. B., & Frey, P. R. (1986). A transfer of training study in the nuclear power industry: From simulation to live performance. *Proceedings of the 29th Annual Meeting of the Human Factors Society* (pp. 1022–1026). Baltimore, MD: The Human Factors Society.

Pellegrino, S. J. (1979). *Modeling test sequences chosen by humans in fault diagnosis tasks.* MSIE Thesis, The University of Illinois at Urbana-Champaign.

Rouse, W. B. (1979a). Problem solving performance of maintenance trainees in a fault diagnosis task. *Human Factors, 21*(2), 195–203.

Rouse, W. B. (1979b). Problem solving performance of first semester maintenance trainees in two fault diagnosis tasks. *Human Factors, 21*(5), 611–618.

Rouse, W. B., & Hunt, R. M. (1984). Human problem solving in fault diagnosis tasks. In W. B. Rouse (Ed.), *Advances in man-machine systems research* (1, pp. 195–222). Greenwich, CT: JAI Press.

TRANSCRIPT OF DISCUSSION

Kevin Bennett: With regard to MITT, were you able to include in that software some type of student assessment module that is able to accumulate responses, interactions with the trainer, the tutor, and come up with some sort of summary indicator of their performance?

William Johnson: Yes we did. With MITT, we kept track of straightforward things such as how many actions they performed. When they made mistakes, were the mistakes made due to not following a procedure (we knew what the procedures were because they were coded in CLIPS), or were the mistakes logical errors? We counted both kinds of errors for consideration in the "instructor module." The instructor module was comprised of CLIPS rules (simple C code) that kept track of the number of times errors were committed. If they made a procedural error so many times, we finally came back and said, "You are not following X procedures." Because we knew where they were in the program, we could tell them the procedure that they should follow to get back on track. We also kept summary information that we gave to them at the end of the simulation. Some of the summary information included the kinds of mistakes made, how many times, and how long it took to complete each problem. And we provided feedback as to how current performance compares to all other students that ever played the particular MITT problem.

Hugh Burns: I have two questions. What are the implications for the automatic test equipment (ATE) world on your designs over this decade, and what have we learned about knowledge engineering for the shell design?

William Johnson: I like both of those questions. Considering automatic test equipment, if that equipment becomes "magic" and it breaks, the broken test equipment has even greater implications for complex diagnosis and repair than the one piece of broken aircraft hardware that is on the test equipment. Perhaps ATE training is one of the best candidates for our simulation-based diagnostic training.

Hugh Burns: Working on the test scan for about 10 years, when the test scan breaks, you have to go back and troubleshoot the test scan. But are there implications for embedded training? Is that going to be a future direction? What about knowledge engineering?

William Johnson: In this audience, we are preaching to the choir when talking about embedded training. Even today, when we talk about people building new airplanes, new avionics systems, you use the word "embedded training." Everybody likes the idea until you go to the avionics engineer and specify how much RAM you need from the prime system, and they cry, "Sorry no computer for you, its all for operational." So I think somehow, maybe with Manpower, Personnel, and Training initiatives, across DoD, embedded training is going to be able to force its way into the prime system. I think we all have that to look forward to.

In terms of knowledge engineering, Dan Fisk talked about characteristics of the knowledge engineer. We have all discussed that for a long time, but it seems that the knowledge engineer really has to go in and understand the operational system and/or training systems to a certain point. The knowledge engineer has to be to willing to listen to the way they are doing the training and the way the system operates. The knowledge engineer also needs to bring a perspective about the software capability of the training system. We experienced this with the bladefold, mentioned by Doug Towne. Sometimes the design of the training system offers things to the operational environment that they haven't even thought of. The knowledge engineer has to go in there and convince the instructors or operational people that, "What about if we took a different look at the way you are doing this and sort of combine your approach with the approach that we are able to offer with this training system?" I think that is the hardest job description to write. Hiring somebody with the right qualifications is hard—the knowledge engineer must understand computer software and hardware as well as be able to learn about the equipment system for which the training is being designed. Knowledge engineering is a combination of engineering, sales, and art.

Hugh Burns: How much of MITT Writer is going to be an authoring tool for us in knowledge engineering?

William Johnson: MITT writer, by the way it is designed, should stand alone for a reasonably motivated subject matter expert that understands the training. MITT Writer will permit a subject matter expert to build the system without having to call Galaxy Scientific or AL/HRD, for that matter. MITT Writer will attempt to deemphasize, or eliminate, the knowledge engineer.

Alan Lesgold: You did such a nice clean job building these trainers. At some level, doing the test, in one form, is sort of a procedural thing. You follow the procedure and you get this result and maybe make a logical decision and go on. But in all the FAULTS that are really hard, testing is really a modeling procedure because only working systems fit the nice clear, logical model. Nonworking systems, in fact, have new models, some of which we have not seen before. I guess one of the things that I want to know is, what evidence do we have that these clean procedural approaches on how to do a test and make logical fault premises, what information do we have that this transfer to the things that machines just don't do very well which is to deal with faults where a new modeling system is required to do it? As an example, if you call up the phone company and say, "My phone doesn't work," they will answer, "Do any of the phones in your house work?" If you say yes, they will say, "Well, it is not our problem." You do the same thing with electricity. They will also tell you it is not their problem. But, in fact, there are some faults that are implicated by the electric company when some of the things, but not all of the things, work. Another example is if one of two hot leads coming in is OK and the other one isn't. That is a kind of fault-finding or interpreting a test. You have to figure out, "What could be going on here that violates my logical model of the system?" This is just one of many things I think we don't do very well. The success of your system in a sense illustrates how close you can come to a sense of all the instructional requirements, and yet I have a nagging feeling that we are not sure how well our guys will do if they had a *real* fault.

William Johnson: As I described our research and development, we went from *context-free*, which wasn't good enough by itself, and have swung the pendulum all the way over to *procedural*, which is equally unacceptable by itself. We must strive for a combination of teaching good logical decision making as well as teaching the procedural rules.

Walt Schneider: If we take the "pendulum swing" issue, where do you think the pendulum should be? Here we are 15 years later. What is the prescription in terms of integrating the issue of fidelity items? The users like it and it helps on some cases. But what is your prescription at this point? I assume it's embedded in this system of intermixing various approaches—you've got to do the procedures because almost everyone who is doing the troubleshooting uses the procedures some of the time. How do you mix time on equipment, time in a simulator, and time in a diagrammatic troubleshooting? What is your prescription, you being the longest running expert in the area?

William Johnson: I don't claim to be. In fact, Rouse edited a book in 1987. The first chapter was by a Professor Doug Towne, who talked about 20-plus years of experience. And a youngster named Johnson (not trying to make you look old, Doug), a couple of chapters back talked about 10 years of experience. And in another chapter someone talked about 30 years of experience.

Your question about pendulum swing is an important one. What I intend to do is swing the pendulum back a little bit, more toward generic approaches and away from the strictly procedural approaches, and test it again. I am going to take the experimental psychologist approach of modifying the software and running another experiment to see what kind of effect it has. Five years ago, I would have argued that high fidelity is not critical to training effectiveness. But every time I go out to see someone delivering real-world training, I see many computer-based training companies selling a lot of crummy (in my opinion) computer-based training that is nothing more than glorified page-turners. The reason they are succeeding in selling these systems is that there is a whole infrastructure of marketing people and the systems have real pretty graphics, thus increasing the fidelity. The fact that they are selling this stuff is embarrassing. It seems that if we are going to be able to get our semismart, or, in some cases, really smart training systems in the market, we are going to have to spend some time and money making the systems look pretty, whether we want to or not. Otherwise, our intelligent systems will never proceed from our book chapters and our journal papers to real training environments.

9

The Use of On-Line Guidance, Representation Aiding, and Discovery Learning to Improve the Effectiveness of Simulation Training

Kevin Bennett
Wright State University, Dayton, Ohio

INTRODUCTION

Complex and dynamic real world domains (e.g., command and control, process control, air traffic control) require individuals to complete tasks that are difficult and involve significant risks. There is a great deal of interest in developing automated instructional systems that will allow an individual to acquire the required expertise without the associated risk and cost of training on actual equipment. One approach to automated instruction for these domains is the provision of a computerized simulation that replicates the domain of interest. A simulation provides one primary requirement for successful instruction: it allows an individual to acquire necessary skills and knowledge while actively solving domain problems. Simulations vary with respect to how well the physical appearance and dynamic behavior of a domain is replicated. In high-fidelity simulations the training system looks and acts just like the actual system. In low-fidelity simulations the emphasis is on providing instruction for the fundamental skills that underlay performance (Johnson, 1987). There are advantages and disadvantages to each end of the spectrum, and it is possible that instructional programs might be made more effective by incorporating simulations with varying levels of fidelity (Rouse, 1982).

One important issue in the design of simulation training environments is how to use the computational power that recent advances in computer science and artificial intelligence have provided. One approach is to develop and incorporate intelligent machine tutors. Intelligent tutors can provide advice, instruction, or explanation that dynamically changes as a function of the current situation and the individual's mastery of the topic at hand. With rare exceptions (e.g., Woolf,

Blegen, & Jansen, & Verloop, 1987), intelligent tutors have not been incorporated into simulations for complex, dynamic domains. This is probably due to both the inherent complexity of these domains and the amount and types of knowledge (declarative knowledge, procedural knowledge, causal reasoning, psychomotor skills, and meta-cognitive skills) required for successful performance. Both of these factors create difficulties for the development of sophisticated student diagnosis and student modeling modules. One challenge that designers of simulation training environments face is how to incorporate this capability.

With the vast potential that intelligent machine tutors provide, it is easy to overlook other uses of computational power that can also improve the effectiveness of automated instruction. One technique is representation aiding (Hollan, Hutchins, & Weitzman, 1984; Woods & Roth, 1988), where machine power is used to create and manipulate representations of the domain. Direct representation and direct manipulation can help an individual find the relevant data in a dynamic environment, to visualize the semantics of the domain (i.e., make concrete the abstract), and to restructure his or her view of the problem. This can be an indispensable aid in facilitating understanding and performance. However, many issues must be resolved in the development of direct representation and direct manipulation interfaces. For example, which conceptual perspectives, of the nearly infinite number of alternatives, should be provided? What design perspectives are available to guide the mapping of information from the domain to the representation aids?

A third use of computational power is the provision of computerized tools and resources that allow discovery learning. In discovery learning, a student is encouraged to actively explore a domain, and computerized tools are provided to assist the student in the formation and testing of hypotheses about that domain (e.g., Shute & Glaser, 1990). The assumption is that actively exploring and experiencing the important domain concepts will result in more effective instruction than passively learning the same material. As with the development of intelligent tutors and representation aids, many questions arise with respect to discovery learning environments. Which of the potential explorations should be provided, and which computerized tools are needed to support these explorations? How should the explorations be sequenced to facilitate learning and transfer of training?

For the last few years, my colleagues (David Woods and Emily Roth) and I have been investigating issues in the design of decision support for complex and dynamic domains. We have chosen a representative domain (process control) and a representative task (the manual control of feedwater) for our investigations. We believe that on-line diagnosis, graphic displays, and discovery learning are three mutually reinforcing techniques that can be used to improve the effectiveness of training. We also believe that a detailed understanding of both the cognitive demands that are produced by the domain and the cognitive resources that skilled domain practitioners have developed to meet these demands is required for these techniques to be used appropriately. Two instructional systems have been developed that illustrate the approach. The first system is a part-task simulation that replicates the fundamental aspects that make the manual control of feedwater difficult. The second system is an on-line advisor that is incorporated within a full-scope simulator. These two systems, their development, and the design rationale are discussed.

THE MANUAL CONTROL OF FEEDWATER TASK AND THE PART-TASK SIMULATION

Any successful attempt to provide automated instruction needs to be based on cognitive analyses of both the domain and expert performance within that domain. Providing this information is precisely the concern of a nascent discipline that has been referred to as "cognitive engineering" (Hollnagel & Woods, 1983; Norman, 1986; Rasmussen, 1986; Woods & Roth, 1988). Cognitive engineering provides a framework for the development of both on-line (real-time) and off-line (training) decision support. The approach can be paraphrased in the following manner. First, the "cognitive demands" that the underlying system places on the user must be determined. Then the user's "cognitive resources" (information processing capabilities, skills, knowledge, and higher-level strategies) that are available to meet these demands must be determined. Two mutually reinforcing, cognitive-based analyses were conducted to provide this information for the manual control of feedwater task (Roth & Woods, 1988; Woods & Roth, 1988). The goals/means analysis determined those aspects of a domain that make successful performance at the task difficult to achieve. The cognitive task analysis provided a description of the knowledge and skills that individuals had developed to overcome those difficulties.

Goals/Means Analysis

An analysis of the domain is crucial because the domain is the ultimate source of the cognitive demands that will be placed on an individual. As its name implies, the goals/means analysis provides a description of the domain in terms of goals that need to be accomplished and the physical resources that are available to accomplish them. Before discussing the details, a general description of the manual control of feedwater task is in order. The manual control of feedwater task (MCF task) is a critical and difficult task that can result in high economic losses when performance is poor. In a study of reactor trip data derived from plant monthly operation data over a 6-year period (1978–1983), it was found that the predominant cause of reactor trips was the manual control of feedwater task (INPO, 1984). This task was responsible for an average of 1.3 trips per plant, per year, and with certain plant configurations this estimate could be as high as five

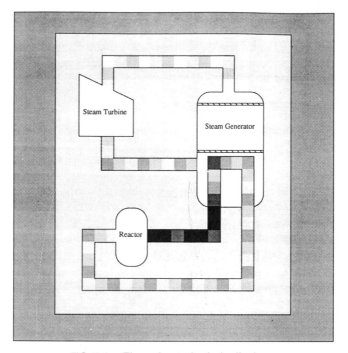

FIG. 9.1.   The animated mimic display.

trips per plant per year. The task itself is embedded in the overall startup of a nuclear power plant and will be explained with reference to Fig. 9.1. During startup the energy produced by the nuclear reactor (in the form of heat) is piped through several boilers or steam generators (only one is pictured) to produce steam. This steam then drives a turbine to produce electricity and is subsequently cooled and returned to the steam generators in the form of feedwater. Controlling the rate at which feedwater returns to the steam generator is the manual control of feedwater task. In addition to the operator who performs this task, there are two more operators who control steam demand and reactor power. The critical performance variable is maintaining the level of water in the steam generators (the indicated steam generator level, ISGL) between an upper trip setpoint and a lower trip setpoint: crossing a setpoint automatically shuts the plant down and the startup must begin anew.

A goals/means analysis of the manual control of feedwater revealed that to accomplish the startup task two conflicting high-level goals must be achieved: (a) maintaining a mass balance by matching the amount of mass entering (feedwater flow) and leaving (steam flow) the steam generator, and (b) maintaining an energy balance by matching steam demand with reactor power production. As an example of how these goals can produce conflicts, consider the following scenario. Imagine that the ISGL is close to the lower setpoint boundary, and that, therefore, a high-priority goal is to raise this level to avoid a plant trip. One of the means available to accomplish this goal is to increase the rate of feedwater flow until the mass flowing into the steam generator is greater than the mass leaving it (steam flow). As one might expect, under these conditions the ISGL will ultimately rise. However, the increase of cold feedwater (relative to the environment inside the steam generator) initially decreases the thermal energy, causing the ISGL to fall (a "shrink" effect), and exacerbates the initial problem. This is one example of how energy effects can cause the initial change in ISGL to be the opposite of the long-term, steady-state effect and how ISGL reflects the true steam generator mass only after a time delay. The highly negative impact of even minimal time delays in tracking tasks is well documented (e.g., Wickens, 1986). Thus, the counterintuitive and time-delayed behavior of the ISGL is one fundamental source of difficulty in performing the task.

The goals/means analysis also revealed several other factors that contribute to the difficulty of the task. Each of the primary variables controlled by individual operators (steam flow, feedwater flow, reactor power) has an impact on the critical performance variable (indicated steam generator level). This high degree of intercoupling demands a significant amount of communication and cooperation between the three operators. In addition, the operators lack information about the critical primary variables: reliable estimates of steam flow and feedwater flow are not available at low power levels (where the startup task occurs) because plant sensors can only detect large volume flows. Finally, from two to four steam generators must be simultaneously controlled, adding a significant time-sharing component to the task.

Cognitive Task Analysis

Although the MCF task is quite difficult, expert operators have developed the knowledge and skills that allow them to accomplish the task. A cognitive task analysis was performed to determine the nature of those skills and knowledge. The cognitive task analysis defines the user's role within the goal/means hierarchy. That is, it determines the decisions and/or actions that the user must perform, and the data or information that is necessary to make those decisions or actions. Expert operators from nine separate utilities attended a 3-day panel session. The operators were asked to describe the major feedwater control maneuvers (with emphasis on what made these maneuvers particularly difficult) and incidents or near-incidents that they had been involved in or were familiar with, and they were also observed on a full-scope training simulator while actually performing the task.

The results of the cognitive task analysis indicated that expert operators had a detailed and rich understanding of the system that they were controlling. One facet of this understanding was the ability to recognize system state, involving the primary task of determining the extent to which current ISGL was due to long-term mass balances or transient energy effects. To accomplish this expert operators were observed to "mentally track" the influences that would eventually have an effect on ISGL, but that had not appeared yet due to the significant time delays. When expert operators lost track of these influences they were observed to perform "experiments"—entering small control inputs to observe the influence on ISGL. The cognitive task analysis revealed that a second facet of their detailed understanding of the system was the ability to predict ISGL response to control inputs. When mismatches between system goals and current system state (e.g., maintain the ISGL away from setpoints or maintain ISGL at a level that prepares for upcoming maneuvers) occur, then control input must be made. Expert operators were able to mentally simulate the system dynamics and choose between alternative control inputs that were most likely to achieve these goals.

In addition, expert operators exhibited specific control strategies that allowed them to avoid or to recover from problematic situations. One strategy to avoid trouble was to make small control inputs, thereby circumventing large oscillations in ISGL. Strategies to recover from trouble involved not only understanding the complex system dynamics, but actually using them to their advantage. Expert operators coordinated changes in the primary variables to produce artificial energy effects (referred to as shrink and swell levers) that would allow the required control inputs for recovery to be made. To recover from the scenario that was described earlier the feedwater operator might ask the turbine operator to increase steam demand, which would then cause a temporary increase in the ISGL (a swell effect), allowing the rate of feedwater to be increased without exceeding the lower setpoint boundary. Perhaps the most defining characteristic of an expert operator was the ability to quickly translate knowledge into action: expert operators were able to recognize a situation, select an appropriate strategy, and execute that strategy in an "automatic" fashion.

Part-Task Trainer

The findings of these two cognitive analyses guided the development of a part-task simulator for the manual control of feedwater task. A control theory expert familiar with nuclear power plants replicated the behavioral dynamics of a single steam generator with high functional fidelity. A set of differential equations were developed to reflect the influence of a number of factors on the ISGL, including steam flow, feedwater flow, and temperature of the feedwater. The simulation is generic in that the relative effects of these variables can be adjusted to represent a wide range of existing steam generators. Thus, the part-task trainer was designed to replicate the critical aspects of the task, as identified in the cognitive analyses described earlier. A significant amount of effort was devoted to developing additional decision support to replicate some of the critical skills and knowledge of expert operators.

Estimates of Steam and Feedwater Flows.   The goals/means analysis and the cognitive task analysis revealed that one major contributor to the difficulty of the task is the lack of information regarding steam and feedwater flows. This information is critical because the relationship between these two variables determines mass balance. The mass flowing out of the steam generator (steam flow) must be replaced by mass flowing into the steam generator (feedwater flow) to maintain ISGL at a constant level. Although this information is not available in the actual plants, it can be obtained from the mathematical simulation and provided to individuals so that they can develop a deeper appreciation of the important relationship between them.

Compensated Steam Generator Level.   The goals/means analysis revealed that two additional contributors to the difficulty of the MCF task are the long time delays between a control input and its effect on ISGL and the counterintuitive energy effects (shrink and swell). A prominent characteristic of expert performance was the ability to estimate the extent to which the current ISGL level was a result of these time delays and energy effects. A "compensated" steam generator level (CSGL) variable was developed that provides an estimate of the critical performance variable, indicated steam generator level. The CSGL variable eliminates the time lags and counterintuitive behaviors (shrink and swell effects) that are characteristic of the ISGL. When mass contributions are balanced (that is, when steam and feed flow are equal) the CSGL estimates the steady-state condition that ISGL will approach, and provides a direct indication of the size and direction of energy effects (shrink and swell).

Predicted Steam Generator Level.   The cognitive task analysis also revealed that an important aspect of operators expertise was the ability to predict the behavior of ISGL. For instance, increasing the rate of feedwater flow could result in a shrink effect that would cause ISGL to cross the lower setpoint boundary. Normally the operators are required to mentally estimate the future behavior of the ISGL based on the current system context and their knowledge of the system dynamics. To assist the operators in this task, a predictor variable was developed that projects the value of ISGL into the future.

Summary

Developing effective automated instruction requires a detailed understanding of the target domain as well as the skills and knowledge that experts have developed to enable them to perform successfully within that domain. Cognitive engineering provides principles and techniques that can be used to discover this information. The analyses that were performed for the manual control of feedwater task provide one example of how the required information might be obtained (Mitchell & Saisi, 1987, describe a similar approach in the design of NASA ground control centers). The goals/means analysis determines the system goals that need to be accomplished, the physical resources (means) that are available to meet those goals, and the resulting cognitive demands that are placed on individuals performing tasks in the domain. The cognitive task analysis identifies the skills and knowledge (the cognitive resources) that individuals have developed to meet those demands. The ultimate goal is to identify instances where the cognitive demands of the domain of application and the cognitive resources of the user are mismatched. When the goal is to develop on-line decision support, these mismatches signal the need to reconfigure the existing interface (collecting or re-representing existing information) or the development of additional information to be added to the interface. When changes to the existing interface are not possible, cognitive demand/resource mismatches signal critical skills and knowledge that must be fostered by the instructional system. Having determined the critical information that is necessary for successful performance of the MCF task (variables, relationships between variables, goals and constraints), and having developed additional decision support to aid successful performance (estimates of steam and feed flows, the compensated SGL, the predicted SGL), the question becomes how to represent this information in the interface.

REPRESENTATION AIDING

One form of decision support that is often overlooked is representation aiding (Woods, 1991; Woods & Roth, 1988; Zachary, 1986) where machine power is used to create and manipulate graphic representations of the domain. Woods (Woods & Roth, 1988) and Rasmussen (1986) have stressed that there can be no neutral representation: any representation that is chosen will necessarily emphasize certain aspects of the domain at the expense of others. When designed appropriately, representation aids can be used to help the human problem solver find the relevant data in a dynamic environment, to visualize the semantics of the domain, and to restructure their view of the problem. This will be especially important during training and instruction, since an individual is explicitly learning about the domain. While technological developments have provided powerful capabilities to generate computer graphics, a clear understanding of how these capabilities can be used to support human cognition is needed.

There are several theoretical perspectives that can be used to guide the development of representation aids. Cleveland and his colleagues (Cleveland, 1985; Cleveland & McGill, 1985) have investigated the visual system's effectiveness in extracting information that has been mapped into various graphical forms (e.g., area of a circle vs. length of a line, etc.). Wickens and his colleagues (Wickens, 1986; Wickens & Andre, 1990; Wickens et al., 1985) have investigated the relationship between the general information-processing capabilities of an individual, the general demands of the task, and the implications for display design. Hutchins, Hollan, and Norman (1986) describe a general theory of interface design that emphasizes the role of direct manipulation (the capability to effect changes in the domain by directly acting upon objects of interest).

A number of researchers have been investigating an alternative approach to display design for complex, dynamic domains. Although their theoretical orientations are slightly different, and the specific conclusions and recommendations may differ, they all share very similar basic beliefs. For these researchers, the success of a representation aid depends upon matching specific perceptual and cognitive capabilities of an individual with specific characteristics of the domain (Bennett, Toms, & Woods, in press; Flach & Vicente, 1989; Rasmussen, 1986; Vicente & Rasmussen, 1990; Woods & Roth, 1988). In particular, the semantics of those domains (the critical variables, the relationships between these variables, and the relevant goals and constraints) must be mapped into the static appearance and dynamic behavior of the representation aid so that critical information can be easily extracted or decoded by the individual.

The principles that these researchers use to guide the design of representation aids for skilled performance are applicable to those for the acquisition of cognitive skills. However, the design of representation aids for automated instruction places additional requirements for integrated sets of displays. Representation aids also need to be designed to facilitate the transition from an initial understanding of the domain semantics to a more advanced conceptualization that approximates that of expert domain practitioners. In addition, when the graphic displays in the training system are not available on the target system, sets of representation aids need to be designed that facilitate the transfer of training to the target system. A set of representation aids that were developed for the part-task trainer is described in greater detail.

Trend Displays

In existing power plants, an operator performs the MCF task with a strip chart that provides the value of indicated steam generator level over time. Figure 9.2 illustrates two "trend" displays that were developed for the part-task stimulus. The upper trend display in Fig. 9.2 contains the critical performance variable ISGL and the CSGL. The current values of these variables are represented by diamonds in the right-hand portion of the screen; the history of these variables across a 5-min time frame is represented in the left hand portion of the screen. The lower trend display in Fig. 9.2 portrays the primary variables that effect ISGL level (steam flow, feed flow, and reactor power).

This representation of the domain semantics facilitates performance of the MCF task in several ways. The cognitive task analysis indicates that an important aspect of performing the MCF task is maintaining an internal record (over time) of the variables that influence ISGL. This is precisely the information conveyed by the trend displays. Variables that are normally available (the ISGL and power level) and some that are not normally available (steam flow, feed flow, CSGL,

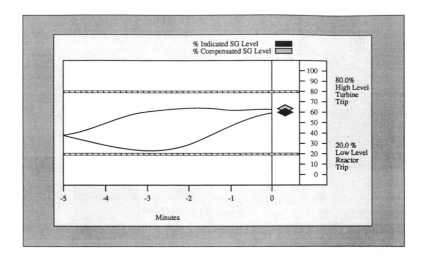

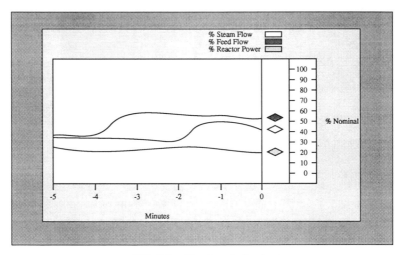

FIG. 9.2.   The trend displays.

ISGL predictor) are collected and placed in the context of the critical performance goals (upper and lower setpoints). In addition, the critical functional relationships between variables (the size and direction of mass and energy balances) are directly represented by color-coding the difference between the variables on the trend displays (this is not shown in Fig. 9.2).

Using the trend display format, two empirical studies were conducted to assess the effectiveness of the decision support that was developed to improve performance at the MCF task (steam/feed flow variables and the compensated level variable). In both experiments, performance with the ISGL alone was compared to performance with the ISGL plus steam and feed flow variables or the ISGL plus compensated SGL. In the first experiment, the dependent variable was the root-mean-square error between the indicated steam generator level maintained by an individual and an optimal steam generator level (Bennett, Woods, Roth, & Haley, 1986). In a second experiment, the dependent measure was how long an individual could maintain the ISGL between the upper and lower setpoint boundaries. The results of both experiments indicated that the addition of either the steam/feed flow variables or the CSGL variable to ISGL significantly improved performance, relative to ISGL alone. There were no significant performance differences between the ISGL plus the steam/feed flow variables and the ISGL plus the CSGL variable.

The Animated Mimic Display

As Hollan, Hutchins, and Weitzman (1984) have argued persuasively, the efficiency of training can be improved by providing alternative conceptual perspectives of the domain. However, Hollan et al. provide very little insight about which conceptual perspectives (of the potentially infinite number available) should be provided. Rasmussen (1986) has developed a methodology to describe complex, dynamic domains that can be used as a framework for the provision of alternative conceptualizations. The "abstraction hierarchy" has five separate levels of description, ranging from the physical form of a system (e.g., What are the system components? What do they look like? Where are they located?) to the higher-level purposes it serves (e.g., What is the system's purpose? What constraints does the system operate under to fulfill this purpose?). Flach & Vicente (1989) and Vicente and Rasmussen (1990) discuss how the abstraction hierarchy can be used as a framework for the design of representation aids.

One type of display that is likely to be effective in providing an individual with an initial understanding of a complex system corresponds to the second level in the abstraction hierarchy, the level of physical function. This level "represents the physical (i.e., the mechanical, electrical, or chemical) processes of the system or its parts" (Rasmussen, 1986, p. 16). A display at this level of description graphically illustrates the important components, systems, or subsystems and the flow of information or resources between them. This should facilitate the development of appropriate mental models of a domain by providing a "continuous graphical explanation" (Hollan, Hutchins, & Weitzman, 1984) that illustrates the causal relationships between important system components. In addition to the pedagogical benefits, this type of graphic display can be used to facilitate diagnostic performance in real time and has a wide range of applicability (e.g., process control, maintenance, troubleshooting).

A graphic display that provides a description of the manual control of feedwater task at the level of physical function is illustrated in Fig. 9.1. This display will be referred to as the animated mimic. The important physical components (the reactor core, the steam generator, and the turbine housing) and the pipes that connect them are represented graphically. The flow of steam (from steam generator to the turbine), feedwater (from turbine to steam generator), and energy (from reactor core to steam generator) is represented by animating the pipes. Apparent motion is produced by systematically changing (cycling) the luminance and chromaticity of adjacent squares inside the pipe.

Despite the intuitive appeal, very little empirical research has addressed issues associated with the implementation of this type of display. Basic research on the perception of motion indicates that the perceptual characteristics of the graphical elements (the squares) will have an impact on how well the apparent motion produced by the display matches the flow rates in the domain. These perceptual characteristics include fundamental frequency, temporal frequency, contrast (chromatic or luminance), shape, and borders. A series of empirical investigations have been conducted: the perceptual characteristics between the graphical elements were altered and observers matched the apparent motion of two horizontal, parallel pipes. The results of one set of experiments indicate that although chromatic contrast could be used to perform the rate-matching task, luminance contrast was much more effective. A second set of experiments revealed that there were optimal combinations of fundamental frequency (the size of the squares) and temporal frequency (the rate at which the squares were cycled). In a third set of experiments the nature of the borders between graphical elements was altered: the borders could be explicit (lines drawn between them) or implicit (no lines, just the contrast between elements) and the borders could remain vertical and fixed (no contours), or increasingly contoured (arrow-shaped) as rates of flow increased. It was found that explicit borders decreased rate-matching performance when no contours were present, but facilitated performance when the contours became more arrow-shaped. Additional details can be found in Bennett (1991a, 1991b).

The Configural Display

The animated mimic is an example of one type of display that has the potential to explain the physical functioning of complex causal systems. However, as Rasmussen (1986) has indicated, to accomplish tasks in complex domains the operator must understand the system at higher levels of abstraction, including system functions that cut across individual components or subsystems. Figure 9.3 illustrates a graphic display that has been developed to explicitly represent a higher-order, functional perspective of the MCF task. This representation corresponds to Rasmussen's fourth level in the hierarchy, the level of abstract function.

This type of display is referred to as a *configural* display. This display maps four variables (feedwater flow, steam flow, indicated steam generator level, and compensated steam generator level) into a single graphical object: a rectangle.

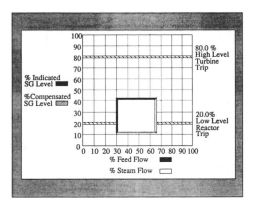

FIG. 9.3. The configural display.

The difference between steam and feedwater flow is mapped in the x axis (therefore, the width of the rectangle represents the degree to which mass input and output is balanced). The difference between the indicated and compensated steam generator level is mapped in the y axis (thus, the height of the rectangle roughly corresponds to the energy balance). The resulting display is a rectangle that changes in size and shape, as well as location inside the display grid. These changing perceptual cues provide direct information about the state of the plant. For example, a rectangle with a large area represents large imbalances in mass and energy and, therefore, an unstable and generally undesirable plant condition. This type of perceptual cue has been referred to as "emergent perceptual features" (Pomerantz, Sager, & Stoever, 1977; Sanderson, Flach, Buttigieg, & Casey, 1989) and does not usually exist with the display of the same information in a separable format (e.g., four bargraphs).

The success of a configural display in improving performance depends upon the extent to which the emergent perceptual features that result from the interaction of the lower-level graphic elements correspond to the demands of the task. When there is a direct correspondence, configural displays have been shown to facilitate performance (relative to separable displays) when information from several variables must be integrated to reach a decision (Wickens, 1986; Wickens & Andre, 1990; Wickens et al., 1985). The results of an empirical investigation that compared performance with the configural display in Fig. 9.3 to performance with a separable display of information (four bargraphs) support this conclusion (Bennett et al., in press). It was found that the configural display facilitated the accuracy (and in some conditions the latency) of responses that required the recall of critical task information: the mass and energy balances. Thus, the configural display provides a high-level conceptual perspective of the MCF task that emphasizes the functional, rather than the physical, aspects of the task that are critical for successful performance.

However, there is a potential cost associated with configural displays. Some research has indicated that displaying information in a configural format can decrease the availability of information related to individual variables. Thus, a critical issue in the design of configural displays is how to prevent this cost. Bennett et al. (in press) found that color-coding the lower-level, configural elements of the display partially offset these costs. Bennett and Flach (in press) review issues in the design of configural displays, including methodologies, associated patterns of experimental results, and relevant theories of design. They conclude that designing configural displays to allow the extraction of information related to both high-level properties and low-level data is a very distinct possibility.

Summary

Representation aiding has a vast potential to improve overall system performance in human-machine systems, due to both our impressive capabilities to process and utilize spatial information and the abundance of hardware and software to produce computer-generated graphics. Graphic displays can collect and integrate information, provide alternative conceptual perspectives, make the abstract concrete, and in some cases transform problem solving from a process that requires limited cognitive resources to one that capitalizes on virtually limitless perceptual resources. This section has outlined one design perspective that can be used to capitalize on this vast potential. One of the key conceptualizations is that the effectiveness of representation aiding depends on the mapping of information from the domain into the perceptual characteristics of the display. To the extent that the relevant information can be easily extracted from the representation, it will be effective.

The displays and decision support that have been developed for the part-task trainer were developed from this perspective. These displays should facilitate the acquisition of skills and knowledge required to complete the MCF task. The steam and feed flow variables and the compensated ISGL variable replicate a large portion of the expertise that expert domain practitioners exhibit. For example, these displays separate the effects of mass and energy balances on the critical performance variable ISGL and eliminate the long time delays associated with control input. Interacting with these displays should facilitate the development of skills such as determining system state, predicting future state, and anticipating necessary actions. Also, by eliminating the need to maintain an internal record of influences on ISGL, the demands on short-term memory are reduced, which allows an individual to concentrate on higher-level aspects of the control task such as control strategies to avoid or recover from trouble.

The trend displays, animated mimic, and configural display provide multiple conceptual perspectives of the domain semantics that pave the way for necessary transitions in knowledge. The animated mimic provides a very concrete, physical perspective of the system components and the causal relationships between them.

This display should be particularly appropriate for the development of an appropriate mental model of the MCF task and provide a basis for causal reasoning. On the other hand, the configural display provides a representation that is a higher-level abstraction of the functional relationships between the primary variables (mass and energy balances). This representation corresponds to one conceptualization that a more experienced operator may have developed after considerable experience at the task. Thus, these displays provide a framework for the transition from novice to expert conceptualizations of the task. In addition, the trend displays provide a conceptual perspective that matches the perspective in the target system and thus provides a means to transition the individuals from the additional decision support that is available on the part-task trainer that is currently available in the actual domain.

DISCOVERY LEARNING

One of the fundamental issues in automated instruction is the degree of learner versus system control of the instructional sequence (Glaser, 1990; Glaser & Bassok, 1989). One approach to automated instruction is to design systems that provide the learner with the opportunity to actively explore a domain. In this type of system a student is provided with tools that assist in the formation and testing of hypotheses about that domain (e.g., Shute & Glaser, 1990). This approach to instruction is based upon the belief that active participation in the learning process will improve the effectiveness of learning.

One of the primary resources that we have to support the discovery learning approach to instruction is representation aiding. As previous discussion has indicated, alternative conceptual perspectives and information that is not normally available can be provided to facilitate understanding and comprehension of complex domains. The discussion emphasized the importance of direct perception, that is, the representation of the domain semantics in a visual form that highlights the critical information necessary to accomplish domain tasks. However, as Holland and his colleagues (Hollan et al., 1984; Hutchins et al., 1986) have emphasized, direct manipulation can also be an important element of discovery learning approaches. Variables can be directly manipulated on the screen, and the resulting effects can provide immediate visual feedback to facilitate understanding.

Several lines of research support the potential of the discovery approach to facilitate learning. For example, Bobrow and Bower (1969) found that asking individuals to generate answers facilitated recall of sentences. Roth, Bennett, and Woods (1987) investigated the effectiveness of performance with an expert system that was designed to replace training on the troubleshooting of an electronic device. It was found that troubleshooting performance was best when technicians actively participated in troubleshooting activities, in direct contrast to the unsuccessful performance that resulted when technicians passively followed the instructions that were given by the system.

Lesh (1987) directly compared discovery and traditional learning approaches for the acquisition of mathematical skills. In subsequent tests, students experiencing the discovery learning approach performed better than those experiencing the traditional approach. In addition, individuals in the discovery learning condition were more likely to understand domain principles that were not directly addressed during instruction. It appears that actively exploring and experiencing concepts in the domain can result in increased structure and interconnections of knowledge in memory. The principles of discovery learning may provide one solution to the problem of inert knowledge (Bransford, Sherwood, Vye, & Rieser, 1986).

The combination of a discovery learning approach and graphic representations providing direct perception and manipulation have a great potential to improve automated instructional systems for complex, dynamic domains. Three key issues in the development of a discovery environment are (a) the nature of the explorations that are provided, (b) the nature of the tools and representations that are provided to support these explorations, and (c) the ordering or sequencing of these explorations. The goal of a discovery learning environment is to provide an individual with the capability to explore the complete range of the situations that might be encountered in a domain and the alternative behavioral responses that are available. A number of potential explorations that might be useful for the MCF task and other complex, dynamic domains will be discussed.

Change System Variables to Perform Experiments.   This exploration is really at the heart of the discovery learning approach. In Smithtown (Shute & Glaser, 1990), individuals manipulate variables to perform experiments and their actions are monitored to see whether they adhere to the scientific method. One issue in this type of exploration concerns which variables should be manipulable. In the MCF task, individuals should be allowed to change any of the primary variables (steam flow, feed flow, and reactor power) or other variables (e.g., the temperature of the feedwater can vary, and this has a significant influence on the size of the shrink and swell effects that occur) that effect the ISGL. However, since ISGL is the critical performance variable that they must learn to control, and since ISGL is influenced by a number of variables, individuals should not be allowed to manipulate it.

Change System Displays.   One important exploration is the capability to add or subtract additional decisional support, and to alternate between various conceptual perspectives. For example, interacting with the additional decision support and alternative conceptual perspectives is likely to facilitate the acquisition of skill at the MCF task. However, because this information will not be available during performance of the actual task, an individual needs the capability to add or subtract this additional support. In this manner, individuals can learn to perform the task with the additional decision support and then gradually "wean" themselves until they can perform the task with the information and conceptual perspective that is available in the real world.

Change Scenarios. In complex, dynamic domains one of the most important explorations that an individual should have is the ability to explore the range of situations that might be encountered. The scenarios should be carefully chosen to present situations that require all categories of the skills and knowledge that are necessary for successful performance in the domain, and ideally, instances within these categories that vary in their degree of difficulty. In the case of the MCF task, this might include standard scenarios with a low degree of difficulty, scenarios with existing trouble that requires the use of specific strategies to recover from trouble, scenarios with impending difficulty where strategies to avoid trouble are required, scenarios where other team members are working at cross purposes, and scenarios where critical aspects are varied (e.g., the temperature of the feedwater is varied to produce larger or smaller shrink/swell effects).

Repeat or Rewind a Particular Scenario. When learning to control a complex process, a learner will benefit from the opportunity to control the process again under the exact same circumstances. For instance, an individual who lost control and crossed a setpoint boundary in the MCF task should be able to immediately "rewind" the scenario and attempt an alternative strategy. Another version of this exploration is to attempt the same scenario with different decision support (e.g., successful completion of a scenario with the CSGL, followed by another attempt with ISGL alone).

Change Role. In complex, dynamic domains teams of individuals must often work together to achieve common goals. This requires an understanding of each team member's role in achieving overall goals. For example, the manual control of feedwater operator often coordinates the actions of the other two operators during the execution of strategies to avoid or recover from trouble (e.g., artificial shrink and swell effects). Thus, an important exploration might be the ability to perform complex tasks while assuming each team member's role.

Step Through or Speed Up Simulation. In complex, dynamic domains there are often multiple events occurring simultaneously, with the end result that an individual may not be able to attend to all events simultaneously. Allowing an individual to slow down the rate at which the simulation updates is an exploration that would allow this to happen. The converse of this exploration is time compression, which is the acceleration of the simulation update rate. In cases where there are significant time delays between a control input and the system's response, reducing the update rate can facilitate the acquisition of skill (e.g., Vidulich, Yeh, & Schneider, 1983).

Predict System Dynamics.   In complex, dynamic domains, particularly those involving causal systems, one important exploration is to allow an individual to predict the behavior of the system or device (e.g., in the MCF task the critical prediction is the behavior of the ISGL). One exploration that might be provided is to allow an individual to make a prediction about the future behavior of the domain and then be provided with feedback regarding the appropriateness of the prediction.

Summary

This section has outlined the rationale behind a discovery learning approach to automated instruction, as well as a number of explorations that might be incorporated into this type of system. The explorations should provide an individual with the opportunity to experience the range of situations that might be encountered in the domain as well as alternative response strategies that are available. Questions concerning how these explorations should be sequenced are closely related to fundamental issues in instructional theory. The strong view of discovery learning requires that an individual be allowed total freedom in the sequencing of explorations. However, there is some evidence that students low in ability or motivation may require explicit coaching to take advantage of this type of learning environment. In addition, there is no guarantee that students will explore all of the domain problem space. At the other end of the instruction spectrum is what has been referred to as the "mastery" approach (Glaser, 1990), where an individual has very little discretion over the sequencing of instructional treatments.

It is likely that an approach located between these two extremes will prove to be the most effective strategy for discovery learning. This has been referred to as a "guided discovery" approach. For example, Shute and Glaser (1990) allow students freedom in their choice of explorations until it is clear that they are not making progress toward instructional goals, at which point more directed instruction is provided. This approach could be extended by allowing an individual freedom within progressive levels of instruction (e.g., an individual might not be provided the opportunity to explore the utility of shrink and swell leverage strategies until success at standard control is demonstrated). Some of the sequencing decisions can be guided by the results of the goals/means analysis, the cognitive task analysis, or even intuition. However, a theory of learning that is adequately detailed to provide guidelines for the sequencing of explorations is needed.

COGNITIVE DIAGNOSIS FOR AUTOMATED INSTRUCTION

The discussion of how explorations should be sequenced serves as an introduction to the role of guidance in automated instructional systems. The approach to instruction that has been discussed to this point emphasizes the role of direct perception, direct manipulation, and discovery learning. When coupled with a simulation of the domain this can provide an effective environment for the acquisition of skills and knowledge for complex, dynamic domains (Hollan, Hutchins, & Weitzman, 1984). However, as Anderson (1988) indicates, this is only part of the expertise that an automated instructional system should provide. An automated instructional system should also guide a student through the acquisition of domain skills, including the provision of advice or instruction in particularly difficult or novel situations, and the adaptation of the instructional sequence based on the student's current level of competency. What are the mechanisms behind the provision of this advice and what form (verbal, graphic) or "grain" (specific or general) should the advice take?

Sophisticated diagnostic and student modeling techniques have evolved to provide guidance in well-constrained domains (Anderson, 1988; VanLehn, 1988). Implementing these advanced techniques requires highly accurate psychological models (e.g., cognitive modeling; Anderson, 1988). With rare exceptions, these techniques have not been incorporated into instructional systems for complex, dynamic domains. In part, this is due to the complexity of the skills and knowledge that are required. Individuals must have detailed declarative knowledge about low-level, physical components of the domain and how they combine to provide higher-level functions of the domain. Individuals must be able to causally reason about the flow of information or resources between components and functions. They must also develop appropriate response strategies to avoid or recover from trouble, contextual knowledge about when these strategies apply, lower-level psychomotor skills to execute these strategies, and monitoring skills for the assessment of progress towards goals. Developing the highly accurate and detailed psychological models of performance that are required to implement more sophisticated diagnosis and modeling techniques would require a tremendous amount of effort (e.g., see Anderson, 1988, and VanLehn, 1988, for discussions concerning the difficulty of, and prospects for, developing diagnostic and modeling techniques for causal reasoning).

An additional aspect of complex domains that would appear to complicate the process of providing guidance is their dynamic nature. Scenarios develop over time, and new events can occur at indeterminate times, thus changing the nature of the problem to be solved. Therefore, the instructional system has the additional burden of assessing the evolving problem solving context to evaluate student actions. However, situation assessment can actually serve as a basis for the provision of instruction. Perhaps the best illustration is the work of Suchman (1987), who emphasizes the importance of "situated action" as the basis of instruction that is tailored for a particular instance and a particular individual. Combining situation assessment with simpler diagnostic techniques is one potential solution to the problem of providing automated instructional environments for complex, dynamic domains. An on-line advisory system was developed for the manual control of feedwater task (Roth, Woods, Elm, & Gallagher, 1987) that utilized situation assessment as one basis for the provision of on-line guidance.

On-Live Advisory System

The on-line advisory system was implemented on a full-scope simulation of a power plant and offers advice that is based on an analysis of expert performance at the MCF task. The design emphasis was to replicate the "cognitive competencies" that expert operators displayed. A portion of this cognitive competency (recognition of system state, the anticipation of future responses, and the separation of mass and energy effects on the ISGL) was provided by the decision support that was discussed earlier. In addition to this information, the on-line advisor provided advice with respect to the acceptable operating ranges for primary variables and also specific strategies for avoiding and recovering from trouble.

Advice on Acceptable Operating Ranges for Primary Variables.   The findings of a cognitive task analysis of the MCF task indicated that expert operators maintained primary variables in a "comfort zone" that minimized the risk of crossing a setpoint boundary. The on-line advisor provides an estimate of the acceptable ranges for the primary variables (steam flow, feed flow, reactor power). One unique feature of this advice is that it is provided graphically, in the form of vertical bars (or operating bands) that are placed adjacent to the current values of the variables. These graphic operating bands change as a function of the current state of the system: when the plant is stable there is a wide range of acceptable values; when the plant is unstable a very narrow range of acceptable values would be provided.

Advice on Specific Strategies.   The system also offers advice on specific strategies to avoid or recover from trouble. This advice takes the form of action scripts that describe the system state, the desired outcome (goal), and general recommendations for control input. The provision of this advice is triggered by an assessment of both current and future system state. The advice that is provided is based on taxonomies of specific plant situations and specific response strategies of operators (obtained from the cognitive task analysis). For example, consider an instance where the ISGL level was dangerously low due to a shrink effect and increasing the feedwater flow would result in crossing the lower setpoint boundary. The on-line advisor recognizes the situation from an assessment of both the current state of the system (ISGL and CSGL variables) and the future state of the system (the ISGL predictor). A response strategy that expert operators were observed to exhibit in this situation is then provided. Initially, an alphanumeric warning appears in an alarm window informing the operator of the adverse plant state ("shrink in progress"), and as the situation worsens the alarm window would direct the operator to consider the advice presented in an action script window. In this example the advice is to create an artificial swell (the goal, "create swell," and the recommended control input, "increase steam flow") and then adjust the mass balance (the goal, "establish net inflow," and the recommended input, "increase feed flow").

Common Frame of Reference.   One obvious feature of the on-line advisory system is that knowledge about the domain is incorporated into a "black-box" expert (Anderson, 1988; Burton & Brown, 1979): the expertise consists of computational algorithms with no attempt to replicate the psychological mechanisms involved. The use of a black-box expert avoids the cost and difficulty of detailed cognitive modeling, which, as Anderson (1988) has emphasized, is formidable even in well-constrained domains. One potential disadvantage of using a black-box expert in instructional systems is the problem of generating explanations acceptable to students. This problem is a particular instance of the more general problem of "opaque device" that has been discussed in the context of expert systems (Roth, Bennett, & Woods, 1987; Suchman, 1987) and computer systems in general (Brown, 1986).

The on-line advisor partially alleviates this problem by integrating advice and the rationale behind it to provide a "common frame of reference" or "mutual understanding" (Roth, Bennett, & Woods, 1987; Suchman, 1987). In the on-line advisor advice is provided as a function of both current situation assessments (ISGL and CSGL) and future situation assessment (the predicted ISGL). This advice is both graphic (recommended operating bands) and alphanumeric (action scripts) in nature, and the grain of this advice is general (high-level recommendations and not specific actions). In addition, the recommended control input is accompanied by a statement of the goal(s) for a particular maneuver. All of this information is directly available to the operator in the interface. This common frame of reference serves as both an explanation of the advice that is provided and a basis for evaluating the effectiveness of that advice.

Issue-Based Diagnosis

The major drawback in using situation assessment as the primary basis for instructional intervention is that instruction cannot be adapted according to an individual's current level of expertise or understanding. One technique that can be used to provide this capability is issue-based diagnosis (Burton & Brown, 1979). Issue-based diagnosis requires an analysis of domain tasks to determine "issues" or fundamental skills that are required for successful performance. The student's performance is monitored with respect to these issues during the process of solving domain problems. The diagnostic module looks for instances where the student has the opportunity to express the skills or knowledge associated with an issue, and maintains a record of whether or not this occurs. After sufficient behavioral evidence has accumulated with respect to an issue either advancement or instructional intervention can be provided. To implement the issue-based approach, the instructional system must be able to assess the evolving problem solving context, and have access to behavioral input within this context (what VanLehn, 1988, has referred to as "intermediate state" input). In addition, a model of expert performance is required for comparison purposes.

One positive feature of this approach to on-line cognitive diagnosis is the fact that detailed psychological models of all critical skills and knowledge may not be required for useful instruction to occur. Burton and Brown (1979, p. 8) state that "the black-box Expert used for evaluation need only be augmented with those incomplete pieces of an articulate Expert which are needed to detect critical or tutorable features of the answers produced by the black-box Expert. The glass-box Expert need not be able to produce the complete solution itself. It needs only to work backwards from the solution to determine the "important" (tutorial) features of the solution. This realization opens up the possibility of constructing coaching systems for domains for which we do not have complete glass-box expertise."

Although the development of the on-line advisor did not concentrate on cognitive diagnosis per se, many of the requirements for the implementation of issue-based diagnosis are present. The issues or fundamental skills that are necessary for the MCF task were identified in the goal/means and cognitive task analyses. Performance with respect to many of these issues can be assessed with direct behavioral measurements. In addition, the student's ability to select and execute appropriate control strategies could be measured by comparing the patterns and timing of their control inputs to those generated by the on-line advisor.

Summary

The MCF on-line advisor utilizes black-box expertise, provides advice that is based on analyses of expert performance, and uses situation assessment as the basis for the provision of this advice. Although this particular system has clear limitations, it provides one example of a broad theoretical approach to cognitive diagnosis (and instruction in general): guided discovery learning (Burton & Brown, 1979). From this theoretical perspective errors and mistakes are viewed as an important part of the learning process. For example, Burton and Brown (1979, p. 6) state that "While the student is making mistakes in the environment he is also experiencing the idea of learning from his mistakes and discovering the means to recover from his mistakes. If the Coach immediately points out the student's errors, there is a real danger that the student will never develop the necessary skills for examining his own behavior and looking for the causes of his own mistakes." There is a fair amount of data that supports the utility of this approach. Some of that data was reviewed in the section on guided discovery learning (e.g., Lesh, 1987; Shute & Glaser, 1990). The range of applicability for issue-based diagnosis is quite large: variations of issue-based diagnosis have been used successfully in a wide variety of domains and for a wide variety of knowledge (Anderson, 1988; Burton & Brown, 1979; Clancey, 1982). Issue-based diagnosis provides one way to cope with the complexity of the skills and knowledge that are required for successful performance in complex, dynamic domains. Although issue-based diagnosis relaxes the requirement to develop complete and highly-accurate psychological models, there is still a need to thoroughly understand the domain and the nature of the skills and knowledge that an individual uses to perform successfully in the domain. The cognitive task analysis and the goals/means analysis described earlier are examples of knowledge engineering methods that are required to support the approach.

SUMMARY

Cognitive diagnosis, student modeling, and other aspects of intelligent tutoring make up one way that instructional designers can use the abundant computational power that is currently available to improve the effectiveness of automated instruction. A second way to use this computational power is to develop representation aiding that allows individuals to envision the characteristics of complex domains through the provision of alternative conceptual perspectives (direct representation) and an improved capability to interact directly with the domain (direct manipulation). A third way to use this computational power is to provide aspects of discovery learning: explorations and computerized tools that support these explorations. Additional insight about how these three mutually interacting and supportive techniques can be used together will improve the effectiveness of automated instruction for complex, dynamic domains.

ACKNOWLEDGMENTS

A number of individuals and organizations have contributed significantly to the ideas and systems that were discussed in the present paper. David Woods and John Flach provided helpful comments. David Woods also conceived and directed the development of the original part-task trainer and the on-line advisor (along with assistance from Emily Roth, Paul Haley, John Gallagher, Lew Hanes, and numerous other individuals at Westinghouse). Funding for the original development was provided by several Westinghouse organizations. Funding for additional research and development was provided by Wright State University (Research Challenge and Research Incentive Grants) and by the Air Force Office of Scientific Research (Summer Faculty Research Program and Research Initiation Program). A special thanks goes to Michael Young and his colleagues at AFHRL/LRG who hosted the SFRP appointment.

REFERENCES

Anderson, J. R. (1988). The expert module. In M. C. Polson & J. J. Richardson (Eds.), *Foundations of intelligent tutoring systems* (pp. 21–54). Hillsdale, NJ: Lawrence Erlbaum Associates.

Bennett, K. B. (1991a). Representational aiding for a complex, dynamic control task. In *Proceedings of the 1991 IEEE International Conference on Systems, Man, and Cybernetics* (pp. 1207–1212). New York: IEEE.

Bennett, K. B. (1991b). *Encoding apparent motion in animated mimic displays.* Manuscript submitted for publication.

Bennett, K. B., & Flach, J. M. (in press). Graphical displays: Implications for divided attention, focussed attention, and problem solving. *Human Factors.*

Bennett, K. B., Toms, M. L., & Woods, D. D. (in press). Emergent features and configural elements: Designing more effective configural displays. *Human Factors.*

Bennett, K. B., Woods, D. D., Roth, E. M., & Haley, P. H. (1986). Predictor displays for complex, dynamic tasks: A preliminary investigation. In *Proceedings of the Human Factors Society 30th Annual Meeting* (pp. 684–688). Santa Monica, CA: Human Factors Society.

Brown, J. S. (1986). From cognitive to social ergonomics and beyond. In D. A. Norman & S. W. Draper (Eds.), *User centered system design* (pp. 457–486). Hillsdale, NJ: Lawrence Erlbaum Associates.

Bobrow, S., & Bower, G. H. (1969). Comprehension and recall of sentences. *Journal of Experimental Psychology, 80,* 455–461.

Burton, R. R., & Brown, J. S. (1979). An investigation of computer coaching for informal learning activities. *International Journal of Man-Machine Studies, 11,* 5–24.

Clancey, W. J. (1982). Tutoring rules for guiding a case method dialogue. In D. Sleeman & J. S. Brown (Eds.), *Intelligent tutoring systems.* (pp. 201–225). New York: Academic Press.

Cleveland, W. S. (1985). *The elements of graphing data.* Belmont, CA: Wadsworth.

Cleveland, W. S., & McGill, R. (1985). Graphical perception and graphical methods for analyzing scientific data. *Science, 229,* 828–833.

Flach, J. M., & Vicente, K. J. (1989). *Complexity, difficulty, direct manipulation and direct perception* (Tech. Report EPRL-89-03). Urbana-Champaign: Engineering Psychology Research Laboratory, University of Illinois.

Glaser, R. (1990). The reemergence of learning theory within instructional research. *American Psychologist 45*(1), 29–39.

Glaser, R., & Bassok, M. (1989). Learning theory and the study of instruction. *Annual Review of Psychology, 40,* 631–666.

Hollan, J. D., Hutchins, E. L., & Weitzman, L. (1984). Steamer: An interactive inspectable simulation-based training system. *AI Magazine, Summer,* 15–27.

Hollnagel, E., & Woods, D. D. (1983). Cognitive systems engineering: New wine in new bottles. *International Journal of Man-Machine Studies, 18,* 583–600.

Hutchins, E. L., Hollan, J. D., & Norman, D. A. (1986). Direct manipulation interfaces. In D. A. Norman & S. W. Draper (Eds.), *User centered system design* (pp. 87–124). Hillsdale, NJ: Lawrence Erlbaum Associates.

INPO. (1984). Reactor trips caused by main feedwater control problems. *Significant Operating Experience Report, 84-4* (July).

Johnson, W. B. (1987). Development and evaluation of simulation-oriented computer-based instruction for diagnostic training. In W. B. Rouse (Ed.), *Advances in man-machine systems research* (Vol. 3, pp. 99–127). Greenwich, CT: JAI Press.

Lesh, R. (1987). The evolution of problem representations in the presence of powerful conceptual amplifiers. In C. Janvier (Ed.), *Problems of representation in the teaching and learning of mathematics* (pp. 197–206). Hillsdale, NJ: Lawrence Erlbaum Associates.

Mitchell, C., & Saisi, D. (1987). Use of model-based qualitative icons and adaptive windows in workstations for supervisory control systems. *IEEE Transactions on Systems, Man, and Cybernetics, SMC-17,* 573–593.

Norman, D. A. (1986). Cognitive engineering. In D. A. Norman & S. W. Draper (Eds.), *User centered system design* (pp. 31–61). Hillsdale, NJ: Lawrence Erlbaum Associates.

Pomerantz, J. R., Sager, L. C., & Stoever, R. J. (1977). Perception of wholes and of their component parts: Some configural superiority effects. *Journal of Experimental Psychology: Human Perception and Performance, 3,* 422–435.

Rasmussen, J. (1986). *Information processing and human-machine interaction: An approach to cognitive engineering.* New York: North Holland.

Roth, E. M., Bennett, K. B., & Woods, D. D. (1987). Human interaction with an "intelligent" machine. *International Journal of Man-Machine Studies, 27,* 479–526.

Roth, E. M., & Woods, D. D. (1988). Aiding human performance: I. Cognitive analysis. *Le Travail Humain, 51*(1), 39–64.

Roth, E. M., Woods, D. D., Elm, W. C., & Gallagher, J. M. (1987). *Intelligent manual feedwater control station* (Tech. Rep. 87-1-C60-HUSCI-R1). Westinghouse Research & Development Center.

Rouse, W. B. (1982). A mixed-fidelity approach to technical training. *Journal of Educational Technology Systems, 11*(2), 103–115.

Sanderson, P. M., Flach, J. M., Buttigieg, M. A., & Casey, E. J. (1989). Object displays do not always support better integrated task performance. *Human Factors, 31*(2), 183–198.

Shute, V., & Glaser, R. (1990). A large-scale evaluation of an intelligent discovery world: Smithtown. *Interactive Learning Environments, 1,* 51–77.

Suchman, L. A. (1987). *Plans and situated actions: The problem of human machine communication.* New York: Cambridge University Press.

VanLehn, K. (1988). Student modeling. In M. C. Polson & J. J. Richardson (Eds.), *Foundations of intelligent tutoring systems* (pp. 55–78). Hillsdale, NJ: Lawrence Erlbaum Associates.

Vicente, K. J., & Rasmussen, J. (1990). *The ecology of human-machine systems II: Mediating "direct perception" in complex work domains* (Tech. Report EPRL-90-01). Urbana-Champaign: Engineering Psychology Research Laboratory, University of Illinois.

Vidulich, M., Yeh, Y. Y., & Schneider, W. (1983). Time-compressed components for air-intercept control skills. *Proceedings of the 27th Annual Meeting of the Human Factors Society* (pp. 161–164).

Wickens, C. D. (1986). *The object display: Principles and a review of experimental findings* (Tech. Rep. CPL-86-6). Urbana-Champaign: Cognitive Psychophysiology Laboratory, University of Illinois.

Wickens, C. D., & Andre, A. D. (1990). Proximity compatibility and information display: Effects of color, space, and objectness on information integration. *Human Factors, 32,* 61–78.

Wickens, C. D., Kramer, A., Barnett, B., Carswell, M., Fracker, L., Goettl, B., & Harwood, K. (1985). *Display-cognitive interface: The effect of information integration requirements on display formatting for C3 displays* (Tech. Rep. EPL-85-3). Urbana-Champaign: Engineering Psychology Research Laboratory and Aviation Research Laboratory, University of Illinois.

Woods, D. D. (1991). Representation aiding: A ten year retrospective. In *Proceedings of the 1991 IEEE International Conference on Systems, Man, and Cybernetics.* Charlottesville, VA: IEEE.

Woods, D. D., & Roth, E. M. (1988). Cognitive systems engineering. In M. Helander (Ed.), *Handbook of human-computer interaction* (pp. 1–41). New York: North-Holland.

Woolf, B., Blegen, D., Jansen, J. H., & Verloop, A. (1987). Teaching a complex industrial process. In R. Lawler & M. Yazdini (Eds.), *Artificial intelligence and education, Vol. 1, Learning environments and tutoring systems* (pp. 413–427). Norwood, NJ: Ablex.

Zachary, W. (1986). A cognitively based functional taxonomy of decision support techniques. *Human-Computer Interaction, 2,* 25–63.

TRANSCRIPTION OF DISCUSSION

Bill Johnson: What kind of reaction did you get when you gave them an independent display, which was not traditional, not what they were used to using all those years?

Kevin Bennett: As I mentioned, we did ask them what types of assistance they could use. We did some informal evaluations and they were generally pleased with the designs and information that we tried to provide them. When they exceed performance setpoints it costs the utility a lot of money. They'd like to have some assistance in performing the task, and the feedback they gave us was relatively positive. With regard to the informal evaluation of the on-line advisor, they said they'd like to have the scope expanded. I know you mentioned in your presentation that sometimes you get a negative reaction to new performance aids. In this case I think the problem is so *big* that they're willing to try a change.

Bill Johnson: What is your reaction when you show pilots glass cockpits and ask, "What should we make this display look like?" And on the glass cockpit they'll draw the old ball and wheel and say "Don't change it, that's what we're used to."

Kevin Bennett: The nuclear power plant control room was designed with a single sensor–single display approach. The operators have to collect and integrate a very large amount of data. So they're in a situation that's not real supportive. In situations like the manual control feed water task, they realize they need help, and are generally receptive.

Doug Towne: What do you find out about people's ability to predict those nonlinear effects individually, even without worrying about representation or comparing them? Just the nonlinear things going on.

Kevin Bennett: We haven't actually done any experiments directly related to that. You can ask Mike Young, and he would tell you that those nonlinearities make the task very difficult.

Doug Towne: Do you have some feeling that maybe there's kind of an assumption on people's part that the world is linear? Or some innate feeling that things ought to be linear?

Kevin Bennett: I wouldn't necessarily say that, but I do think that they have a difficult time keeping track of the influences on SGL that are "in the pipeline." It is a very difficult thing to maintain those influences in memory, and then predict the effect that those influences will have on the steam generator level. First, an operator has a high memory load in terms of keeping track of these effects, and then has to calculate or simulate the systems.

Hugh Burns: On the action windows, the action scripts, did you run any experiments on their comprehensibility?

Kevin Bennett: Well, as you can see the system was developed prior to 1986. I left Westinghouse in 1987. To my knowledge, only informal evaluations were done. That could have changed since then.

Hugh Burns: Let me ask you the "issue question" then. Back in the days of STEAM-ER and the mathematical model that ran the simulation, are there any things going on here that show that a written explanation of procedures can support or enhance that graphical display? In other words, the mixture of graphics and language rather than just graphics alone. I don't know if there is or not.

Kevin Bennett: I believe that ONR has sponsored some research along those lines. I know of an article that John O'Hare was the contract monitor on, and the name of the authors escapes me for the moment (Palmiter, Elkerton, & Bagget [1989], University of Michigan Technical Report C4E-ONR-2), but they did a comparison of animated demonstrations and written instructions and found that animated demonstrations alone might not be sufficient. In this case, I think there are some advantages to offering the information graphically. In particular, they don't have to read the words and follow the action scripts. I think that's a unique feature of the on-line advisor; it presents advice in a graphic form that people can easily comprehend and react to.

Val Shute: There's an experiment you could do if you still have access to the systems. It may be that those people who do best with variations of the graphical depictions are those who have higher spatial aptitudes. These high spatial persons would then be able to abstract more information from displays than less spatial folks. I like graphical displays, but I know other people who, if you are trying to describe a functional system, prefer verbal descriptions over complex displays. In other words, there may be an aptitude–display type interaction where declarative descriptions suit some people better than graphical representations. Maybe that actually would "buy" you some statistical significance as far as your outcome measure—if you considered verbal or spatial aptitudes.

Kevin Bennett: That's a good point.

Alan Lesgold: You have mentioned that the real-life task is done by several people. And they really have to communicate. I'm curious, do you have any observations on what it takes to support the communication?

Kevin Bennett: At the moment this information is scattered throughout the control room and the operators are physically separated. In fact, this is part of the problem. There is a need for a high degree of communication. In fact, good operating teams will orchestrate their performance: "I'm going to increase the feedwater flow so you need to increase the steam flow." Usually the feedwater operator is in charge of this orchestration. Mike Young, Lorraine Duffy, and I have talked about providing a common frame of reference, essentially a display to facilitate communication.

Mike Young: The Air Force is going to distributed decision making. Where you used to have all the people altogether, in these new systems they are literally about a half mile apart, communicating through fiber optics. AFHRL/LRC is very interested in this task and group decision making and how it can be mediated by computers.

Alan Lesgold: The next question is that it seems to me there have to be some nouns and verbs that map onto some of these illustrated phenomena that get passed back and forth between people. A big piece of cognitive task analysis in a group task is, for example, suppose the first person who controls the manual feed water wants feed water, but realizes that a compensation has to be made in the increase of the steam body, and that requires the involvement of the steam person. But then the steam person says, "No, no, what we need is more water, you turn up the water." What happens in these conflict situations if they arise?

Kevin Bennett: Since the manual control of feedwater is the most difficult of the three tasks, that individual, at least in the expert teams, orchestrates the startup process. No one takes a move without first informing him. The whole problem arises because you have conflicting goals in terms of mass and energy across the primary and secondary system. The way they have learned to deal with it is through cooperation and communication.

Jim Pellegrino: Here's a related question. What is the extent to which all three operators have to share the same understanding? Does the person who is manually controlling the feedwater have the full representation of the situation because he is the one orchestrating it?

Kevin Bennett: I believe that they are "interchangeable parts." One person may be a steam turbine operator one day and a manual control of feedwater operator the next.

Jim Pellegrino: Given that they assume alternative roles, it is essential that they all have the same underlying representation, since they are going to be in the lead role. This could create some problems with communication back and forth.

Kevin Bennett: Lorraine Duffy is interested in the issue of group decision making. She is interested in doing research on that very aspect.

Author Index

245

Subject Index